# THE MEDIÆVAL CHURCH ARCHITECTURE OF ENGLAND

BY

CHARLES HERBERT MOORE

WITH TWENTY-THREE PLATES IN HALF-TONE AND ONE HUNDRED
AND FORTY-NINE ILLUSTRATIONS IN THE TEXT

 BOOKS FOR LIBRARIES PRESS
FREEPORT, NEW YORK

First Published 1912
Reprinted 1972

INTERNATIONAL STANDARD BOOK NUMBER:
0-8369-6738-0

LIBRARY OF CONGRESS CATALOG CARD NUMBER:
74-37900

PRINTED IN THE UNITED STATES OF AMERICA
BY
NEW WORLD BOOK MANUFACTURING CO., INC.
HALLANDALE, FLORIDA 33009

# PREFACE

THIS book is critical, but it will not be found captious. Its purpose is to set forth the character of mediæval church architecture in England in the light of a structural analysis and comparison with the French Gothic art, and of the conditions and influences under which it was produced. If the results of this investigation point to conclusions that have not hitherto prevailed, I believe it will be found that they are just, and I have confidence that English fairness will ensure their recognition. I think it must be acknowledged that much English writing on this architecture has been too uncritical, and that without a properly critical spirit it is impossible to form a just estimate of any art.

In my treatise on *Gothic Architecture*, first published in 1890, I had occasion to compare the mediæval architecture of the Ile de France with that of other countries, in order to illustrate the distinctive nature of the French art. My treatment of the other styles was necessarily summary, and I have since felt that the mediæval architecture of England, at least, ought to be more adequately set forth, both to demonstrate its essential difference from the French Gothic (notwithstanding that it drew largely and constantly from the French source), and to do justice to what I consider its finer qualities. I have been impelled to the present work more especially since much of what I have formerly written has been challenged by some critics, and because it appears to me that great misunderstanding of the real character of the art of England, and its relation to that of the Continent, has been shown by recent, no less than by earlier, English writers. This misunderstanding is, I think, due largely to two causes: first, to a fragmentary method of study of architectural systems, with consequent failure to grasp them as wholes, and second, to what may be called the patriotic point of view. The fragmentary method is inadequate, and the patriotic bias is fatal to impartial judgment.

Writers on mediæval architecture have not hitherto recognized the fact that in the pointed art of the Ile de France we have a style of building fundamentally different in structural character from all other styles. It appears to be generally assumed that there was in the Middle Ages a common pointed style, current in all parts of Europe, which, though differing in minor ways in different localities, was essentially the same everywhere. I do not think that a discriminating study and comparison of the various forms of mediæval pointed architecture will justify this view. The vigorous spirit of the Northern races was, indeed, widely operative, but under varying circumstances, and with different results according to local conditions. In the Ile de France alone[1] did racial and other conditions conspire to produce an essentially new art, the principles of which were never grasped elsewhere.[2]

As to the name by which this French art should be called, I have no wish to impose any preference of my own, but it appears to me that things so different as the pointed architecture of the Ile de France in the twelfth and early thirteenth centuries, on the one hand, and all other varieties of pointed building, including that of England, on the other, ought not to be called by the same name; for this implies similarity of character and leads to confusion. I think there are solid grounds for calling the French art Gothic, since it is the consistent manifestation of the Northern, or Gothic, genius that differentiates it from all other art. In it alone are the elements of the older systems creatively and fundamentally transformed, and adapted with logical consistency, to a new architectural organism. In all other art of western Europe in the Middle Ages, we see the Gothic spirit variously influencing, without essentially changing, the ancient structural forms.

To call the French art Gothic does not, of course, mean that

---

[1] What I consider the true Gothic art was not, indeed, confined strictly within the limits of the Ile de France. The remarkable artistic activity of that centre naturally extended, more or less, as I said long ago (*Development and Character of Gothic Architecture*, second edition, p. 58), into portions of a few contiguous provinces.

[2] Violet le Duc (*Dictionnaire*, etc., s.v. *Construction*, p. 35) says: "Il y a des arcs brisés, au XIIe siècle, par toute l'Europe occidental. Il n'y a de construction Gothique, à cette époque, qu'en France, et sur une petite partie de son territoire actuel." The affirmation applies equally to all later epochs.

it was produced by barbarian Goths. Far otherwise. It was a product of that highly civilized French people, of mingled Latin and Teutonic blood, who derived from the Gothic source those elements of character that were needed to quicken artistic genius in new directions. No other people of the Middle Ages had the same happy ethnographic constitution, or the same fine balance of Southern artistic aptitude and Northern vigour and imagination. I would, therefore, for the sake of clearness, as I said long ago,[1] restrict the use of the term "Gothic" to the French art, using the general term " Pointed" for that architecture of the Middle Ages, whether in England or elsewhere, in which the pointed arch, and other new details, are merely applied to forms of building that retain the structural character of the older art.

But the question of names is of secondary importance. The primary consideration is whether such a fundamental difference as I affirm really exists between the pointed architecture of the Ile de France and all other pointed styles. The question can be determined only by a systematic examination and comparison such as I have attempted in this book.

Since the main body of a mediæval church edifice of the organic type consists of a series of compartments, or bays, which are substantially all alike, in so far as the building is of one epoch, a single bay embodies the essential structural system, and is enough for consideration. I have, therefore, for the sake of limiting the field, confined attention primarily to this structural unit, taking the parts in the order of their importance: the vault,[2] the main supports, the buttress system, the character of the openings, the profilings, and lastly the ornamental carving. I have not, of course, been able to examine every mediæval church in England, but I have examined the greater part of the more important among them, as will be seen. The most admirable architecture of the Middle Ages, both in England and in France, is, in my opinion, that of the twelfth and early thirteenth centuries. After 1250, at latest, the sobriety and monumental simplicity of the early art gave place, more

---

[1] *Ibid.*, p. vii.
[2] Though many mediæval churches were never vaulted, possible vaulting must be considered, since it is with reference to this feature, in logical organic building, that all other parts of the system were designed.

and more, to useless complexity of structure and excessive exuberance of unrefined ornament. I have, however, followed the English art through its various stages of decline, but I have not dwelt on what I regard as its decadence with the same fulness that I have given to its prime. I have not, indeed, treated any part of the subject exhaustively; that would be a task of great magnitude, but I have, I think, done enough to set forth the character of English church architecture in the Middle Ages with substantial thoroughness, and enough to show that the difference between it and the contemporaneous art of the Ile de France is so great, and so fundamental, that the two styles cannot be ranged in the same category on any right principles of classification.

The illustrations in the text are, save in a few cases which are indicated, from my own drawings and from photographs. In the plans, elevations, and sections, I cannot affirm that the measurements are always strictly exact. Measurements on a large scale are difficult to make, especially when one works single handed. Many parts of a great monument are difficult, if not impossible, to reach, and such parts I have taken by eye, helped by reference to other parts that could be measured. For the larger dimensions, as the heights of vaulting, and clerestory and triforium levels, I have used a plumb line — a hole through which it may be dropped being almost always found at the crown of a vault. For lesser heights, I have used a pole or a jointed fishing rod. Only rough measurements can, of course, be got in this way, but such measurements may be accurate enough for illustration. As to irregularities, both of plan and elevation (which are constant, and often surprising, in mediæval work), it is impossible to represent them exactly without great expenditure of time and labour. In a few cases I have given such irregularities with substantial correctness; but for the purely diagrammatic illustrations I have, for the most part, made the usual mechanical drawings. It should, however, be understood that such drawings do not truly represent mediæval architecture, in which there is hardly ever a straight line, or any kind of mechanical exactness. Mediæval building was not done with any scrupulous use of instruments of precision. The setting out and carrying up were governed largely by what is called "rule of thumb." Thus the T-square, the ruling pen, and the compass cannot express the real character of mediæval architecture.

I regret that this book has not had the advantage of revision such as was formerly so freely given by my friend, the late Professor Norton, of Cambridge, Massachusetts. I trust, however, that, whatever its imperfections, it will be found clear in statement and substantially correct.

Wellfield, Hartley Wintney,
    Winchfield, Hants, June, 1912.

# CONTENTS

## CHAPTER I

### THE NORMAN ROMANESQUE

The far-reaching influence of the Norman Romanesque in England — Roman and Saxon building undeveloped architecturally — Slight influence of such building on the Anglo-Norman Romanesque — Transformation of the Norman Romanesque into so-called English Gothic art — Structural inconsistencies of the Norman Romanesque — The vaulting of the nave rare in Norman Romanesque churches — Variety of Norman systems — Uniform and alternate systems in Norman architecture — These systems equally logical, but rarely carried out with consistency in Norman building — Vaulting shafts improperly used in Norman churches — Their manifold structural inconsistencies show that the Normans were not inventive builders — The admirable qualities of Norman architecture qualified by lack of logic — Further examination of the structural character of Norman art — Character of early Norman vaulting in St. Albans, Worcester, and Canterbury — The vaulting of Norman apses — Character of Norman ribbed vaulting in Canterbury, Peterborough, and elsewhere — Survival of Roman features in Anglo-Norman vaulting — Difference between the ribbed Norman vaulting and the ribbed vaulting of the Ile de France — The vaulting of Peterborough compared with that of St. Étienne of Beauvais — The vaulting and system of Durham Cathedral — Imperfect development of supports for ribbed vaulting in Durham — The system of Durham compared with the systems of St. Ambrogio of Milan and the cathedral of Le Mans — The semicircular groin rib in Durham not of Gothic tendency — Neither has the pointed arch in the Durham vaulting any significance in connection with the beginnings of Gothic construction — Composition of the Norman pier — The Norman buttress — The Norman clerestory — The Norman triforium — Norman capitals and bases — Norman profiling — The Norman cornice and corbel-table — Circular Norman buildings . . . . . . . . .   1

PAGE

## CHAPTER II

### POINTED NORMAN

Early changes in the Norman style — No structural significance in the early-twelfth century use of the pointed arch, save in the Ile de France — The pointed arch in England first found in the

Cistercian churches of the North — Its use at Fountains and Kirkstall has little structural significance — No logical system of vault supports connected with it — The aisle vaulting of Malmesbury Abbey — This vaulting compared with that of St. Denis — The system of Roche Abbey — The west bays of Worcester Cathedral — Analysis of the aisle vaulting of these west bays — The vaulting and system of St. Cross, Winchester — French capitals and bases of St. Cross — St. Mary's, New Shoreham — Peculiarities of the system of St. Mary's — Glastonbury Abbey — Combination of French and Anglo-Norman characteristics in the system and details of Glastonbury — Pointed Norman features of the nave of Wells Cathedral — Resemblance of the details of Wells to those of Glastonbury — The choir of Ripon Minster — Transept and nave of Ripon — The Temple Church, London — Lightness of construction in the Temple Church — Analysis of its aisle vaulting — This aisle vaulting compared with that of the apsidal aisle vaulting of Paris — The essentially Norman structural character retained in all pointed Normal design — No complete organic system developed in any pointed Norman structures . . . . . . . . . .   45

## CHAPTER III

### The Choir of Canterbury

The choir of Canterbury — The early French Gothic system largely embodied in this work — Relation of Canterbury to Sens — The French architect handicapped by the Norman remains — No exact conformity with Sens — The vaulting of Canterbury compared with that of Sens — The system of supports not so logical as that of Sens — Improvements eastward of the transept — The compound pier of William of Sens derived from French sources — The pier of coupled columns — Other peculiarities of the work east of the transept — The vaulting of the aisles — Awkwardnesses in this vaulting resulting from the Norman remains — Use of the round arch in the aisle vaulting and in the archivolts opening into the transept — Irregularities resulting from lack of conformity of the new piers with the Norman responds — The triforium arcade compared with that of Sens — The Norman passageway in the clerestory — Analysis of the cross-section of the choir — Peculiarities of the buttress system — Survival of the tribune gallery in the south triforium — Profiling not of purely French type — Exceptional forms of capitals and bases in the Eastern transept — The whole work, though of mixed character, dominated by the early French principles of design and construction — Withdrawal of the French architect . . . . .   70

## CHAPTER IV

### TRINITY CHAPEL

Evidence that the eastern extension of Canterbury was planned by the French architect — Remarks of Willis on the work of the English architect — Relation of the east end of Canterbury to that of Sens — French character of the corona — Remarks of Gervase on the corona — First work of English William — Slight resemblance of the eastern crypt to the work of William of Sens — Plan and system of the eastern crypt — Evidence that it was begun by William of Sens — French conformation of the vaulting — Peculiarities of the vaulting of the apse — Peculiar features of the apsidal aisle vaults — Comparison with those of Sens — French profiling of the vault ribs — Style of Trinity Chapel — This style follows that of William of Sens in the choir — Plan of Trinity Chapel — Character of its vaulting and vault supports — Round archivolts in the great arcade of English William — The triforium arcade follows that of the French architect in the easternmost bay of the choir — Features of the apsidal aisles of Trinity Chapel — Round arches in the vaulting of these aisles — The aisle vaulting of Sens compared — Peculiarities of planning in the imposts of the great archivolts of the apse — Imposts of Sens compared — Vaulting of the corona — French capitals and bases of the whole eastern extension — Mistaken affirmations of English style in the work of English William . . . .  90

## CHAPTER V

### BEGINNINGS OF EARLY ENGLISH

Further changes of style in the rebuilding of Chichester Cathedral — Strong Anglo-Norman character manifest in the new details of Chichester — Vaulting of the nave — Compound pier at east end of this work — Mingled French and Anglo-Norman features of this pier — First use of corbels to support vaulting shafts — Earliest examples of Early English capitals — St. Hugh's rebuilding of the east end of Lincoln Cathedral — Some of the finest features of the Early English style developed here — Plan of St. Hugh's choir and transept — Demolition of the apse — Vaulting and vaulting system of the transept — The ground-story piers derived from Canterbury — Profiling and foliation of St. Hugh's capitals — Purity of style in the exterior of this transept — Its derivation from Canterbury — Vaulting and system of St. Hugh's choir — New rib profiling — Cross-section of this choir compared with that of Canterbury — The ground-story pier in its original form — The aisle vaulting — Features from Canterbury embodied in this aisle — Corbelling of vaulting shafts in this aisle — Mingled French and Anglo-Norman features in the wall arcade — The triforium scheme — Superfluous shafts in this triforium — Survival of Norman character in the clerestory — Likeness of the buttress system to that of Canterbury — Mistaken notion that St. Hugh's choir exhibits a new and independent architectural style — Short-sighted remarks of Freeman, Viollet le Duc, and Parker — Further development of the Early English style in the details of the east end of Rochester Cathedral — Norman characteristics of this east end — Vaulting of the Presbytery and transept . . . . . . . . . . . 109

## CHAPTER VI

### The Early English Style

The nave of Lincoln — Its marked expression of Anglo-Norman proclivities in design — Multiplication of superfluous ribs in its vaulting foreshadowing the Perpendicular style — The characteristic misadjustment of vaulting shafts established — The ground-story pier not provided with members for the ribs of the high vaulting — Increase of ornamental elaboration — The five-celled vaulting of the aisles shows improvement on that of the choir — The cross-section reproduces that of the choir save for curtailments tending away from the principles of Gothic — The profiling follows that of the choir with some variations — Multiplication of fillets in the foliation of capitals — Salisbury Cathedral — The scheme of Lincoln traceable in Salisbury — Close similarity of plan — No organic skeleton in Salisbury — Its Norman wall construction associated with Early English details — The vaulting not of Early English character — Degradation of profiling in the bases of the ground-story piers — The triforium scheme a variant of that of Lincoln nave — Crossing piers variants of those of Canterbury — Vaulting of the aisles and treatment of the aisle walls — Homogeneous style of the interior as a whole — No buttress system of a Gothic kind — Excessive attenuation of supports in the east end — Beverley Minster — Vaulting and internal system of Beverley — Prevalence of the moulded capital in this work — Differences of springing level in Early English vaulting discussed — The Buttress system of Beverley — Worcester Cathedral — Worcester east end the purest example of Early English style — Yet it is essentially a Norman Romanesque structure — Deplorable mutilation and restoration of Worcester — Vaulting and system of its Early English part — Members without function in the ground-story pier — Features of the triforium and the clerestory — Extensive use of moulded capitals — Character of the openings — Sculpture of the arcades — Profil-

# CONTENTS

PAGE

ings — Scheme of the choir — The buttressing — York Minster — Features of the transept derived from Lincoln and Salisbury — Scheme of Whitby choir — The Early English style culminates in the foregoing monuments — The features of Lincoln nave form the basis of them all — Exceptional scheme of Pershore Abbey — Peculiarities in the vaulting of Pershore — External features of the Early English style . . . . 132

## CHAPTER VII

### THE CHOIR OF WESTMINSTER

Strong and direct French influence manifest in Westminster — A work, however, of Anglo-Norman builders — Influence of Reims and Amiens on the choir and transept — Planning of the apse and apsidal chapels — The elevation French in leading lines and proportions, and Early English in details — French Gothic character of its high vaulting — Construction of the vaulting imposts — Illogical adjustment of the vault supports — Early English character of the ground-story piers — Analysis of the cross-section — Survival of the tribune gallery in the triforium — This feature inconsistent with the bay scheme of developed Gothic Art, which is reproduced in Westminster — Peculiarity of the triforium arcade — Comparison of the structural forms of the triforium and clerestory with those of French Gothic monuments — The ground-story enclosure compared with that of Reims — Anglo-Norman character of the great arcade of the apse — The mullioned openings — The profiling . . . . . . 149

## CHAPTER VIII

### THE LATER POINTED ART

Slight influence of the larger features of Westminster on subsequent architectural design in England — The presbytery of Lincoln — The finer inspiration of the early art not manifest in this work — General decline of architecture after the early part of the thirteenth century — Analysis of the structural system of the presbytery — Proneness of English builders to work away from organic structure shown further in the buttress system — Mullions and tracery of the presbytery derived from Westminster — The Norman clerestory with the passageway — The great eastern opening — Contrast of the ornate design of the presbytery with the monumental simplicity of the earlier work — Character of the foliation — Merits of the exterior — Sculpture of the south portal — The nave of Lichfield Cathedral — Its proportions — Ravages of restoration — Omission of the transverse rib in its vaulting — Supports rise from the pavement — But no complete organic system developed — Clerestory openings derived from the triforium of Westminster — Redundance of ornamental details — Degradation in the forms of capitals — Transept of Hereford Cathedral — Influence of Westminster — Analysis of its vaulting — Its segmental arches — Resemblance of its clerestory to that of Lichfield — System of the west side — Pier and vaulting shafts of the east side — Profiling of pier bases — Choir and east end of old St. Paul's Cathedral — Influence of Westminster on this work — The choir of Exeter — Approach to fan vaulting in the conoid section — Possible forms of conoid governed by the number, curvature, and adjustment of the ribs in vaulting — The nave of York Minster — Combination of clerestory and triforium in its bay scheme — French origin of this peculiarity — Remarks of Willis — Increase of ornamental elaboration — Sinuous tracery in openings of the west front — The nave of Worcester — New feature in its vaulting — Further growth of factitious and florid character in the Octagon of Ely — The wooden ceiling of this octagon not on Gothic principles — Incongruity of the enlarged space at the crossing of such a building — Its possible derivation from Siena — Analysis of details — Vaulting of Ely choir — Details of the choir system . . . . . . . 161

## CHAPTER IX

### THE PERPENDICULAR STYLE

Havoc wrought in the fourteenth century on the buildings of earlier epochs — Summary of features in the earlier art leading toward the perpendicular style — Remodelling of the transept and choir of Gloucester — Perpendicular vaulting of the choir — Details of the choir elevation — The great eastern opening — Rebuilding of the choir of York Minster — The eastern enclosure — New features of the exterior — Buttressing of the choir — Remodelling of the nave of Winchester — The work of Bishop Edingdon — The work of William of Wykeham — Influence of Gloucester choir on Wykeham's design — New form of window arch — New form of profiling — Analysis of Wykeham's alterations in the Norman bays — The vaulting — Forms of capitals — The buttressing — The nave of Canterbury — Its probable derivation from Winchester — Homogeneous character of the work — Survival of Romanesque tradition — New rib profiling — Analysis of the cross-section — Form of the pier — The aisle openings — General proportions — The church of St. Mary Redcliffe, Bristol — Character of its vaulting — Composition of the pier — Features of the archivolts — The triforium and clerestory — The vaulting of Norwich Cathedral — The vaulting of St. George's Chapel, Windsor — Development of fan vaulting in the cloister of Gloucester — Willis's definition of fan vaulting — The designer now governed by science of construction — Vaulting in the Perpendicular style is architectural jugglery — The van vaulting of Peterborough — The vaulting of King's College Chapel, Cambridge — The vaulting of Sherborne nave — The bay scheme of Sherborne — Vaulting and system of Bath Abbey — External aspect of Bath Abbey — Vaulting of Henry VII's Chapel, Westminster — Involved construction and vulgar ornamentation of this vaulting — The choir vault of Oxford Cathedral . . . 182

## CHAPTER X

### TIMBER ROOFS

Timber roofs of the Middle Ages of three kinds — Analysis of the truss — The function of the tie beam — Truss of Grasmere — English tendency to omit the tie beam — Truss of Charney, Berkshire — Variety of ornamental framing in English roofs of the Middle Ages — Truss of Ely transept — Omission of collar beams in English trusses — The hammer beam — Truss of Brinton, Norfolk — Truss of St. Stephen's, Norwich — Unreasoned composition of the truss of March, Cambridgeshire — Truss of Wandswell Court, Gloucester — Use of knee timbers — Truss of Sutton Courtenay, Berkshire — Truss of Nursted Court, Kent — Truss of Malvern Priory — Wastefulness of forms which omit the tie beam — The roof of Westminster Hall — True principles of timber construction embodied in the roofs of the basilican churches of Rome — Properly trussed roofs require neither thick walls nor buttresses — Truss of St. Michael's Coventry — Truss of St. Margaret's, Westminster — True form of truss at Chipping Norton, Oxfordshire — No need for shafts to support timber roofs — Use of corbels and templates under trusses — Truss of San Francesco of Siena . . . . . . . 208

## CHAPTER XI

### CONCLUDING SUMMARY

Persistence of Norman principles in the art of England — Merits of the Early English style — The Early English style not a copy of French Gothic — Relation of Lincoln to Salisbury — Rickman's description of the Early English style — Sharpe's description of the same — Summary of the distinctive features of the Early English style — The ideal of Early English — The Early English style never completely embodied in any single monument — Duration of the Early English style — Its essential difference from the Gothic of the Ile de France illustrated by a comparison of Amiens and Salisbury — The possibilities of the Early English style never fully worked out — Decline of Mediæval art in England . . . . . . . . . . 218

## LIST OF ILLUSTRATIONS

| FIG. | | PAGE |
|---|---|---|
| 1. | St. Albans — Plans of Aisle Vaults | 5 |
| 2. | Worcester — Plan of Vault of Crypt | 6 |
| 3. | Worcester — Capital and Impost of Crypt | 6 |
| 4. | Worcester — Profiles of Bases | 7 |
| 5. | Worcester — Part Plan of Crypt | 8 |
| 6. | Canterbury — Plan of Crypt Vault | 9 |
| 7. | Canterbury — Cross-Section of Crypt Vault | 10 |
| 8. | Canterbury — Plan of Apsidal Aisle Vault of Crypt | 12 |
| 9. | Canterbury — Cross-Section of Apsidal Aisle Vault of Crypt | 13 |
| 10. | Tower of London — Plan of Apsidal Aisle Vault, St. Joseph's Chapel | 14 |
| 11. | Canterbury — Vault of St. Andrew's Chapel | 15 |
| 12. | Romsey — Vault of Apse | 17 |
| 13. | Christchurch — Plan of Apse Vault | 17 |
| 14. | Christchurch — Vault of Apse | 18 |
| 15. | Christchurch — Imposts of Apse | 19 |
| 16. | Christchurch — Plan of Crypt | 20 |
| 17. | Christchurch — Part Elevation of Crypt | 20 |
| 18. | Canterbury — Plan of Vault under Treasury | 21 |
| 19. | Canterbury — Cross-Section of Vault under Treasury | 22 |
| 20. | Diagram of Vault Construction | 27 |
| 21. | Geometrical Diagram of Vault Construction | 28 |
| 22. | Durham — Longitudinal Section of Nave Vaulting | 29 |
| 23. | Norwich — Section of Main Pier of Nave | 31 |
| 24. | Norwich — Elevation of Nave Pier | 31 |
| 25. | Norwich — Section of Intermediate Pier of Nave | 32 |
| 26. | Ely — Cross-Sections of Nave Piers | 32 |
| 27. | Peterborough — Section of Nave Pier | 33 |
| 28. | Romsey — Section of Nave Pier | 33 |
| 29. | Canterbury — Infirmary Pier | 33 |
| 30. | Malvern — Impost of Nave Pier | 34 |
| 31. | Rochester — Sections of Nave Piers | 35 |
| 32. | Jumièges — Section of Clerestory | 36 |
| 33. | Abbaye aux Hommes — Section of Clerestory | 37 |
| 34. | Romsey — Triforium Opening | 38 |
| 35. | Lincoln — Early Norman Capitals | 39 |
| 36. | Christchurch — Capitals of Crossing Pier | 40 |
| 37. | Christchurch — Capitals of Triforium | 40 |
| 38. | Abbaye aux Hommes — Profile of Base | 41 |
| 39. | Tewkesbury and Canterbury — Profiles of Bases | 41 |
| 40. | Durham — Base of Main Pier of Nave | 42 |
| 41. | Peterborough, Durham, and Christchurch — Rib Profiles | 42 |

## LIST OF ILLUSTRATIONS

| FIG. | | PAGE |
|---|---|---|
| 42. | Profiles of Norman String Courses . . . . . . | 43 |
| 43. | Fountains — Vaulting of Aisles . . . . . . | 46 |
| 44. | Kirkstall — Vaulting of Aisle, from photograph published by Bilson | 48 |
| 45. | Malmesbury — Plan of Aisle Vault . . . . . . | 49 |
| 46. | Malmesbury — Cross-Section of Aisle Vault . . . . | 50 |
| 47. | St. Denis — Vaulting and System of Apsidal Aisle, from photograph | 51 |
| 48. | Worcester — Clerestory of West Bay . . . . . | 52 |
| 49. | Worcester — Capital of West Bay . . . . . . | 53 |
| 50. | Worcester — Plan of Aisle Vault of West Bay . . . | 54 |
| 51. | Worcester — Section of Conoid, Vault of West Bay . . | 55 |
| 52. | Worcester — Springing of Aisle Vault, West Bay . . . | 56 |
| 53. | Worcester — Plan of Vault in Cloister Passageway . . . | 58 |
| 54. | Worcester — Springing of Vault in Cloister Passageway . . | 58 |
| 55. | St. Cross — Rib Profiles . . . . . . . | 59 |
| 56. | St. Cross — Ribs of Vault . . . . . . . | 59 |
| 57. | St. Cross — Section of Transverse Rib . . . . . | 60 |
| 58. | St. Cross — Section of Vault Supports . . . . . | 60 |
| 59. | St. Cross — Capital of North Aisle . . . . . | 60 |
| 60. | St. Cross — Base of North Aisle . . . . . . | 61 |
| 61. | New Shoreham — Capital of Pier . . . . . . | 61 |
| 62. | New Shoreham — Compound Pier Capital . . . . | 62 |
| 63. | Glastonbury — Rib Profile . . . . . . . | 63 |
| 64. | Wells — Rib Profile . . . . . . . . | 64 |
| 65. | Wells — Base Profile . . . . . . . . | 65 |
| 66. | Temple Church — Archivolt Profile . . . . . | 67 |
| 67. | Temple Church — Plan of Aisle Vault . . . . . | 68 |
| 68. | Canterbury — Plan of Choir and East End, from Willis . . | 72 |
| 69. | Laon — Pier of Nave, from Viollet le Duc . . . . | 76 |
| 70. | Sens — Triforium Arcade, from Viollet le Duc . . . | 80 |
| 71. | Canterbury — Cross-Section of Choir . . . . . | 82 |
| 72. | Senlis — Rib Profiles . . . . . . . . | 83 |
| 73. | Sens — Rib Profiles . . . . . . . . | 83 |
| 74. | Canterbury — Rib Profiles . . . . . . . | 84 |
| 75. | Canterbury — Anglo-Norman Capitals of Transept . . | 85 |
| 76. | Canterbury — Anglo-Norman Profiling of Archivolts . . | 86 |
| 77. | Canterbury — Base of Choir . . . . . . . | 87 |
| 78. | Canterbury — Anglo-Norman Base of Transept . . . | 88 |
| 79. | Canterbury — Rib Profiles of Eastern Crypt . . . . | 93 |
| 80. | Canterbury — Plan of Apsidal Aisle Vault, Eastern Crypt . | 94 |
| 81. | Canterbury — Cross-Section of Apsidal Aisle Vault, Eastern Crypt . | 95 |
| 82. | Sens — Plan of Apsidal Aisle Vault, from photograph . . | 96 |
| 83. | Canterbury and Sens — Rib Profiles . . . . . | 96 |
| 84. | Canterbury — Plan of Trinity Chapel . . . . . | 98 |
| 85. | Canterbury — Cross-Section of Trinity Chapel . . . | 102 |
| 86. | Canterbury — Plan of Apsidal Aisle Vault . . . . | 103 |
| 87. | Canterbury — Cross-Section of Apsidal Aisle Vault . . | 104 |
| 88. | Sens — Plan of Impost of Apse Pier . . . . . | 105 |

# LIST OF ILLUSTRATIONS xxi

| FIG. | | PAGE |
|---|---|---|
| 89. | Canterbury — Base of Trinity Chapel | 106 |
| 90. | Canterbury — Profile of Base, Trinity Chapel | 107 |
| 91. | Chichester — Section of Vault Conoid | 110 |
| 92. | Chichester — Rib Profiles | 111 |
| 93. | Chichester — Section of Vaulting Shafts | 111 |
| 94. | Chichester — Capital of Aisle | 112 |
| 95. | Lincoln — Plan of East End | 114 |
| 96. | Lincoln — Outline of Clerestory Arch | 116 |
| 97. | Lincoln — Profile of Base | 116 |
| 98. | Lincoln — Capital of East Transept | 118 |
| 99. | Lincoln — Plan of Choir Vault | 119 |
| 100. | Lincoln — Rib Profiles | 120 |
| 101. | Lincoln — Cross-Section of Choir | 121 |
| 102. | Lincoln — Pier of Choir, from photograph | 122 |
| 103. | Lincoln — Section of Choir Pier | 122 |
| 104. | Lincoln — Capital of Choir Aisle | 124 |
| 105. | Lincoln — Capital of Choir Aisle | 125 |
| 106. | Lincoln — Profile of Triforium Archivolt | 126 |
| 107. | Rochester — Plan of Eastern Transept and Presbytery | 130 |
| 108. | Lincoln — Plan of Nave Vault | 133 |
| 109. | Lincoln — Section of Vault Conoid | 133 |
| 110. | Lincoln — Pier Sections | 134 |
| 111. | Lincoln — Capital of Triforium of Nave | 136 |
| 112. | Salisbury — Rib Profiles | 137 |
| 113. | Salisbury — Triforium and Clerestory, from photograph | 138 |
| 114. | Salisbury — Profile of Base | 139 |
| 115. | Worcester — Rib Profiles | 145 |
| 116. | Reims — Part Plan of East End, corrected from Viollet le Duc | 149 |
| 117. | Westminster — Part Plan of East End, from Lethaby | 150 |
| 118. | Amiens — Part Plan of East End, from Viollet le Duc | 151 |
| 119. | Westminster — Cross-Section of Choir, inner part from Vacher | 154 |
| 120. | Westminster — Pier Section at Triforium Level | 156 |
| 121. | Reims — Cross-Section of Aisle Enclosure, from Viollet le Duc | 157 |
| 122. | Amiens — Springing of Apsidal Aisle Vault, from Viollet le Duc | 158 |
| 123. | Lincoln — Rib Profiles and Impost Plan of Presbytery | 163 |
| 124. | Hereford — Rib Profiles | 167 |
| 125. | Hereford — Section of Vault Conoid | 168 |
| 126. | Hereford — Pier Section | 169 |
| 127. | Hereford — Profile of Base | 170 |
| 128. | Diagrams — Showing Possible Forms of Conoid Sections | 171 |
| 129. | St. Germain des Prés — Clerestory, from photograph | 173 |
| 130. | Worcester — Vaulting Conoid of Nave, from photograph | 175 |
| 131. | Ely — Plan of Choir Vault | 179 |
| 132. | Winchester — Brace Profile of Nave | 189 |
| 133. | Winchester — Bays of Nave, from Willis | 190 |
| 134. | Winchester — Plan of Norman Nave Pier, from Willis | 191 |
| 135. | Canterbury — Rib Profiles of Nave | 193 |

## LIST OF ILLUSTRATIONS

| FIG. | | PAGE |
|---|---|---|
| 136. | Canterbury — Cross-Section of Nave | 194 |
| 137. | Canterbury — Plan of Nave Pier | 195 |
| 138. | Gloucester — Vaulting Conoid of Cloister | 199 |
| 139. | Sherborne — Plan of Nave Vault | 202 |
| 140. | Westminster — Section of Vault, Henry VII's Chapel, from Willis | 205 |
| 141. | Diagram of Trussing | 208 |
| 142. | Grasmere — Truss | 209 |
| 143. | Charney, Berkshire — Truss, from Viollet le Duc | 210 |
| 144. | Ely — Truss, from Viollet le Duc | 211 |
| 145. | March, Cambridgeshire — Truss, from photograph published by Bond | 212 |
| 146. | Diagram of Truss, from Viollet le Duc | 213 |
| 147. | Wandswell Court, Gloucester — Truss, from Parker | 213 |
| 148. | Hall of Sutton Courtenay, Berkshire — Truss, from Parker | 214 |
| 149. | Malvern Priory — Truss, from Viollet le Duc | 215 |

# LIST OF PLATES

| PLATE | | PAGE |
|---|---|---|
| I. | Apse Vault of St. Germer de Fly | 19 |
| II. | Aisle of St. Étienne, Beauvais | 23 |
| III. | Aisle of Peterborough | 24 |
| IV. | Nave of St. Ambrogio, Milan | 26 |
| V. | Nave of Durham | 27 |
| VI. | Nave of Le Mans | 30 |
| VII. | Glastonbury Abbey | 62 |
| VIII. | Temple Church, London | 67 |
| IX. | Clerestory of Canterbury Choir | 74 |
| X. | Pier of Canterbury Choir | 75 |
| XI. | Triforium of Canterbury Choir | 78 |
| XII. | Eastern Crypt of Canterbury | 92 |
| XIII. | French Pier, Canterbury Crypt | 94 |
| XIV. | Apsidal Aisle of Trinity Chapel, Canterbury | 103 |
| XV. | Apsidal Aisle of Sens | 104 |
| XVI. | Capital of Wall Arcade, Lincoln | 123 |
| XVII. | System of Lincoln Choir | 124 |
| XVIII. | Presbytery of Rochester | 128 |
| XIX. | System of Lincoln Nave | 133 |
| XX. | Eastern System of Worcester | 142 |
| XXI. | System of Lincoln Presbytery | 161 |
| XXII. | Nave of York Minster | 172 |
| XXIII. | Choir of Gloucester | 182 |

# MEDIÆVAL CHURCH ARCHITECTURE

## CHAPTER I

### THE NORMAN ROMANESQUE

WHEN by the Conquest of 1066 the primitive church building of England was brought to an end, and a new style of Architecture was introduced by the conquerors, a far-reaching influence was established in the country. The Norman Romanesque of the eleventh and early twelfth centuries not only covered the land with monuments of imposing grandeur, but gave ideas and methods of design and construction which became deeply rooted, and from which the English builders of the Middle Ages never wholly departed. It was long before this foreign art was even superficially modified either by new continental influences or by local ideas.[1] The older church building of the island — Roman and Saxon, both of rude provincial basilican type — was too undeveloped architecturally to act with material effect on the stronger art from overseas. About the middle of the twelfth century, however, new influences began to operate, and thereafter superficial changes were wrought which at length transformed this architecture into the pointed style commonly called English Gothic. Thus in order to understand this pointed style (a style, as we shall see, fundamentally different in character from the true Gothic art, which I conceive to be exclusively French) it will be necessary to examine the Anglo-Norman Romanesque to follow the changes wrought on its primitive forms, to discover what we can of the influences that governed

---

[1] Such modifications of plan as monastic requirements — Benedictine, Augustinian, or other — gave rise to constitute no essential change in the architectural system.

these changes, and to observe how radically the art differs at all stages of the transformation from the French Gothic art.

The Norman Romanesque, notwithstanding its grandeur, and even its nobility, from many points of view, has not the consistent character of the most logical types of that widely distributed Romanesque of Western Europe of which it is a variety.[1] Its structural inconsistencies are manifold, and are found in the most important members and adjustments. For instance, the naves of Norman churches are rarely vaulted, yet in most cases they are furnished with shafts which have no use apart from vaulting, and these shafts are, as a rule, carried up to the top of the wall, where vaulting could not spring, and are thus without function.

The structural schemes of Norman churches are of considerable variety. In some instances we find a uniform system of piers and vaulting shafts; the members, magnitudes, and groupings of which are the same throughout the series, as at Winchester,[2] Peterborough, and Romsey.[3] In others there is a difference in the magnitudes and members of the piers in rhythmical alternation, as at Ely, Norwich, and Waltham; while in still others, as at Gloucester, Southwell, and Tewkesbury, no vaulting members occur, and the nave, like that of a basilican structure, has no division into bays and no organic composition. The uniform and alternate systems in vaulted buildings of the

[1] What is called Romanesque Architecture in Western Europe is broadly divided into two types, which may be called respectively the inorganic and the organic. The inorganic type is that in which the structural forms of the timber-roofed basilica, with its unbroken walls and continuous arcades, survive, while the organic, in its complete development, has ribbed vaulting on functionally compound supports, breaking the building into a series of compartments, or bays. Both are of many varieties, but of the latter type only two, I believe, are strictly organic, *i.e.* have a complete system of functional members, logically related and extending through the whole building; namely, the Lombard Romanesque and the Romanesque of the Ile de France. Such others as the Rhenish, the Burgundian, and the Norman, are incompletely and imperfectly organic, and their manifold inconsistencies appear to me to show that they were largely short-sighted imitations of the true organic types.

[2] The nave of Winchester in its original form.

[3] There is often a break in the Norman uniform system, as in the nave of Peterborough, where at the west end a double bay occurs with its main piers of larger magnitude than the others of the series; and in the nave of Romsey, where the pier next to the crossing pier is a plain round column reaching into the triforium, while the others are compound.

Middle Ages are equally logical, and depend respectively on the form of vaulting to be provided for. The uniform system arises where each compartment of the high vaulting covers only one bay of the structure, and the alternate system comes into being where vaults, each embracing two of these bays, are to be supported. But in Norman monuments the logic of these respective systems is not often observed. For not only are vaulting shafts seldom used for vaulting, being, as we have seen, carried up so high that they could not, without alteration, be so used, but they are frequently introduced in other illogical ways. In the nave of Ely, for instance, the piers are alternately large and small, and for the only kind of vaulting for which they are adapted (that could, at the time of its construction, have been thought of), namely quadripartite vaulting in compartments, each embracing two bays, no shafts would be required in the smaller piers, since these piers would take no part in the support of such vaulting. Yet shafts are attached to these piers precisely as in the larger ones — the vaulting members in each consisting of a pilaster strip and an engaged column. In other words, we have at Ely the vaulting members of a uniform system incorporated with the piers of an alternate system, which is illogical. A consistent alternate system for quadripartite vaulting is found in the nave of the Cathedral of Durham where no shafts occur in the smaller piers.[1] But in Norman alternate systems the logic of Durham is seldom found. In Waltham Abbey, for instance, the logic of the scheme is violated by the introduction of a vaulting shaft in the smaller pier rising from the triforium string,[2] and in the nave of Norwich a shaft rising from the pavement is incorporated with the smaller pier.[3] This last is, however, not a vaulting shaft, but a shaft for the support of the first order of the triforium arcade, such as we find in some of the Rhenish Romanesque churches. These, and many other structural inconsistencies show, I think, that the Normans were

---

[1] The vaulting of Durham does not, however, conform to the alternate scheme, as will be seen further on.

[2] For sexpartite vaulting this shaft would be, of course, entirely logical.

[3] M. Ruprich-Robert (*Architecture Normande*, p. 144) says of Norwich: " Les dispositions generales de ce dernier monument font voir d'une maniere certain qu'il a ete construit pour recevoir des voutes sexpartite." I think he is mistaken, for the shaft here introduced in the smaller pier is, as stated in the text, a mere arcade shaft.

not inventive builders, but that their art was, on its structural side, an imperfect imitation of a more logical system the principles of which they did not comprehend.[1] Builders who had themselves invented such members as we find in Norman monuments would, I think, know better how to use them. They would neither make their shafts useless for vaulting by carrying them so high, nor make such extensive preparation while so rarely constructing high vaults. However this may be, the facts are as we see.

But Norman architecture has admirable qualities, notwithstanding that it is so extensively lacking in structural logic. Among these qualities are, it appears to me, noble proportions, robust dignity of expression, and monumental breadth of appropriate, effective, and thoroughly architectural enrichment, where enrichment is given. These are qualities of great art, but in the greatest art such qualities are based on logic of construction, as they are not in Norman architecture. To an eye quick to perceive functional relations the great merits of Norman buildings are thus materially qualified, however much, in respect to their finer qualities, we may admire them.

Let us examine somewhat more fully the structural characteristics of this architecture in order to understand better what they really are, and to see, later on, how far these characteristics survive in the pointed style which followed it. We may begin with such vaulting as occurs. While vaulting is rare over naves, there is much of it in crypts, in aisles, and in a few cases vaulted apses of noteworthy character are found. The most of it is groined vaulting, in which the ancient Roman idea of intersecting cylindrical surfaces so far prevails as to give nearly level crowns and approximately semi-elliptical groins. These vaults are built of ragstone, and are usually covered with plaster. In execution they exhibit little precision — the

[1] I think there can be little doubt that Norman architecture from the middle of the eleventh century, was mainly derived from the Lombard Romanesque, and that the earlier Norman alternate systems, as those of Jumiéges and the Abbaye aux Hommes, show a direct influence from Lombardy. M. Ruprich-Robert (op. cit., p. 74) has affirmed this, and given substantial grounds for it. The objections to this view that have been raised by M. Lefèvre-Pontalis and others, appear to me without force, and inconsistent with the evidence afforded by the monuments themselves.

groins being very irregular on plan, as at A, Fig. 1, from the north choir aisle of St. Albans, where they do not meet at the crown. It will also be seen that in this, and in the plan B from the south aisle, the groins are irregularly sinuous. In these instances the crowns of the cells incline downward a little from the bounding arches to the centre of the vault. The compartments are slightly oblong, measuring roughly 5 by 5.18 metres, and are separated one from another by shallow and very wide transverse ribs. The ribs are carried on pilaster strips with a second order supporting the groins. These vaults are, I believe, among the earliest Norman vaults in England,

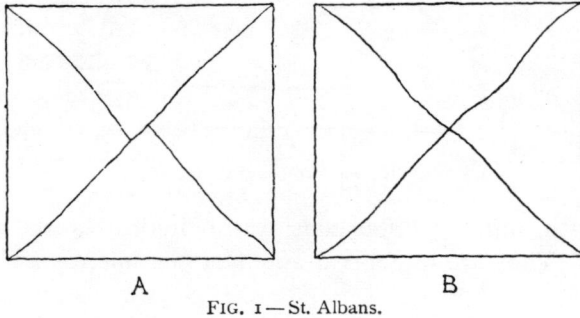

A        B
FIG. 1 — St. Albans.

but more or less of the same rudeness of construction characterizes all Norman vaulting.

Other examples of this vaulting are found in the great crypts of Winchester, Worcester, Gloucester, and Canterbury. These crypts all have eastern apses with apsidal aisles, and the vaults of the aisles exhibit peculiarities, growing out of the curved plan, some of which we may notice presently. The rectangular vaults are very irregular in the setting out (as most mediæval work is), and their opposite sides are rarely of equal length. The vault, Fig. 2, of the crypt of Worcester, for instance, is as nearly square on plan as will usually be found, but there is a difference of 19 centimetres in the lengths of its axes. The compartment is enclosed by ribs of rectangular section, which are roughly semicircular in elevation and somewhat stilted, or of horseshoe form. The rib A of this compartment has a radius of $87\frac{1}{2}$ centimetres, while its crown is 1.07 metres above the capital, and it is stilted on one side and horseshoe shaped, as at *a*, on the other. The ribs vary greatly in width at different parts of

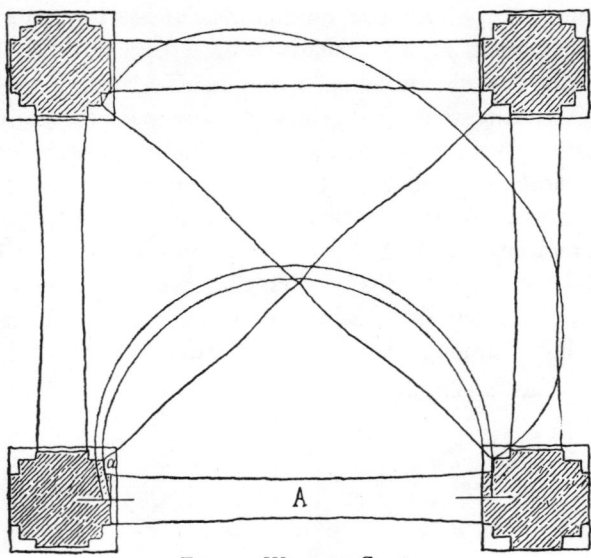

FIG. 2 — Worcester Crypt.

their length, and they differ considerably in this respect one from another. They are in general about 25 centimetres wide at the springing, and narrow irregularly to about 20 centimetres at the crown. The vault at the point of intersection of the groins is 2 centimetres lower than at the outer ends of the cells, and the groins are, as usual, irregularly sinuous on plan, and distorted semi-ellipses in elevation. A single round column supports each angle of the compartment in common with the corresponding parts of the adjoining compartments, and the capitals of these columns are of the common Norman cushion form, varied in some of them by having the rounded part hollowed under the angles

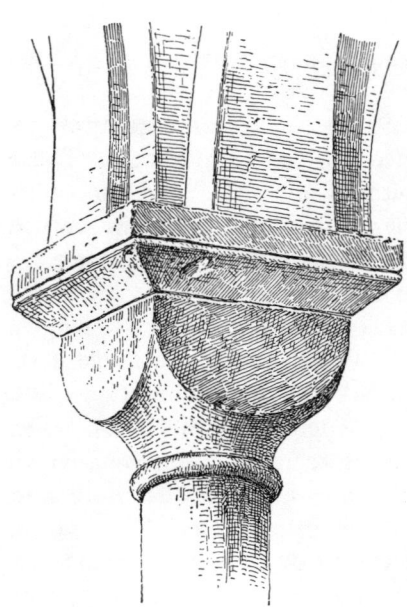

FIG. 3 — Worcester Crypt.

so as to produce an ogee outline in the oblique view (Fig. 3). The base profiles are, for the most part, as at A, Fig. 4, but some of them are more elaborately moulded, as at B. Since the vaulting of the crypt supports the pavement of the choir and apse of the church above,[1] it requires (Fig. 5) a central row of columns from which the compartments of the apse radiate. Of these apsidal compartments those of the inner series are thus triangular on plan, and the others trapezoidal. The radiating

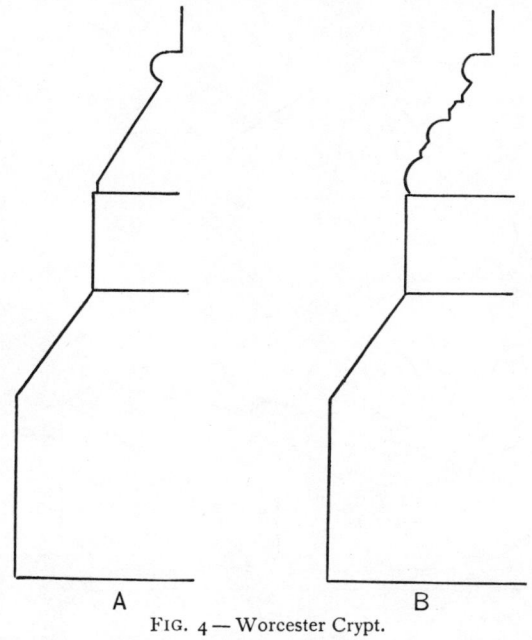

FIG. 4 — Worcester Crypt.

ribs follow the shapes of the compartments, their sides being radii of the curve on which the apse is set out. They are thus narrow on plan where they start from the easternmost column, and widen outward. The abaci of the capitals of the columns standing on the curve between the two series of compartments are wedge-shaped in conformity with the general plan. It will be seen that the trapezoidal compartments are straight on plan on their inner and outer sides, instead of curving with the apse as such vaults usually do — the arches on these sides being in planes like those on the other two sides;

[1] The Norman east end of the church was apsidal in correspondence with the crypt.

but the groins, since they are produced by the interpenetration of cone-shaped surfaces with those of an annular barrel vault, are sinuous curves on plan. The vaults of the inner series are naturally tripartite, and thus each has a straight groin from the central column to the centre of the compartment, and two curved ones. It will be noticed also that, in consequence of the shapes of the respective interpenetrating surfaces, the points of

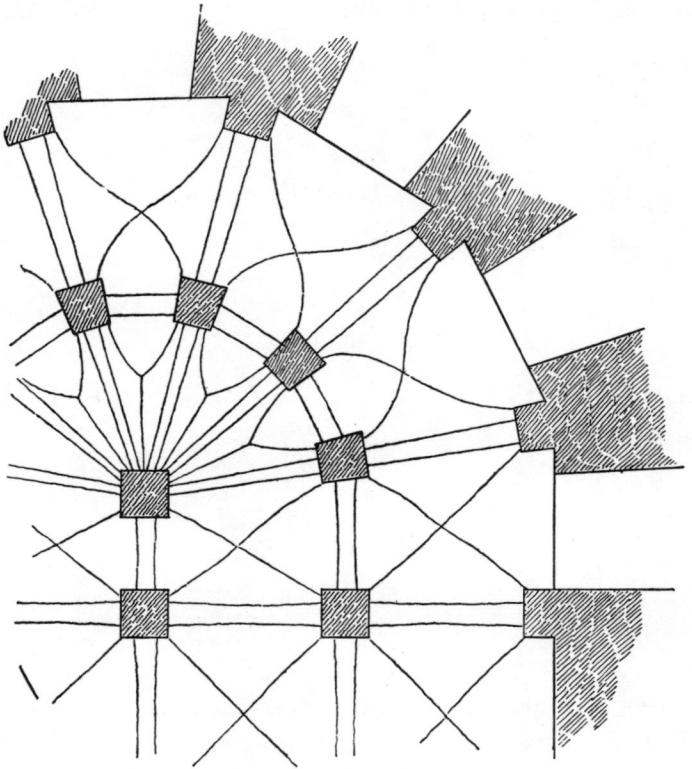

FIG. 5 — Worcester Crypt.

intersection of the groins of the quadripartite compartments are nearer the inner than the outer sides of these compartments. The arches on the narrow sides are stilted in order to bring their crowns up to about the same level as the crowns of the wider spanned ones on the opposite sides, and the points where the triangular vaults meet the central column are placed at the same level, so that the crowns of both series of vaults, in the direction of the radii, are in nearly straight horizontal lines. In other respects the apsidal aisle vaults are like the rectangular ones already described.

The vaults of the Norman crypt of Canterbury are generally less rude in construction than those of St. Albans and Worcester. They are for the most part in square compartments, and present no peculiar features, but an oblong one at the west end of the central aisle[1] has some noticeable peculiarities. This compartment (Fig. 6) measures 3.85 by 2.37 metres on plan from centre

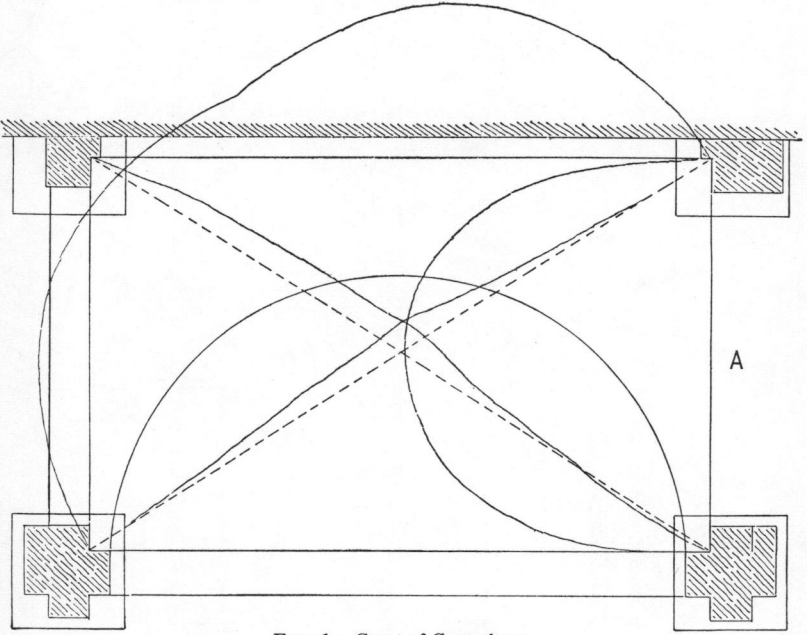

FIG. 6 — Crypt of Canterbury.

to centre of its supports. The vault has little of the character of oblong vaulting with strictly cylindrical surfaces, in which the narrow cells are stilted, and the groins are sinuous on plan. The idea of a straight groin, as in the Byzantine form of oblong vault, appears to have actuated the builders, but this idea is imperfectly carried out in execution — as will be understood from the plan, in which the actual groins, indicated by the rough and indirect lines, depart widely from the true diagonals of the rectangle ruled in together with them in dotted lines. The

[1] The crypt of Canterbury is larger than that of Worcester, and has a double row of columns in the middle, forming a central aisle.

rudeness of the work is such that the groins intersect considerably to one side of the centre, and they are thus broken on plan so that their opposite sides meet at an angle, but from the point of intersection to the points of springing they are as straight as the rude workmanship could make them. A semicircular arch spans the narrow side A, and upon it are laid two supplementary courses of voussoirs against which the cell of the

FIG. 7 — Crypt of Canterbury.

vault abuts, tracing an oval, or elliptical, curve, as shown in the cross-section, Fig. 7. This elliptical curve would naturally result from board centring running straight from the groins, but the vault surface is not straight, it is slightly and irregularly concave, as if shaped on a mould of earth laid upon the centring. In elevation the groin is roughly elliptical, and consists of two curves meeting at the crown in an obtuse downward point, as shown in the elevation folded down on the plan. The wall ends of the cells are slightly unequal in height, and the arches on the long sides of the rectangle are not full semi-circles, but are struck from centres a little below the springing level. Thus this vault exhibits a considerable survival of the ancient Roman oblong form, — in which the groins, resulting from the interpenetration of cylindrical surfaces, are necessarily elliptical in elevation — but it departs from this form in having a groin approximately straight on plan (the Roman groin being in oblong vaults, necessarily sinuous), and in shaping its surfaces to the straight groin and the elliptical wall arch. What it retains of the Roman form is the approximately level crown and the elliptical groin. The idea of the groin straight on plan in oblong vaulting was, I suppose, derived from the domical vaulting, of Byzantine origin, that was common on the Continent, even before the introduction of the groin rib — as in the nave of Vezelay and the aisles of Morienval. This domical vaulting (which, in its groin straight on plan, opened such possibilities to the builders of Northern Europe) does not appear, I believe, in Norman architecture before the introduction of the groin rib, and never became general in Norman work. Yet this vault of the crypt of Canterbury, though not in a proper sense domical, is slightly, and I suppose unintentionally, raised at the crown, notwithstanding the downward point of the groin. The greater part of Norman vaulting, even after the introduction of the groin rib, as that of the aisles of Peterborough, retains the level crown; and where the crown is not level, as in the choir aisles of Durham, the centre of the vault is still kept comparatively low by striking the curves of the groin ribs from points far below the springing level.

Passing now into the apsidal aisle of this Norman crypt of Canterbury we find vaulting that presents some other points worthy of notice. These trapezoidal compartments are separated one from another by ribs of rectangular section which, like those of Worcester, are shaped on plan in approximate conformity with the radii of the curve of the apse — so that they widen considerably outward. But in the free-hand work of the Middle Ages, as in natural organisms, irregularities are constant, and no two parts are exactly the same. Thus of the two ribs A of one compartment (Fig. 8)[1] one tapers considerably more

[1] I regret that the line marking the outer side of the compartment is wanting in this cut. It should be a curve concentric with that of the inner side.

than the other. The piers B are wedge-shaped on plan, their sides roughly coinciding with the radii of the apse, and with the curved stylobate on which they stand, and are of two orders in conformity with the archivolts which they support. It will be seen that the point of intersection of the groins is in the middle of the compartment instead of being toward the narrow end, as in the corresponding vaults of Worcester crypt, and that thus the triangular cells are made more nearly equal in magni-

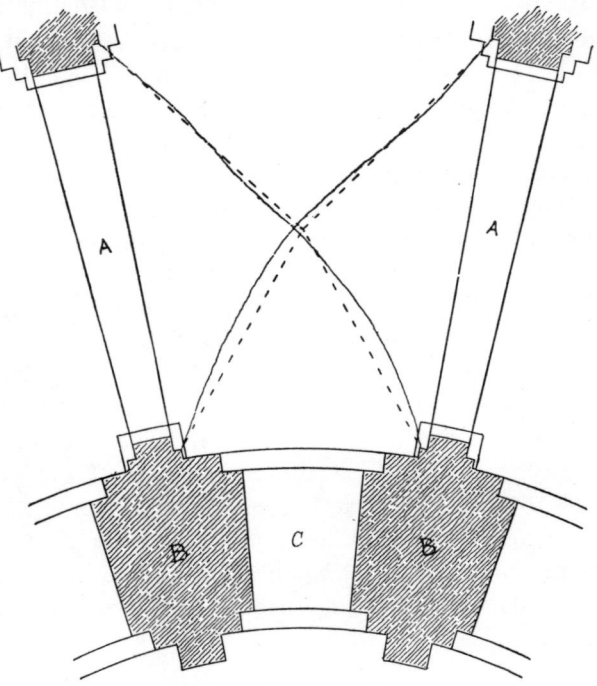

FIG. 8 — Crypt of Canterbury.

tude. It is further noticeable that although the groins are somewhat irregularly sinuous, they are so nearly straight as to show that the mind of the builder was largely emancipated from the idea of interpenetrating conical surfaces with those of an annular barrel vault. This shaping of the vault to groins, independently established, instead of letting the groins result from the forms of the interpenetrating surfaces, was one of the first progressive steps toward Gothic principles in mediæval vaulting. To find Norman vaulting without ribs thus formed is remarkable. To keep the crown of the vault level the great archivolt C, of two orders, is stilted, so that its springing is 1.26 metres above the springing of the transverse ribs; and it is worthy of notice that the mason has gone a little too far with his stilting, and has got the point D (Fig. 9) a little higher than the point E — the height at D being 4.55, and the height at E 4.41 metres. The thick archivolt C, like the vault itself, is slightly cone-shaped — since the sides of the piers from which it springs are not parallel, and the span, and consequent height, are greater on one side than on the other. The archivolt has thus a winding surface, and it was, of course, to avoid a more

FIG. 9 — Crypt of Canterbury.

pronounced winding that the piers were made wedge-shaped on plan.[1] On the wall side the responds have three members, which are more than enough, since there are no wall ribs, and thus only the transverse ribs and the groins of the vault spring from them. The system is therefore here illogical. In the earlier work of St. John's Chapel in the Tower of London the compartments (Fig. 10) of the apsidal aisle show several points of difference. Here the abaci of the great supports, in the form of round columns, are square — giving the maximum of twist to the soffits of the stilted archivolts, though at the crown these

---

[1] In the shaping of the piers and archivolts of apses the builders of the Middle Ages made many experiments before reaching a solution of the difficulties growing out of the curved plan. But as the apse never became a characteristic feature of mediæval architecture in England, it is unnecessary to consider these points further.

soffits are kept level. The transverse ribs widen outward much more than they do in Canterbury—the rib A measuring 37 centimetres where it springs from the pier, and 1.15 metres at the respond. Thus these ribs taper so much that their sides do not nearly coincide with the radii of the apse. This form would appear to have been given them in order to shorten the long side of the compartment, and so reduce the inequality of the magnitudes of the cells of the vault. The groins do not, in

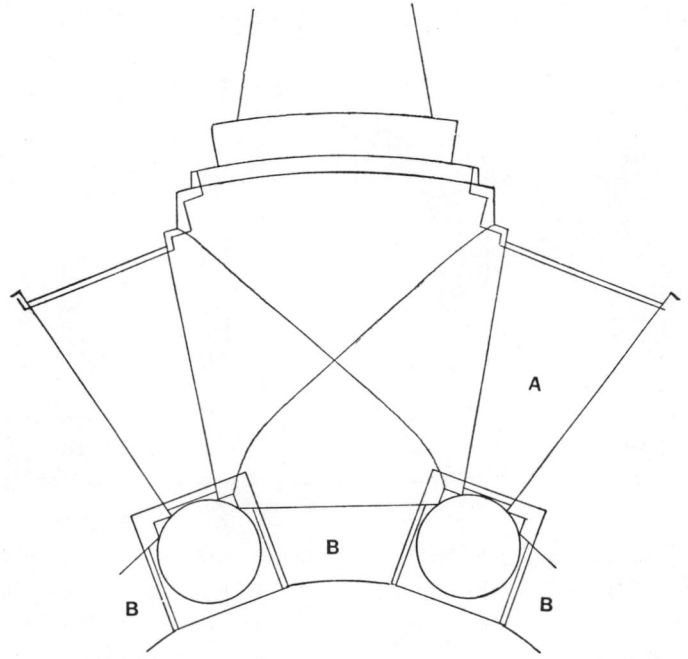

FIG. 10—St. John's Chapel, Tower of London.

this case, intersect in the middle of the compartment, but at a point nearer the narrow side, as where a vault of this plan consists of regular interpenetrating surfaces. Yet they are kept roughly straight on plan from the haunches upward. The great archivolts B are curved on plan on the inside, but are straight on the side of the aisle. As in most early Norman vaults, the transverse ribs are of slight projection, and are not entirely independent arches, and thus they are not effective in preventing ruptures arising in one compartment from extending into others.

Cracks have in several places passed through the ribs into adjoining compartments.

Coming back to Canterbury, little of the Norman work above the crypt remains complete, but the Chapels of St. Andrew and St. Anselm have survived, and each of them has a small apse with vaulting that is worthy of notice. The perspective drawing (Fig. 11) of St. Andrew's Chapel shows the form of this vaulting. It will be seen that it is divided into three cells, the

FIG. 11 — Apse of St. Andrew's Chapel, Canterbury.

crowns of which, at the ends that abut against the wall, are about as high as the point where they meet on the crown of the great arch. This is a characteristic of Gothic apse vaulting, but this vault has no tendency in a Gothic direction; and it will be seen that it is formed on a different principle. The French Gothic apse vault appears to have grown out of the half dome of the primitive apse by first breaking it into shallow cells, (meeting in groins supported on ribs), the crowns of which, at the wall ends, were not far above the springing of the groins; and then, by successive steps, raising these ends until they reached a level equal to that at which the groins meet on the crown of the great transverse arch.[1] Here at Canterbury, however, the surface of a semi-dome is merely broken with three such cells as we have found in the vaults of the crypt, leaving intervening portions of the rudely spherical surface tapering downward toward the springing with irregularly sinuous outlines.

A further development occurs at Romsey in the small apse

[1] Cf. my *Gothic Architecture*, p. 70, and *Renaissance Architecture*, pp. 56–59.

at the east end of the North Choir aisle (Fig. 12), where the spherical surfaces disappear, and groins are created, furnished with heavy ribs of square section which, together with the sub-order of the great transverse arch on the crown of which they meet — the keystones of this arch being extended and shaped to meet them — form a rib system on which the vault cells are turned. This is a peculiar vault. It will be noticed that the groin ribs spring from a higher level than that from which the great arch springs, and that the chords of their arcs are therefore not steeply inclined. The cells are in consequence more shallow than those of the vault of Canterbury.

The apse vault of the Norman chapel in the south transept of Tewkesbury is more advanced in character. Here the groin ribs spring from the same level as the transverse rib, the cells are consequently more developed, the ribs are lighter, and their edges are bevelled.

But the most remarkable Norman apse vault is, I believe, that of Christchurch, Hants. This apse (Figs. 13 and 14) is on the east side of the south arm of the transept.[1] Though superficially mutilated in the thirteenth century, and lately worked over by a modern architect, this apse remains substantially intact. As will be seen in the perspective view (Fig. 14) no alterations have been made in the bay to the left. In the middle bay an awkwardly shaped pointed arch has been inserted in front of the Norman window arch, but in the bay to the right the wall has been broken through, and a window inserted, while the soffit of the opening has been shaped to the form of a diminutive vault on a system of pointed ribs. The Norman work at Christchurch is commonly said to have been begun by Bishop Flambard of Durham about 1099. There appears, however, no clear evidence that it was commenced so early, and the character of this apse is such that I do not think it could have been constructed much before the middle of the twelfth century. For it is hardly conceivable that any contemporaneous work at Christchurch should be so much in advance of Canterbury. The apse vault of St. Andrew's Chapel there, though not earlier

---

[1] There was a corresponding apse in the north arm of this transept, but it was demolished in connection with later alterations. In the small crypts under the transept, to be presently noticed, there still remain two small vaulted apses substantially like the one described in the text.

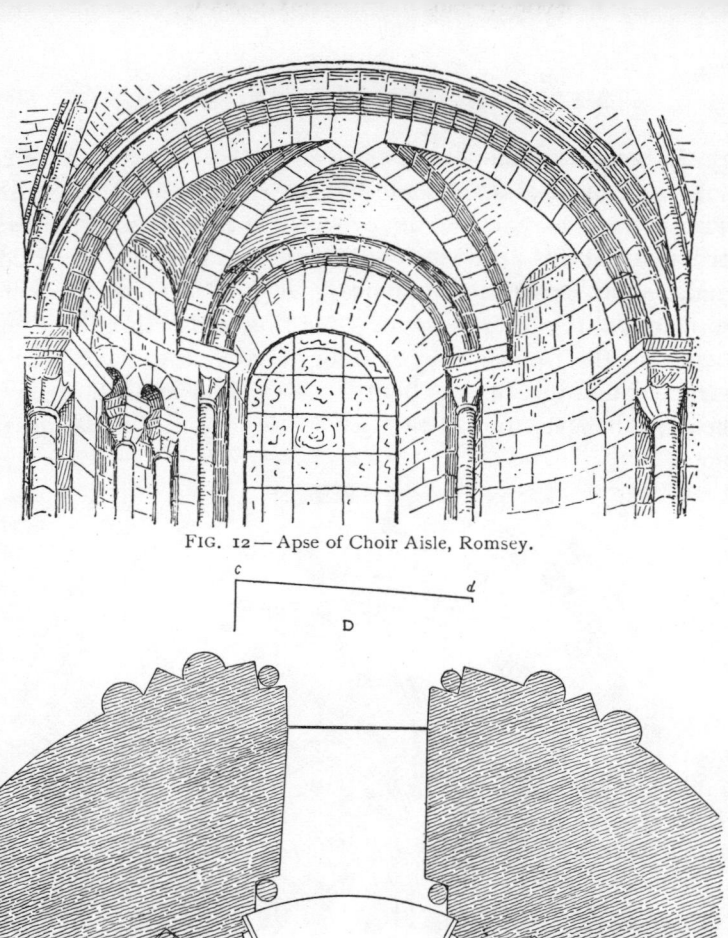

FIG. 12 — Apse of Choir Aisle, Romsey.

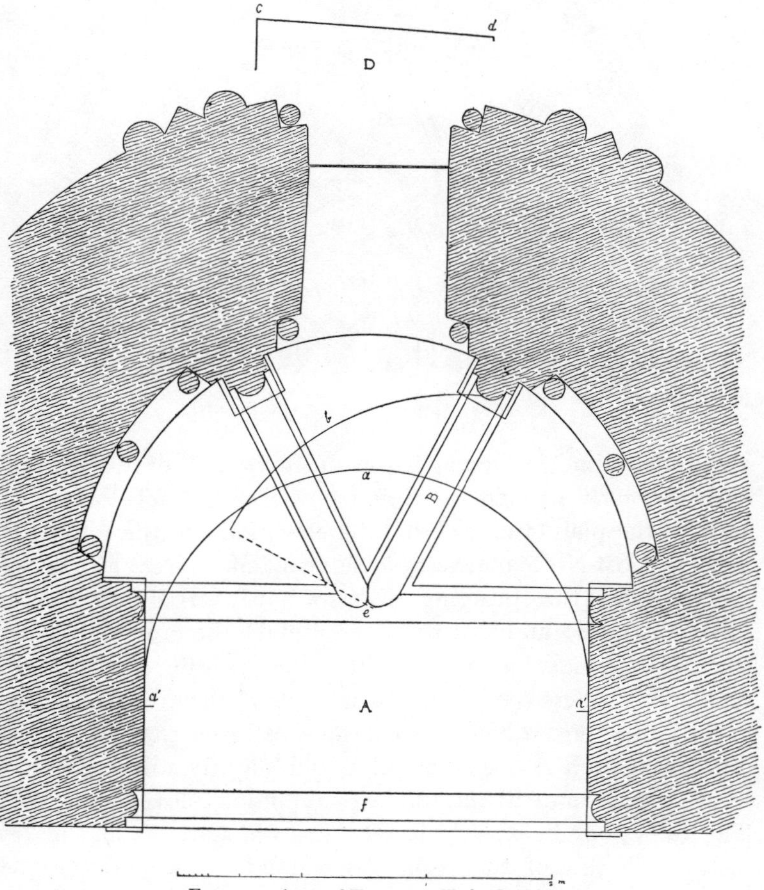

FIG. 13 — Apse of Transept, Christchurch.

than the first decade of the twelfth century, is, as we have seen, very rude in character, and without ribs. The later apse of Romsey, too, is rude, and undeveloped in comparison. However this may be this apse vault of Christchurch is very exceptional, and, so far as I know, unique in Anglo-Norman architecture. Celled vaulting of apses, with groin ribs, and with cells of nearly equal height from end to end, do not appear to have been constructed in France before about 1130 — the earliest extant example being, I believe, that of St. Germer de Fly, Oise, dating from

FIG. 14 — Apse of Transept, Christchurch.

about that time. A comparison of this vault of Christchurch with the early French example may be useful here. It will be seen on the plan (Fig. 13) that the elevation $b$ of the groin rib B is, as in most Norman vaults, a segment of a circle struck from a point below the springing level, so that it starts from the capital at an angle: and that the line $cd$ at D, the crown of the middle cell, is almost horizontal. It slopes a little, however, from $c$, the point where the groin ribs meet, to $d$, the crown of the wall arch — the point $d$ being 13 centimetres lower than the point $c$. The great arch A is semicircular and slightly stilted, as shown in the elevation of its intrados $a$ — the impost level being at $a'$. The roll $e$, on the apse side of this arch, starts from the level of the springing of the groin ribs, which is considerably higher; but the roll $f$, on the transept side, is brought down to the main

PLATE 1

St. Germer de Fly.

impost as shown in the perspective view. The several imposts, as seen from the apse side, are shown in their relations to each other, on a larger scale, in Fig. 15, where *a* is the impost of the great arch, *b* that of the apse vaulting, and *c* that of the wall arcades. In the apse of St. Germer de Fly (Plate I) the groin ribs are quarter circles, thus no angles are formed at the springing, and the crowns of the wall arches are on about the same level with the point of intersection of the groin ribs. The Christchurch apse is small, and its vault has but three cells, while that of St. Germer is relatively large, and has five cells, but this constitutes no material difference between the two works. I do not think there can be any question that the apse of Christchurch was built under French influence, though with little exact knowledge of French models. It looks like a rough Norman imitation of an early French vault, such as Anglo-Norman builders would be likely to attempt. Had such vaulting of apses been independent inventions they would, I think, have become more general, and would have been carried farther, as time went on, instead of coming to an end. Such invention does not seem to me in line with the character of Norman Art.

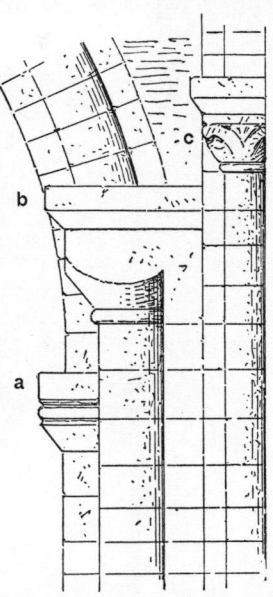

FIG. 15 — Imposts of Apse of Christchurch.

A small barrel vaulted crypt under each arm of the transept of Christchurch is worthy of notice, and each of these crypts has, as before remarked, a vaulted apse similar to the one in the transept just described. Fig. 16 gives the plan, and Fig. 17 a part longitudinal section, of the crypt under the north transept arm. This crypt measures roughly 10.25 × 4.08 metres on plan, and its vault is of segmental section — the curve being struck from a point far below the springing level, as shown in the elevation folded down on the plan. The vault is turned on two very wide transverse ribs supported on stumpy pilaster strips, both arches and supports having their edges rounded, and the supports being furnished with plain bevelled bases, and equally plain impost members, as shown in the section (Fig. 17). These arches and supports differ considerably in width, and both arches and vault are roughly built of ragstone, with edges of ashlar to

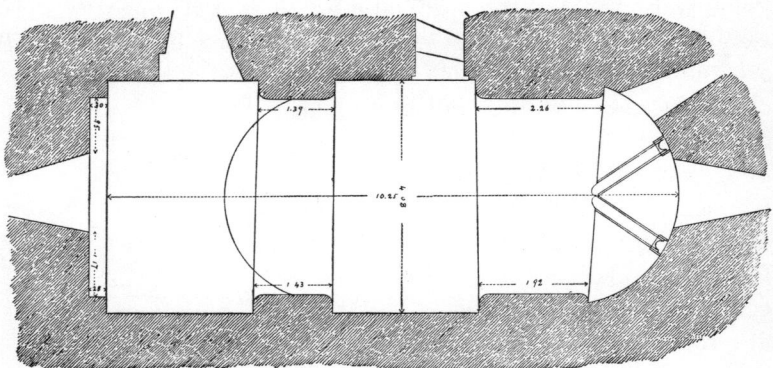

FIG. 16 — Crypt of Christchurch.

the arches. The irregularities of construction are very marked, the eastern arch, or rib, being 1.92 metres wide on the south side, and 2.26 metres wide on the north side — which makes its eastern side adjoining the apse very oblique on plan. It will be seen

FIG. 17 — Crypt of Christchurch.

that this crypt bears a rude resemblance to the barrel vaulted structures of Southern France, in which the vaults are furnished with salient transverse ribs. The barrel vault is not very common in Norman building, and where it occurs elsewhere, so far as I know, as notably in the Chapel of St. John in the Tower of London, its surface is unbroken by ribs.

Coming back to quadripartite vaulting, the later vaults with groin ribs are worthy of special attention, and some instructive examples are found under the treasury adjoining St. Andrew's Chapel at Canterbury. This basement is open on two sides, and has four small, and nearly square, vault compartments, one of which is shown in plan in Fig. 18, and in cross-section in Fig. 19. Though apparently intended to be square it is slightly

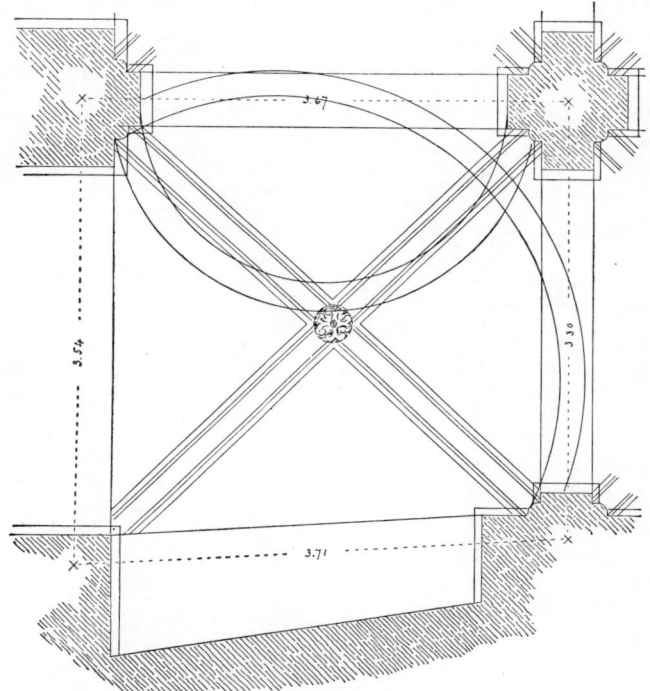

FIG. 18 — Vault under the Treasury, Canterbury.

oblong, and no two of its sides are of the same length, two of them being so unequal that the third side is very much askew. The arches on the sides are nearly semicircular, but the groin ribs are segmental, yet high enough to raise their crowns above those of the bounding arches so as to make the vault distinctly domical, as shown in the cross-section. The crowns of the cells are, however, in nearly straight inclined lines, though in some of them there is a slight arching, giving a rise of less than 2 centimetres in a length of 1.30 metres. The groin ribs are filled out in some places with ragstone in order to raise the vault surface, as we shall see later on was done at Peterborough, Worcester, and elsewhere. The supports are compound, and consist of rectangular members with engaged colonettes. These supports provide for the bounding arches only, the groin ribs springing from the reëntrant angles of the grouped abaci, and in order to find room they interpenetrate the bounding arches so that only the rolls of their soffits are free at the impost. The bounding arches are of plain square section, and, like those of the earlier vaults, are made up of voussoirs that do not run through their thickness, but consist of short stones worked square on the edges of the arch and un-

FIG. 19 — Vault under the Treasury, Canterbury.

shaped at their inner ends, with an interval filled with bits of ragstone and mortar. The groin ribs are, however, composed of single, and perfectly shaped, voussoirs, well faced and closely jointed, and have each a roll and two fillets on the soffit, while a well-cut ornamented boss is placed at their intersection.

As I have already said, the domical groined vault is uncommon in Norman architecture. The Norman builders do not appear to have perceived its advantages in giving freedom in the shaping of vaults to oblong areas, without the awkwardness and weakness inseparable from vaulting in which the Roman traditional forms survive. The capital advantages of the domical groined vault are: (1) that the groin, being an arch in a vertical plane, is naturally straight on plan, and thus indepen-

St. Étienne, Beauvais.

dent of those intersecting surfaces which give the sinuous curves to the groins of oblong vaults on the Roman model; (2) that the crown of the groin being higher in proportion to its span than that of the elliptical Roman groin the thrusts are diminished; and (3) that the arching of its surfaces brings their bearing more effectively on the ribs. There is no reason to suppose that the domical form was sought for itself. It was a natural result of the use of what was found to be the most efficacious form of groin arch, and in the Romanesque of the Ile de France the elevation of the crown above the crowns of the bounding arches was reduced to a minimum by stilting the narrow spanned arches. Thus the advantage of the semicircular groin was secured without the excessively domical form that results where the narrow spanned arches are not stilted.[1]

The great difference between the Norman ribbed vaulting of England and the Romanesque ribbed vaulting of the Ile de France does not appear to be enough appreciated. A comparison of the aisle vaulting of St. Etienne of Beauvais (Plate II), dating from about 1130,[2] with that of the aisle of Peterborough (Plate III), dating from the second half of the same century, will illustrate this difference. In the vaulting of St. Etienne, which is in compartments measuring about 4.45 × 5.75 metres from centre to centre of its supports, the groin ribs are nearly full semicircles rising gracefully from their supporting shafts, and giving a distinctly domical form to the vault, notwithstanding that the transverse ribs are much stilted, so as to raise their crowns to a level nearly equal to that of the wider spanned arches. The great archivolt, however, which is narrowed in span by the thickness of the piers, is also stilted enough to bring its crown up to the height of the groin ribs, and thus this vault presents the peculiarity of a level crown in the cell on the nave side.[3] The piers are composed of members per-

---

[1] The Gothic builders improved on this by substituting the pointed arch for the round arch.

[2] This is not the earliest vaulting of St. Etienne. That of the easternmost bay on either side of the nave appears considerably earlier, and has heavy groin ribs of rectangular section with bevelled edges. This earlier vaulting is figured in my *Development and Character of Gothic Architecture*, second edition, p. 54.

[3] I have not measured this later aisle vaulting of St. Etienne myself, but my friend Mr. John Bilson (on the authority of M. Lefèvre-Pontalis who caused it to be measured for him) has kindly given me the following figures: height of vault

fectly corresponding to the ribs of the vault, and these members are furnished with bases and capitals of considerable elegance of form. It will be noticed, too, that the shafts supporting the groin ribs have their bases and capitals set obliquely in conformity with the directions of these ribs. In contrast to this the vaulting of Peterborough has ponderous groin ribs of low segmental form rising from their supports at an angle. The conformation of the vault is like that of the oblong groined vault of the Roman builders in having a level crown and stilted arches over the narrow spans. (The surfaces are, however, of course necessarily warped out of the Roman cylindrical form by the necessity of shaping them to the segmental groin rib straight on plan.) Though the transverse rib is stilted in both St. Etienne and Peterborough, there is a significant difference between them as to the purpose of the stilting. In St. Etienne it is done merely to avoid an excessively domical form arising from the use of the semicircular groin rib,—the vault still remaining domical, while in Peterborough it is employed, as in the Roman vault, to bring the level crown of the narrow spanned surface to the height reached by the wider one. In other words, in Peterborough the ribs are shaped awkwardly to fit a vault with level crown, while in St. Etienne they are established independently, and the vault is shaped to them. This independent character of the rib system of St. Etienne was a long step in the direction of Gothic vault construction, whereas the vaulting of Peterborough, like most other Norman vaulting, shows that the minds of its builders were largely preoccupied with the Roman tradition, and that they were striving to conform to the Roman model so far as the use of the groin arch straight on plan would allow.

In the eastern aisle of the transept of Peterborough, and in the aisles of the transept of Winchester, are vaults in which the groin ribs become more nearly semicircular, and the surfaces are a little domical; but such vaults, as before remarked, are uncommon in the Norman architecture of England.

An exceptional instance of Norman vaulting over a nave oc-

surface at the intersection of the groin ribs 8.60 metres, height of vault surface at the crown of each transverse rib 8.25 metres, height of vault surface at the crown of the wall arch 8.42 metres, height of vault surface at the crown of the great archivolt 8.60 metres.

PLATE III

Peterborough.

curs in the Cathedral of Durham. This vaulting has been made the subject of important papers by Mr. John Bilson,[1] who writes with ability, and argues in an admirable spirit, in favor of a very early date for this vaulting. The dates (1104 for the original choir vaults — which, though long ago destroyed, are supposed by him to have been similar to those now extant in the north transept — and 1128–1133 for the existing vaults of the nave) which Mr. Bilson thinks established by both documentary evidence and the character of the monument, have been questioned by a distinguished French archéologist,[2] but his arguments appear to me inconclusive. It is remarkable, indeed, if it be true, that vaulting like that which we now see in the north transept should have been built over the choir so early as 1104, but it does not seem to me impossible that the vaulting of the nave should have been completed by 1133. I find no difficulty in accepting this date. I see in it, however, no significance in connection with the beginnings of Gothic architecture. Stupendous as it is, no part of Durham Cathedral has, in my judgment, any tendency in a Gothic direction. It does not belong to that class of consistent organic Romanesque monuments of the Middle Ages which were quick with the germs of Gothic development.

Mr. Bilson considers that the semicircular groin rib and the pointed transverse arch in its vaulting give it a rudimentary Gothic character. But the beginnings of Gothic construction, as distinguished from Romanesque construction, do not consist in the use of the semicircular groin rib, or even in that of the pointed arch as it is employed in the vaulting of Durham. The semicircular groin rib is a feature of organic Romanesque, and the pointed arch of Durham is not used in what I consider a Gothic way — that is to say, no structural advantage is gained by it that the round arch would not give, as I think we shall presently see.

That Durham Cathedral is not a building of true organic Romanesque type will be seen, I think, on comparing its system

---

[1] *The Beginnings of Gothic Architecture*, by John Bilson, F.S.A., published in the *Journal of the Royal Institute of British Architects*, March 11 and 25, 1899, and May 10, 1902.

[2] M. le Comte de Lasteyrie. — *Discours sur les Origines de l'Architecture Gothique*, Caen, 1901.

with that of a monument which has the true character; namely, the church of St. Ambrogio of Milan, in which the remarkable Lombard system, the first, I believe, to have a consistent organic character, culminates, and the earlier date of which is, I believe, beyond question.[1] The vaulting of the nave of St. Ambrogio (Plate IV) is in nearly square compartments, and each compartment is furnished with a complete system of ribs of which those on the groins are semicircular as well as those on the sides. The vaults are thus very domical, and bear on the ribs as they would not in vaulting with level crowns.[2] That is to say, the masonry being arched from rib to rib, as at A (Fig. 20), is supported by the ribs more effectively than it would be if laid flat, as at B in the same figure. The strength of the vault is thus

[1] Concerning the date of St. Ambrogio, Sig. Cattaneo (*L'Architettura in Italia dal Secolo VI al Mille Circa*, Venice, 1888, p. 210) adduces evidence that the vaulted nave of this church was built during the second half of the eleventh century. This is confirmed by Sig. Rivora (*Le Origine della Architettura Lombarda e delle sue Principale Derivazione nei Paese d'Oltr' Alpe*, Rome, 1901, vol. I, pp. 242–243) who assigns it to the pontificate of the Archbishop Guido — 1046–1071. This author, however, in his second volume (Rome, 1907, p. 188), modifies this opinion to the extent of holding only that the structure must have been completed by the year 1098. The conclusions of Cattaneo and Rivora are, however, based primarily on written documentary evidence, and such evidence is hardly ever conclusive, since it is rarely unmistakable, and almost never affords means of determining whether what we see in a given monument is that to which the document refers. The character of a building itself furnishes more trustworthy evidence of the epoch to which it belongs, and that of St. Ambrogio points clearly, I think, to the eleventh century as the time of its production. Works of repair may have been executed later, and the atrium is commonly, and I believe correctly, assigned to the twelfth century. The sculptured details of the atrium are in advance of those of the nave. To suppose that this nave was derived from any architecture north of the Alps, as some recent writers have suggested, appears to me impossible. For no Romanesque architecture of the north, save the later Romanesque of the Ile de France, has the logical character of the Lombard as embodied in St. Ambrogio, and it does not appear to me credible that a logical system could have been derived from an illogical one.

[2] In St. Ambrogio, on account of the nearly square plan, and semicircular ribs, they bear less on the groin ribs than they do on the transverse ribs. I regret that, when on the spot, I have not noticed just how far groins are developed in this very domical vaulting. If the compartments were perfectly square on plan, and the surfaces spherical, there would, of course, be no groins. The vault would be merely a spherical dome intersecting on the bounding arches, and the diagonal ribs would have no structural function. As it is, the groins are very obtuse, and above the haunch they appear to die away completely. Vaulting very similar in this respect is noticeable in some early Gothic churches in France, as in the triforium gallery of Senlis.

St. Ambrogio, Milan.

PLATE V

Durham Cathedral.

made to reside primarily in the rib skeleton, and the masonry of the cells may be materially lightened. The principle of sustaining groined vaulting on such a skeleton, with appropriate supports from the pavement, was, I believe, the great contribution of the Lombard builders to the architecture of the Middle Ages. The Byzantine constructors had opened the way for this by making the form of the groin arch independent of intersecting cylindrical surfaces, but without the Lombard addition of the rib skeleton, the Byzantine innovation must have remained fruitless of the far-reaching consequences that followed.

The vaulting of St. Ambrogio is carried on compound piers, in which each rib is provided with its own supporting member. The aisles have each two small vault compartments to every larger one in the nave, giving rise to a small pier, between each pair of great piers, for the support of the transverse rib that divides the two-aisle compartments one from another. An alternate system is thus produced having a logical relationship to the vaulting of both nave and aisles, and this internal system is supplemented on the outside of the building by vigorous buttresses set against the lines of thrust. All the parts of an organic system, in logical combination, are thus present in St. Ambrogio.

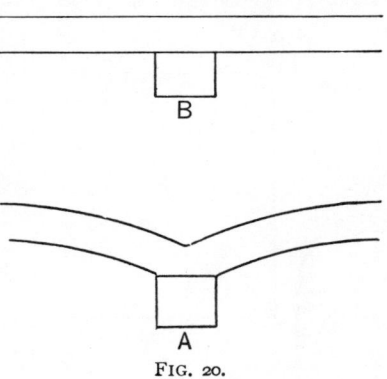

FIG. 20.

In the nave of Durham, on the other hand, we have, as we have already seen, a very pronounced alternate system, which calls for vaulting in compartments each embracing a double bay, as in St. Ambrogio. But the builder has not made his vaults conform to this system. He has built them in compartments each covering a single bay. That is to say, the nave of Durham (Plate V) has the vaulting of a uniform system on the supports of an alternate system, which is illogical. Moreover, while the scheme of supports is consistent in its alternate character, it is not so with reference to any kind of vaulting on groin ribs, since no shafts for such ribs are provided. The great piers carry transverse arches of two heavy, and awkwardly pointed, orders, and are furnished with shafts for these orders only. This would suggest that no vaulting was originally intended, but that the main piers and their arches were meant to carry walls reaching to the rafters of the timber roof, as in some unvaulted naves of the Continent. However this may be, no other scheme, save that of plain groined vaulting in compartments each covering two bays, would be logical. When the present vaulting was decided on, corbels for the groin ribs had to be inserted, as we see (Plate V) in the triforium spandrels. The vaults have thus no organic connection with the piers, and in themselves they are backward in idea, since they show a strong survival of the Roman tradition. The surfaces have not, indeed, the cylindrical form of Roman vaulting, as of course they could not have

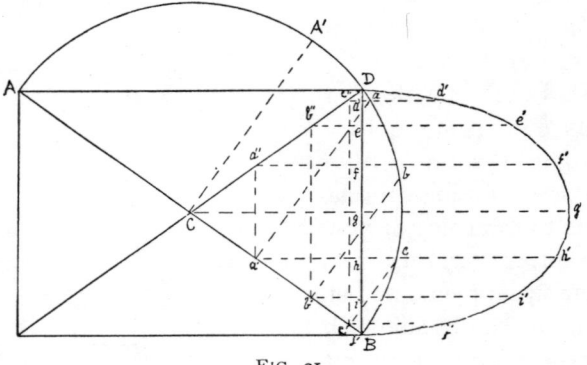

FIG. 21.

with the semicircular groin ribs, and the pointed transverse arches. They are essentially like the small oblong vault of the crypt of Canterbury above described (pp. 9-10), save for the use of the semicircular groin rib; and in so far as the lateral cells are shaped by straight board centring it makes them trace elliptical curves against the clerestory wall — since this curve results when points are projected from semicircular groin ribs in lines perpendicular to the clerestory wall, as in Fig. 21. In this figure AB is the plan, and AA'B the elevation, of one groin rib. Dividing A'B, half of the semicircle, into any number of equal parts, as A'$a$, $ab$, $bc$, $c$B, and from the points marking these divisions, letting fall perpendiculars to the line CB, the half plan of this groin rib, we obtain the points $a'$, $b'$, $c'$. Projecting these points on the line CD, the half plan of the other groin rib, we obtain the points $a''$, $b''$, $c''$.  Drawing from these points, in both diagonals, lines perpendicular to the line DB, the narrow side of the rectangle, we get the points $d, e, f, g, h, i, j$, and erecting perpendiculars from these points, and laying off on them lengths corresponding to the lengths of the perpendiculars from the half diagonal CB, we obtain the points $d', e', f', g', h', i', j'$ through which the curve of the arch on the narrow side of the rectangle must pass. This semi-elliptical curve is, then, the form that the clerestory arch of a vault constructed on straight centring from semicircular groin ribs must necessarily take.  The vaulting of Durham is not, however, shaped strictly on this principle, as Norman vaulting generally is not.  Its surfaces are not perfectly straight from the

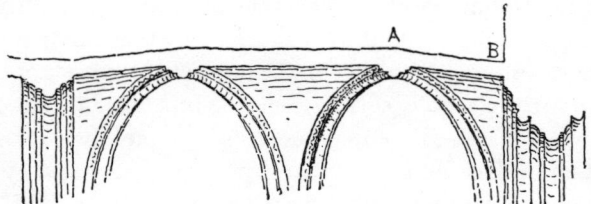

FIG. 22 — Longitudinal Section, Vault of Durham.

groin ribs to the clerestory wall.  They are a little ploughshared near the springing, and a straightedge perpendicular to the wall would hardly coincide with them anywhere unless possibly at the crown.  But the work has enough of the form that would result from the process illustrated in Fig. 21 to show that the builders were largely governed by the idea of vaulting on this principle.[1]

In the longitudinal direction the crown of the vault of Durham is not level, since the crown of the great semicircular arch of the crossing, and the crowns of the pointed transverse arches, are lower than those of the groin ribs.  From the crown of the crossing arch to the point of intersection of the first pair of groin ribs (AB, Fig. 22) there is a rise of about 30 centimetres. Between this point and that of the intersection of the second pair of groin ribs, the crown of the vault is level.  From this last point it falls a little to the crown of the first pointed transverse arch. This difference of level between the crowns of the groin ribs and

---

[1] The persistence in the Early English style of this, and other Norman characteristics of construction, will be noticed later on.  The clerestory arch of the nave of Lincoln has very much the shape of that of Durham.

those of the transverse arches is found in every compartment, but it is greater in some of them than it is in others.[1]

It is hard to see why the transverse arches were pointed, and why they were so awkwardly formed of curves struck from centres below the springing level. Round arches would require but little stilting to bring them to the same height, and would avoid the unsightly angle at the springing which these segmental curves make.

It will be seen that the two vault compartments between each pair of these transverse arches are not separated one from the other by a transverse rib. This omission marks another lack of progressive character in the work, for the first step in the development of groined vaulting was that of placing a transverse rib between one compartment and another, so that any rupture that might arise in one of them should not extend into another, and so endanger the whole series. In organic Romanesque, and in Gothic, vaulting each compartment is completely enclosed. In the system of Durham the great transverse arches would properly enclose such vaulting as the piers naturally call for, namely, quadripartite vaulting without groin ribs, each compartment covering two bays of the substructure. But with two compartments in each double bay another transverse rib is required to give proper enclosure.

It may be useful to compare another continental alternate system with that of Durham. The nave of the Cathedral of Le Mans (Plate VI), in its present form, was begun about 1143 and consecrated in 1158.[2] Its vaulting appears to be derived from that of Angers, and is very domical. Unlike Angers, however, it has aisles, and an alternate system, probably derived from the Ile de France, though properly without the members in the intermediate pier that were introduced by the builders of that locality to meet the needs of sexpartite vaulting, for which alone they employed the alternate system. The work has thus the nature of a pasticcio, but it is nevertheless for the most part a very logical composition. The vaults are in nearly square com-

---

[1] I am indebted to Mr. W. G. Footitt of Durham for these facts — having failed to observe them myself. Mr. Footitt, at my request, kindly took the trouble to examine the upper surface of the vaulting with regard to these levels.

[2] Cf. M. Eugène Lefèvre-Pontalis, *Etude Historique et Archéologique sur la nef de la cathédrale du Mans*, Mamers, 1889, p. 16.

PLATE VI

Le Mans Cathedral.

partments in conformity with the main supports, and have a full system of ribs, all of which are pointed, and have their curves struck from the springing level, except the transverse ribs — which are a little stilted. A great shaft from the pavement supports the transverse rib, a smaller one on either side takes the groin rib, while the longitudinal rib springs from one of the rectangular members of the pier. The intermediate pier is, as at Durham, a single round column confined to the ground story, since it has no function to perform in connection with the high vaulting. Thus between St. Ambrogio and Le Mans on the one hand, and the nave of Durham on the other, the difference in point of consistency and completeness of organic composition must be apparent.

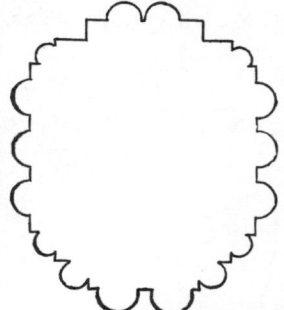

FIG. 23 — Norwich.

We may now give some further attention to the composition of the Norman pier — a member of great significance in the architecture of the Middle Ages, — and then notice some other characteristic features of the Anglo-Norman Romanesque which largely survive in the Early English style, as we shall see.

In the most logical vaulted building the composition of the pier corresponds, as in St. Ambrogio and Le Mans, with the members of the vaulting, so that from the pier alone the character of the vaulting can be understood as to its general form. But in Norman architecture this is rarely the case. The Norman pier is hardly ever so composed as to manifest an intention of vaulting in a logical manner. Shafts for groin ribs in the high vaults do not, I believe, ever occur, as we have seen that they do not in the nave of Durham.

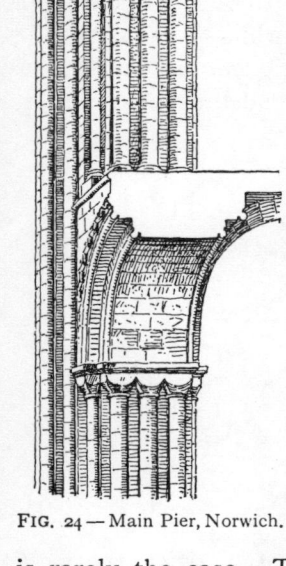

FIG. 24 — Main Pier, Norwich.

In the system of Norwich, for instance, the main piers (Figs. 23 and 24) have each a pilaster strip with a pair of engaged shafts rising from the pavement.[1] On either side of this group another shaft (the one noticed on pp. 3 and 4) rises to the impost of the triforium arcade, a level from which it could take no part in vaulting, so long as the other shafts are carried higher, as they are here. Yet this shaft occupies the place that should, in a structure with vaulting on ribs, be taken by the support of the groin rib. The subordinate members of this pier — those relating to the aisle vaulting and to the arcades of the ground story and triforium — are logical, as such parts frequently are in Norman monuments. The archivolts, however, of the ground story and triforium are so wide that three shafts are set on each side of the pier to carry them. The intermediate pier (Fig. 25) has a very small portion of a great cylinder engaged on either side, and these single members carry both orders of the great archivolt, while on the nave side a shaft on either side of the main vaulting group rises no higher than the impost of the triforium arcade, and thus, as before, it could not carry vaulting.

FIG. 25 — Norwich.

 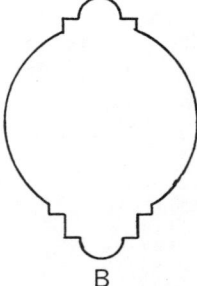

FIG. 26 — Piers of Ely.

The piers of Ely are variants of those of Norwich, the main piers having the section A (Fig. 26), and the intermediate pier

---

[1] These members now carry the fifteenth century vaulting, but they were formerly, I suppose, carried to the top of the wall in the usual Norman manner.

the section B of the same figure.[1] But no tall shafts occur here that could not be used for vaulting by cutting them down to the proper level. The

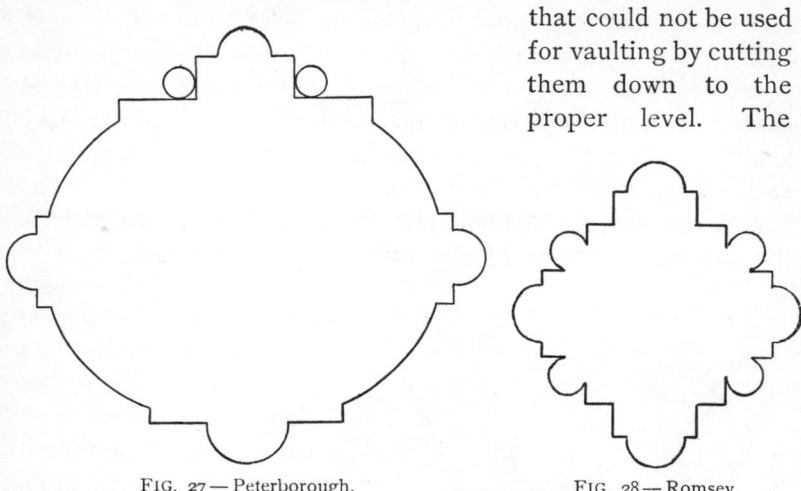

FIG. 27 — Peterborough.   FIG. 28 — Romsey.

system of Ely is, however, illogical, as we have seen (p. 3), in having uniform vaulting members with piers of alternately large and small magnitudes.

The uniform system of Peterborough has, on the nave side, in each pier but a single shaft without any pilaster strip, and the first and second orders of the triple archivolts are not provided with separate shafts. On the aisle side, as will be seen in the section (Fig. 27), shafts for the groin ribs, as well as for the transverse rib of the existing vaults, are provided — making a logical system here. It is thus clear that

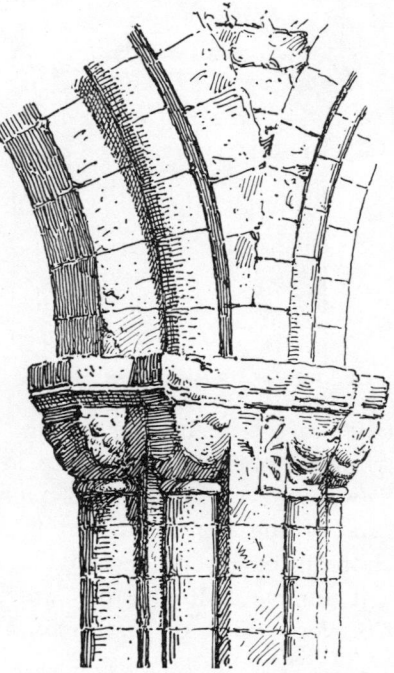

FIG. 29 — The Infirmary, Canterbury.

[1] Piers similar to those of Norwich and Ely occur across the channel in the churches of Oystreham and Berniers sur mer. Cf. Ruprich-Robert, *L'Architecture Normande.*

high vaulting was never intended over the nave of Peterborough, as I believe that it generally was not in Norman naves.

The piers of the uniform system of Romsey have the usual pilaster-strip as well as an engaged shaft on the nave side of each pier, and a separate member on the aisle side for each vault rib, while the great archivolts of the ground story have each a supporting shaft (Fig. 28).

Another form of compound pier is one that does not reach above the ground story. Such piers are composed of members answering to the arch orders, and to the vaulting of the aisles only — the walls above having no division into bays, as in the remains of the Infirmary at Canterbury (Fig. 29). Piers of this kind survive in a variety of forms, in the most characteristic Early English monuments, as we shall see in the nave and Presbytery of Lincoln, and in Salisbury, Worcester, and Exeter.

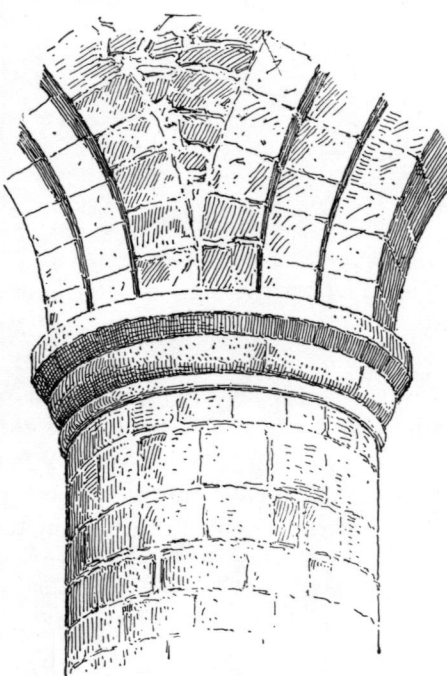

FIG. 30 — Priory Church, Malvern.

Where the pier has the form of a plain round column, as in the Priory Church, Malvern (Fig. 30), it is of massive proportions, and in some cases of great height, giving lofty aisles, and crowding the triforium and clerestory into low spaces, as at Gloucester and Tewkesbury. This form of pier is rare in the Norman architecture of the Continent, but it occurs on a small scale in the churches of Étretat, Écranville, and a few others.[1]

The nave of Rochester Cathedral, as it has come down to us, has piers (A, B, C, Fig. 31) of a variety of forms in which the

[1] Such round columns occur in some of the Romanesque architecture of Burgundy, as at Tournus, Chapaize, St. Hippolite, and elsewhere.

component parts have no logical relationship either to possible vaulting or to the arch orders. A single engaged shaft starts from the impost in each of them and reaches only to the triforium string; but this shaft may in the first construction have been carried higher. Even so, however, it would not provide properly for groined vaulting.

Many variants of these leading forms may be found in the Norman work of England, but I am unacquainted with any

A　　　　　　　　　　B　　　　　　　　　C

FIG. 31.—Piers of Rochester.

that are logically composed for groined vaulting over naves, with shafts that terminate at a level from which such vaulting could spring.

As for the buttress in Norman architecture, it is rarely more than a flat pilaster strip, as at St. Albans, and in the clerestories of Ely, Winchester, and Romsey — and in this form it is sometimes of two orders, as in the aisles of Winchester and Romsey. In some cases it takes the form of an engaged shaft, as in the clerestory of Peterborough, or of a shaft on a pilaster strip, as in the aisles of Ely. As a rule, the Norman pilaster buttress is too shallow for offsets. It usually does not project beyond the face of the wall cornice — the corbel-table, where it occurs, being flush with it. It is, however, sometimes more salient, and then it is weathered at the top, as in the clerestory of Norwich and the aisle walls of Romsey. In a few instances an abutting arch is sprung in the triforium gallery, as in the choir of Durham and formerly in the nave of Christchurch. In the triforium of the nave of Durham (cf. Plate V) and in that of the choir of Gloucester, flying buttresses occur which have been taken by some recent writers to be the earliest of such members, and thus inventions of the Norman builders. I do not think that this view can be justified, for it is not in line with the general character of Norman building. It seems to me more reasonable to suppose that these examples were derived, as I believe the well-known ones of Caen were, from the more logical and progressive art of the Ile de France. Precisely when and where the flying buttress, in its rudimentary form under the aisle roof, first appeared in the Ile de France cannot be confidently affirmed; but I believe no earlier instance than that of the choir of St. Germer de Fly,[1] dating from about 1130, has yet been found. To suppose that the Norman instances are earlier, and were invented by the Norman builders, appears to me inconsistent with the character of Norman art. When we consider that the flying buttress never became a characteristic feature of either Norman or Early English architecture, the notion that it was a Norman invention appears to me untenable. The invention of such a member is, on the other hand, entirely in line with the other remarkable developments of the builders of the Ile de France, and to look elsewhere for the origin of this, or any other distinctive feature of the Gothic style, appears to me futile.

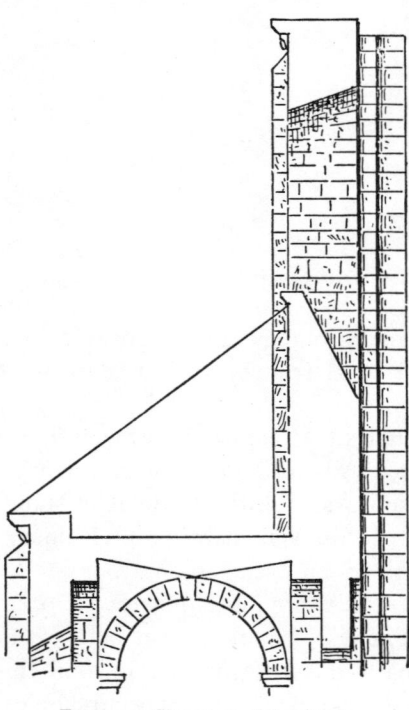

FIG. 32 — Clerestory of Jumièges.

We may now consider such features as the clerestory, the triforium, wall arcades, and details of capitals, bases, and profiling, which characterize the Norman art and survive in the pointed style which followed it. The Norman clerestory is peculiar in

---

[1] Cf. My *Development and Character of Gothic Architecture*, pp. 78, 79. The precise date of the choir of St. Germer de Fly has not been determined, but its architectural character appears to mark it as earlier than St. Denis. M. Eugene Lefèvre-Pontalis, in his *Étude sur la Date de l'Eglise de St. Germer (Bibliothèque de l'École des Chartres*, vol. XLVI, p. 429) concludes that while it may be later, the weight of evidence is in favor of the date 1130 circa.

having a passageway in the thickness of the wall (cf. Plate V). In the smaller early churches of Normandy, and in some of the larger ones, as the Abbey church of Jumièges, the clerestory has a solid wall with a deeply splayed opening (Fig. 32). But in the more typical Norman architecture, which took form soon after the middle of the eleventh century in the two great churches of Caen — the Abbaye aux Hommes, and the Abbaye aux Dames — the clerestory wall is double, with an interval forming a passage for circulation (Fig. 33). In the Norman monuments of England this latter form of clerestory is practically constant in the larger structures, as at Ely, Peterborough, and Durham. The outer wall has a single opening in each bay, and in some cases, as at St. Albans, there is but one opening in the inner plane also. In general, however, the inner plane has three shafted openings, as at Durham (Plate V), and on the outside of such clerestories a blind arch is often worked on either side of the opening, making a composition corresponding to the divisions of the triple opening of the interior.

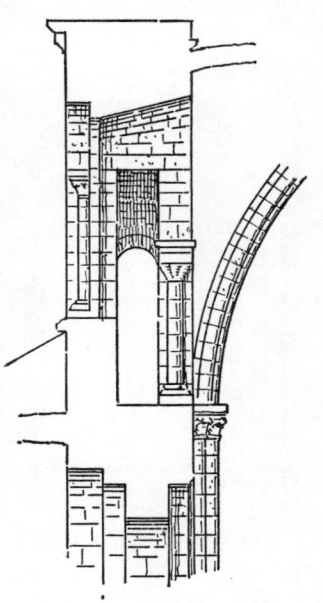

FIG. 33 — The Abbaye aux Hommes.

The triforium in Norman architecture is less peculiar. Most of the larger churches have triforium galleries, as in the Lombard Romanesque. Their openings into the nave are usually compound, and consist of two arches embraced by a larger arch. The triforium gallery is often very high, as at Ely, Norwich, and Romsey; but in many cases it is low, as at Durham, Southwell, and Waltham, and sometimes, as at Norwich, Southwell, and Waltham, it is undivided. An exceptional form of compound triforium opening occurs at Romsey — where the tympanum is open, and has a diminutive colonette, with its capital reaching to the intrados of the encompassing arch, set between the two smaller skeleton arches (Fig. 34). In the transept of the same building a variant of this scheme occurs in which three small arches are embraced by the larger arch, and intersecting skeleton arches occupy the Tympanum space. The Norman triforium is not walled in, and thus the timber roof is open to view from the pavement of the nave. This characteristic is, as we shall see, carried over into the Early English style.

Wall arcades, both internal and external, are common in the richer Norman churches. They form an effective and appropriate surface decoration, and present a variety of treatment — the arches often intersecting and thus producing subordinate pointed arches, as on the external walls of the chapel of St. Andrew and St. Anselm at Canterbury. These arcades are in some cases severely plain, as in the aisles of Durham and Peterborough (cf. Plate III), while in other instances they are richly ornamented with carving. West fronts are not seldom profusely adorned with such arcading, as at Castle Acre, which foreshadows the magnificent Early English arcade work of the west front of Lincoln.

FIG. 34 — Triforium of Romsey.

Coming now to smaller details — capitals, bases, the profiles of vault ribs, archivolts, and string courses — we find the Norman art marked by a fine monumental quality. And, however richly ornamented, as in the western portals of Lincoln, and the wall arcades of Christchurch, these details never fail to have breadth and architectural effectiveness. The most common form of Norman capital in England is that which is shaped out of a more or less cubical block of stone by rounding off the lower part to a circular outline, so as to fit it to the round column, a half round neck moulding being worked on the lower edge, and a plain square bevelled abacus laid upon it, as in Fig. 7, p. 10, from the crypt of Canterbury. Where archivolts of several orders spring from a great round column, this form of capital sometimes becomes compound, with parts answering to the arch orders, as in the choir of Peterborough. But in general the great cylindrical columns have single round capitals, as in the naves of Gloucester, Tewkesbury, and the Priory church at Malvern (Fig. 30, p. 34). Later Norman capitals often have the lower part scalloped (Fig. 52, p. 56), and they are sometimes adorned with carved ornament. In Normandy a rude Corinthianesque form prevails, as in the Abbaye aux Hommes at Caen,

FIG. 35 — Lincoln.

and this is reproduced in what remains of the work of Remegius at Lincoln (Fig. 35). In the later Anglo-Norman works many variants of this type appear which are sometimes of great elegance, as at Canterbury, at Lewes, and in the triforium of St. Bartholomew's, Smithfield, while a few in the western portals of Lincoln are of almost classic elegance. In the nave of Christchurch a variety of forms occur, some of which are of great richness. These have for the most part a convex outline, and

FIG. 36 — Christchurch.

a group of exceptional elaboration is found in the northwest crossing pier (Fig. 36). This richer carving of Christchurch must, I think, have been done at a time considerably subse-

FIG. 37 — Christchurch.

quent to that of the original construction, and evidence of reworking appears in many parts of the fabric, especially in the north triforium, where on the inside of one group (Fig. 37) a capital, not seen from the nave, retains the cubical form, as if it had been left unaltered when the rest were recut. But this is a conjecture.

The early Norman base is in some cases only a bevelled ring on a square plinth, as in the Abbaye aux Hommes at Caen (Fig. 38). In the crypt of Worcester, as we have already seen, the profiles A and B (Fig. 4, p. 7) occur, and these are repeated with minor variations in other bases of the same crypt. Other characteristic profiles are A and B (Fig. 39) from the nave of Tewkesbury. The profile B, it will be seen, is a rude form of that of the Attic base, and C, from the crypt of Canterbury, is a common variant of it. Bases of this form are found at Winchester also, and elsewhere. In the nave of Durham the great piers have bases consisting of a narrow bevelled ring at the foot of each shaft on a common square plinth of three courses of which the middle one projects beyond the others (Fig. 40).

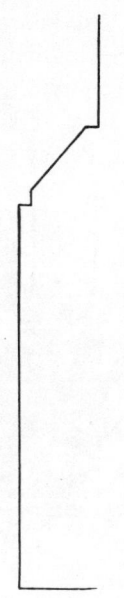

FIG. 38.—Abbaye aux Hommes.

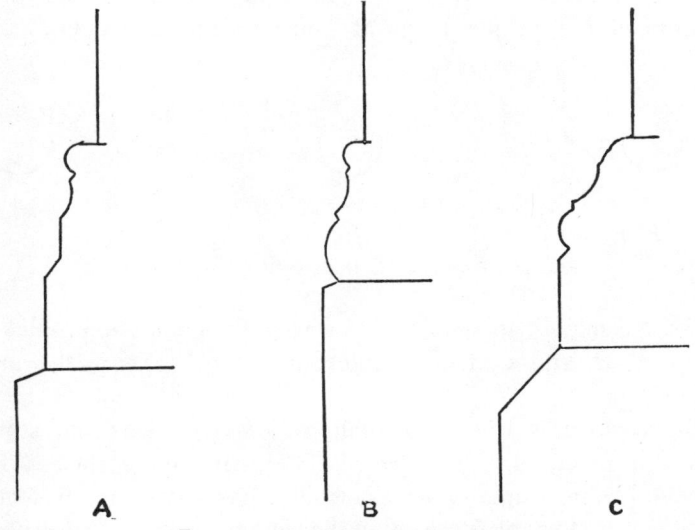

FIG. 39.—Tewkesbury and Canterbury.

The characteristic profilings of Anglo-Norman vault ribs have been sufficiently described above in connection with the vaulting. Archivolts, except in wall arcades, are usually of several orders, and may be of plain square section, as in the nave of the Priory church, Malvern (Fig. 30, p. 34), and in the transept of Winchester, or they may have a roll on the edge, as at Ely and Norwich (Fig. 24, p. 31). In many cases a great roll is added to the soffit of the sub-order, as at Peterborough (A, Fig. 41) and at Romsey. Sometimes, as at Durham, the square section of the sub-order is further broken up by having, in addition to the roll on the soffit, hollowed chamfers on its edges (B, Fig. 41), and in other cases the sub-order has a pair of rounds on the soffit, as in the naves of Gloucester and Christchurch (C, Fig. 41). Nearly all of these profiles we shall find carried over, with many variations and amplifications, into the subsequent pointed style. Triforium archivolts are often profiled with variants of the profile B, as at Durham and Christchurch.

FIG. 40 — Durham.

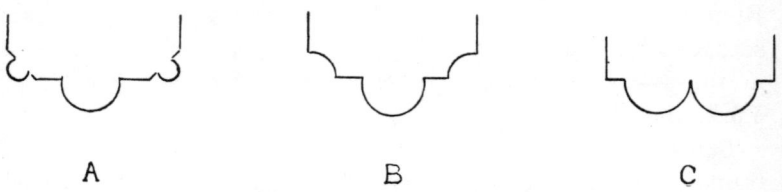

A        B        C

FIG. 41 — Peterborough, Durham, and Christchurch.

The Norman string-course has a variety of simple profiles of which A, B, and C, from Canterbury (Fig. 42), are the most common.

The cornice is usually a plain salient course of flat stones with the lower edge bevelled, often resting on corbels. The corbel-table in England, as elsewhere, has a variety of forms. In the clerestory of Romsey corbels alone occur, in the clerestory and aisle walls of Peterborough the corbels carry diminutive monolithic arches, at Winchester the small arches are segmental, and in the aisles of Romsey there are pairs of arches.

As a whole, the Anglo-Norman building, in its rude massiveness, has a monumental dignity that is hardly found in any other architecture of the Middle Ages; and while it differs from the Norman art of the continent in no essential way, it has a local stamp and a distinctive expression. The exterior, in its integrity, is especially noteworthy, the structural inconsistencies of the interior not appearing here.

The Anglo-Norman exterior is, however, nowhere to be seen in its original completeness. It is only in parts, mainly transepts, that we find it unmutilated enough to enable us to realize

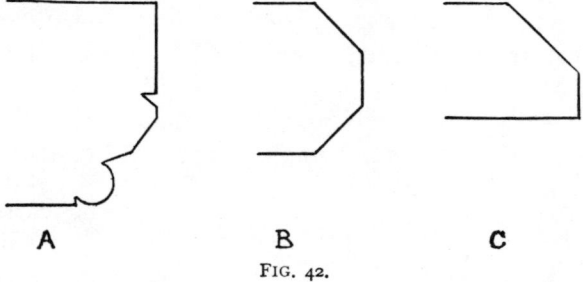

FIG. 42.

its real grandeur. Such transepts as those of Winchester, of Romsey, and of New Shoreham, gave the model, as we shall see, for what is finest, as to the larger features and proportions, in the Early English transepts of Lincoln, of Worcester, of York, and of Beverley.

Before passing to the consideration of the early stages of transformation of this Norman art into the pointed style we must notice two exceptional forms of Norman building in England; namely, the circular form without internal divisions, and the circular church with a concentric aisle. An example of the first of these is the Chapter House of Worcester. It is about 20 metres in internal diameter, and has a round central column from which spring ten radiating ribs, of half round section, breaking the surface of an annular barrel vault into as many compartments. On the wall side these ribs are carried by shallow shafts, each engaged with a pilaster strip. Over the central column the vault is pinched up between each pair of ribs into a groin, which is sharp at the springing, but becomes obtuse above, and dies away just above the haunch. On the outer part it now has pointed interpenetrations over large openings with dividing members in the Perpendicular style. The unaltered parts correspond in style with the primitive Norman work at the west end of the nave, of which only a few fragments remain, as will be seen in the next chapter. This Chapter House of Worcester gave the model for those later ones which became so characteristic of the Early English style.

The second form of circular building is found in St. Sepulchre of Cambridge, where the central area is covered with a hemispherical vault, with surface ribs springing from corbels in the triforium spandrels, and converging on the crown. This vault springs from the top of the wall, but it is fortified by stepped rings of masonry after the manner of the Roman Pantheon. The great arcade is carried on massive round columns, like those of St. John's chapel in the Tower of London. The aisles have groined vaults on ribs, and the structure as a whole foreshadows the more elegant Temple Church of London to be noticed in the next chapter.[1]

[1] I do not know St. Sepulchre at first hand. I take this description from M. Ruprich-Robert's plates in *L'Architecture Normande*.

# CHAPTER II

### POINTED NORMAN

WE have now to consider the beginnings of those changes which ultimately transformed the Norman Romanesque architecture into what is known as the Early English style. These changes are commonly spoken of as constituting a transition from the Norman to the Gothic style. But since in the transformation no essential change was wrought in the structural system — such as was developed in what I consider the true Gothic art — this seems to me an improper way of speaking. The only changes effected were superficial and consisted chiefly in the substitution of the pointed arch for the round arch, together with the introduction of a new style of ornament. This was the case also in many other parts of Europe. Indeed, the use of the pointed arch in the greater part of the architecture of the continent in the twelfth century appears to have arisen from æsthetic motives only, and is thus unaccompanied by a proper development of that consistent organic system which distinguishes the true Gothic style. In the hands of the builders of the Ile de France alone — I must repeatedly affirm — does it appear to have been employed, in connection with appropriate supports, primarily, and creatively, for structural ends. Its advantage in the narrow spanned arches of groined vaulting had, in the course of structural experimentation, been recognized by these builders early in the twelfth century, and before the middle of that century it was employed by them systematically in the forming Gothic style.[1] It appears, indeed, to have been used elsewhere in Europe quite as early, if not earlier, but only in buildings having no progressive character of the kind that distinguishes that peculiar structural and artistic evolution of the Ile de France in which it was so important a factor.

[1] Cf. my *Development and Character of Gothic Architecture*, pp. 59 *et seq.*

In England the pointed arch occurs first, I believe, in the Cistercian churches of the north not long before the middle of the twelfth century, and it appears here to have been an importation from Burgundy. It was not, however, in the Cistercian architecture, either of Burgundy or of England, accompanied by any change in the general system of construction. The

FIG. 43 — Fountains Abbey

Cistercian churches of England are essentially Norman in structural character. Fountains Abbey, for instance (begun in the year 1135), resembles the small church at Étretat in having massive round piers, no vaulting members, no triforium openings, and a heavy walled clerestory with no passageway. But the great pier arches are pointed, and the aisles are covered with a series of pointed barrel vaults (Fig. 43) having their axes perpendicular to the long axis of the building, after a common Burgundian manner. These vaults are supported on transverse round arches sprung from corbels let into the piers on one side, and the wall on the other, at a considerable distance below the arcade impost. The great archivolts are of three orders on the nave side, and of one order on the side of the aisle. To conform with this impost plan the great abaci are made polygonal on the nave side and square on the other, each angle of the square being supported by a shaft engaged with the pier. Externally the flat Norman buttress breaks the clerestory wall, and two string-courses, one at the level of the window sills and the other at that of the window arch imposts, are returned around the buttresses — the upper one being bent to form hood moulds to the windows. Thus apart from the pointed arches, and the Burgundian aisle vaulting, the nave of Fountains is thoroughly Norman Romanesque of the least organic kind.

The nave of the daughter church of Kirkstall Abbey, begun after 1152,[1] resembles that of Fountains in its larger features. There is the same absence of any provision for high vaulting, and although the surfaces of the piers are subdivided into small members, these members have no relation to the archivolts and aisle vaulting which they support. Thus from a structural point of view the piers remain substantially like the plain round columns of the mother church. The aisles, however (Fig. 44), have groined vaulting of advanced Anglo-Norman character, with semicircular groin ribs and acutely pointed transverse ribs. The cells on the nave side are shaped to the pointed archivolts of the great arcade, and those of the wall side, where there are no ribs, trace pointed arches against the wall. All the ribs are brought up to about the same height, and the crowns of the cells are in nearly straight lines. In other respects this vaulting is like the earlier ribbed Norman vaulting — the cells being of ragstone in courses measurably straight in the upper parts, but variously inclined below, and the surfaces being slightly warped in shaping themselves to the semicircular groins and pointed transverse arches. The rib profiling is, with variations, like that of the basement of the Treasury at Canterbury. Notwithstanding the pointed ribs in the vaulting, this aisle of Kirkstall has no complete and logical system of supports from the pavement such as we find in the Ile de France even before the in-

---

[1] Cf. Mr. John Bilson's admirable monograph, *The Architecture of the Church of Kirkstall Abbey*, Leeds, 1907.

troduction of the pointed arch, as we have already seen in St. Étienne of Beauvais. The system is less organic as a whole than that of the round arched aisle of Peterborough. This lack of organic character in Kirkstall is shown further in the east end, and in the transept. The two compartments of high vaulting over the east end are of substantially the same form as that

FIG. 44 — Aisle of Kirkstall Abbey.

of the aisles of the nave. Springing from corbels in the wall, they have no independent supports from the pavement. There are, indeed, shaft groups at the crossing, but the vaults have no connection with them. The westernmost transverse rib of the vaulting is separated by a considerable interval from the crossing arch — the intervening space being filled with a narrow section of pointed barrel vaulting like that of the aisles of Fountains. On the east side of the transept a series of rectangular chapels are each covered with a barrel vault springing from unbroken partition walls. There is thus neither in Fountains nor in Kirkstall any indication of an independent spirit of structural invention tending in the direction of an organic system. On the contrary, such disjointed composition shows, I think, that the principles of organic construction were not grasped by the Anglo-Norman builders.

Pointed vaulting, with supports of a more logical character occurs, however, in the aisles of Malmesbury Abbey, dating apparently from not long after the middle of the twelfth century.[1] This

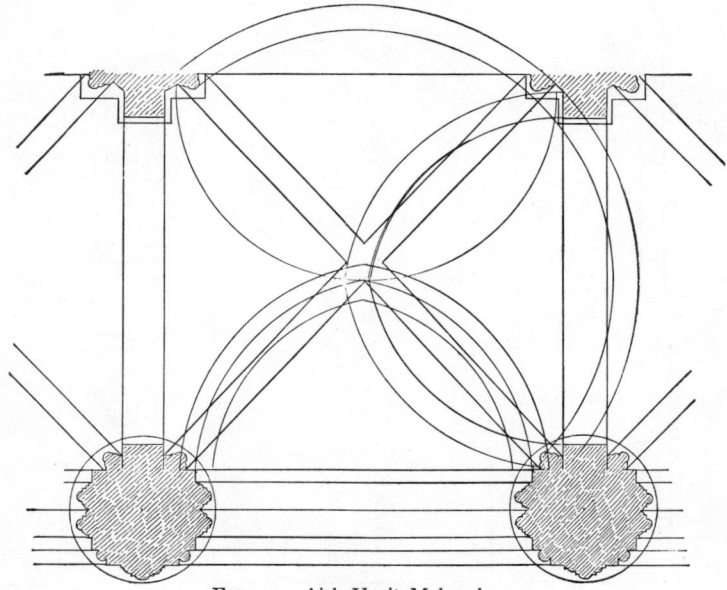

FIG. 45 — Aisle Vault, Malmesbury.

is more like the round arched vaulting under the Treasury at Canterbury (Fig. 18, p. 21). The compartments (Fig. 45) are nearly square, the vaults are domical (Fig. 46), and the pointing of the transverse ribs is less acute than at Kirkstall. The surfaces are, I believe, slightly concave, though I have not been able to reach the vault in order to verify this.[2] An impor-

[1] The date of the Malmesbury vaulting has not been determined. In the brief account of the pointed architecture of England given in my *Development and Character of Gothic Architecture*, I accepted the then generally received opinion that it was contemporaneous with St. Denis. I do not think that any one would maintain this now.

[2] It is very possible that in the cross section (Fig. 46) I have given too much curvature to the crown of the vault.

E

tant point to notice is that we have here, on the wall side, a group of supports from the pavement logically related to the ribs of the vaulting. These aisles of Malmesbury have been held by some English writers to be contemporaneous with St. Denis of France, and to show that England was then as far advanced in the development of the Gothic style as France itself. A comparison will show, however, that this claim could not be

FIG. 46—Cross Section, Aisle of Malmesbury.

justified even if the buildings were contemporaneous. The difference between the two works is vast. In St. Denis[1] (Fig. 47) we have a new art almost wholly freed in structural character, from the influences of Romanesque tradition; in Malmesbury we have a ponderous Norman construction with its aisle vaulting alone shaped in part after early French models.

The small church of St. Peter's in the East at Oxford, which appears to have followed not long after Malmesbury, has vault-

[1] The apsidal aisles, with their radial chapels, are all that remain of the east end of St. Denis as built in the twelfth century. The two piers at the left in the illustration (Fig. 47) belong to the alterations of the thirteenth century. All the rest is the original work dating from 1137–1140.

ing of a similar kind. The system has suffered some alterations, but what remains intact has more elegance than Malmesbury, though in other respects it is substantially of the same character.

The remains of the Cistercian Church of Roche Abbey show a fuller introduction of the members of an organic system, in-

FIG. 47 — Apsidal Aisles, St. Denis.

cluding high vaulting. The date of this work is uncertain, but from its architectural character I do not think it can be earlier than the close of the twelfth century. Of the vaulting only portions remain, but the clerestory wall on the east side of the north arm of the transept is nearly intact, and shows plainly a direct influence from the Ile de France in the important feature of the stilted longitudinal arch. But the Anglo-Norman tendency to break the continuity of supports appears in the use of corbels, instead of shafts, for the groin ribs — the transverse rib only having a supporting shaft from the pavement. There is a well-developed triforium with a pair of blind pointed arches in each bay, and in the choir these arches are profiled in the French manner, and have small angle shafts with capitals of a French Gothic type. The vaulting capitals, and those of the ground story piers, have square abaci and plainly moulded bells of concave outline.

The two western bays of the nave of Worcester Cathedral, assigned by Willis,[1] I believe correctly, to the last quarter of the

FIG. 48 — Clerestory, Worcester West Bay.

twefth century, exhibit on a large scale a remarkable instance of pointed Norman architecture. This was, I think, clearly a completely vaulted structure, though the two south aisle compartments alone retain the original vaulting, the great vaults, and those of the north aisle, having been reconstructed in the fourteenth century, when the rest of the nave was rebuilt in its present form. That there was twelfth century vaulting over

[1] *Architectural History of Worcester Cathedral.* By R. Willis, London, 1863.

these bays appears from the work as it now exists. A scar (Fig. 48) beneath the longitudinal rib of the existing vault shows where the Norman rib was, and the shafts for its support still remain in the system below, but are now without function, since all the ribs of the present vaulting are gathered on the three other shafts which formerly carried, it would appear, only the transverse and groin ribs of the Norman vaults. Thus the system of these west bays included vaults on a full rib system, with five shafts in the pier — one for each rib — the first instance of this that we have met with in England. The structure as a whole is of massive Norman character, having ground story piers of great bulk, heavy archivolts and enclosing walls, and a ponderous clerestory with the Anglo-Norman passageway. But within this heavy structure the vaulting system is of remarkable lightness and elegance.[1] The scar of the former wall rib on the clerestory wall shows that this rib was acutely pointed, and somewhat stilted, though not enough to give much of the French Gothic form to the vaulting conoid. There can be no doubt that the transverse ribs were pointed, but what was the nature of the vault masonry

FIG. 49 — Worcester West Bay.

there appears no means of determining, though it would seem likely that it was like that of the aisles to be presently noticed. In the inner wall of the clerestory the great central round-arched opening is flanked by a small pointed opening on either side, while the triforium has a pair of pointed arches each embracing three small round ones of two orders, the first order being shafted and taller than the sub-order. The archivolts

---

[1] The lightness of these vault supports, not in keeping with the ponderous walled construction, appears to me a clear indication of direct, though partial, imitation of French Gothic models. It does not seem to me that such slender supports would be a natural Norman development. In taking them over from the French Gothic, where they are duly proportioned to the true skeleton system of construction, the Norman builders were inconsistent. Such attenuation with them was inappropriate.

of the great arcade are pointed, and of four orders of square section.

The capitals of these bays are of great variety, and above the ground story they are of thoroughly French Gothic form (Fig. 49). Those that crown the high vaulting shafts have great elegance, and some of them are richly ornamented with foliate carving. The capitals of the ground story are variants of the Norman scalloped type, the bell having a finely concave outline.

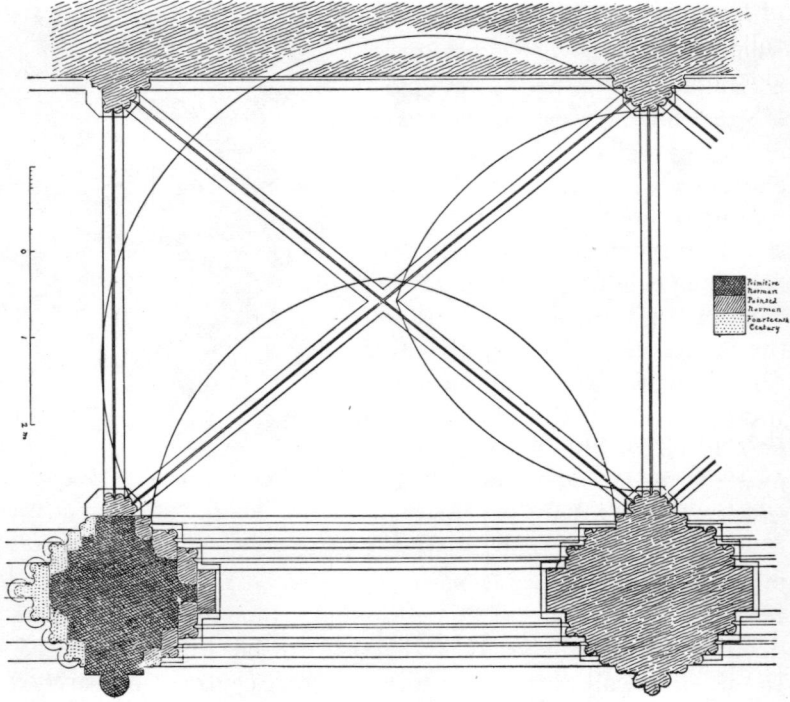

FIG. 50 — Aisle Vault, Worcester West Bay.

The base profiles (B, Fig. 52) are of French Gothic type, but the angle spur does not occur. A strong influence from the French Gothic is thus manifest in the details of the west bays of Worcester, but no structural change differentiates it from the older Norman art.

The Norman character of the work is shown further in the two compartments of vaulting which remain of the original construction in the south aisle. It will be worth while to make a detailed examination of this vaulting. Each compartment is on plan (Fig. 50) a wide oblong rectangle measuring 5.95 × 6.20 metres from centre to centre of the supports. The vault is furnished with a complete system of ribs, of which those on the groins are segmental, and those on the sides are pointed. We shall presently see, however, that these ribs are not used altogether as the ribs in true Gothic vaulting are. The groin ribs and the transverse ribs are of the same magnitude, and the same profiling (A, Fig. 52) — each having the common French form of two roles separated by a sunk fillet, with a quirk above each roll. The curves of the groin ribs are struck from centres considerably below the springing level, so that they form angles at

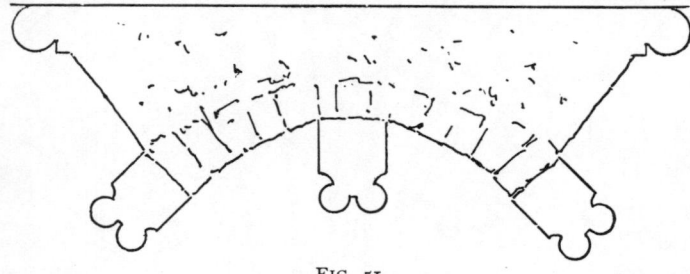

FIG. 51.

the springing after the common Norman manner. The transverse ribs are acutely pointed, the wider spanned longitudinal ribs is obtusely so, and thus all the ribs are brought to nearly the same height — the intrados of the groin ribs being 2.86 metres above the springing level, that of the transverse rib 2.91, that of the great archivolt member 2.88, and that of the wall rib 3.05. These forms and adjustments of the ribs bring about irregularities in the vault surfaces with which the builders appear to have experienced some difficulties, as we shall see.

The segmental form of the groin rib makes its haunches low, while the haunches of the narrow spanned and pointed transverse ribs are relatively high. Moreover, the transverse rib is set on the abacus very little in advance of the groin ribs, and, rising more steeply, it is, in the horizontal section (Fig. 51), considerably drawn in. If the courses of rough masonry of the vault filling were laid directly from extrados to extrados of the ribs (as they are in French Gothic vaulting) very oblique surfaces, from the springing to the haunch, would be developed.

To avoid this, as far as possible, the builder has started his filling (Fig. 52) with stones laid from the extrados of the groin rib to the roll of the transverse rib, and as the courses rise they meet this rib farther back against its side until

FIG. 52—Conoid of Aisle Vault, Worcester West Bay.

they reach the extrados and are then laid upon it. From this point upward the transverse rib, embedded below, becomes free, as shown in cell C of the illustration. Then finding, in cell D, that the very low haunch of the segmental groin rib would warp the vault surface excessively if the courses were continued to its extrados, the builder has pieced out the rib with rough stones so as to raise the vault in that part. It will be seen that where the piecing of the rib begins the upper bed surface of the last stone running to the extrados is left, for the most part, uncovered, and that the first stone above this slants at an angle which coincides neither with the upper nor the lower vault surface. These rude makeshifts are very common in the Anglo-Norman ribbed vaulting, and their presence here in the west bays of Worcester shows how far behind contemporaneous French work it is.[1] The wall arch in this aisle vault is not, as before remarked, used as it would be in Gothic vaulting. That is to say, the vault masonry does not rest upon it. It is, in fact, not properly a vault rib, independent of the wall, but rather a wall arch against which the vault abuts, tracing an irregular curve, as shown in the illustration. The courses of rough masonry in this vaulting appear slightly arched, giving a little concavity to the surfaces, but they are of great irregularity, and in some places appear nearly straight.

On the outside against this south aisle of Worcester is a walled passageway covered with several small compartments of nearly square vaults of the same general character as those of the interior just described. The ragstone filling is here very rough, the crowns of the cells are in nearly horizontal straight lines, and the lower surfaces are much warped, giving the horizontal section shown at A on the plan (Fig. 53). The ribs are of plain bevelled section, and spring from corbels (Fig. 54).

Other important buildings showing pointed Norman features are: St. Cross, Winchester; St. Mary's, New Shoreham; Glastonbury Abbey; Wells Cathedral; Ripon Minster, and the Temple Church, London. These are all, I believe, nearly

---

[1] The plaster, with which the surfaces of Norman vaults were covered, hides these irregularities to a great extent, yet they may often be seen through the plaster, as in the aisles of the nave of Peterborough. The piecing out of a vault rib was sometimes resorted to in the experimental works of the primitive French Gothic builders, as at Bury, and in the vaulted chamber over the porch of St. Leu d'Esserent (cf. my *Development and Character of Gothic Architecture*, second edition, pp. 66, 67, 69), but this was confined, I believe, to the transverse ribs, where its purpose was to raise the crown of this rib in order to avoid an excessively domical form in the vault. The early Gothic builders would not have occasion to raise the haunch of a groin rib, because this rib with them was not a segmental curve struck from below the springing level.

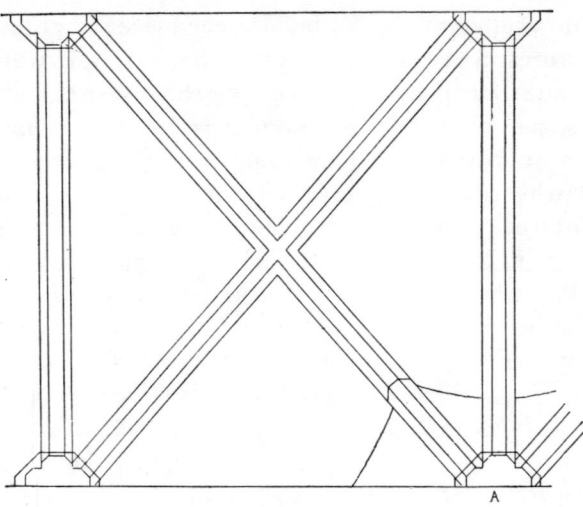

FIG. 53 — Worcester.

contemporaneous with the west bays of Worcester, but their chronological order is uncertain, and we may take them in the order in which they are here named.

FIG. 54 — Worcester.

The east end of St. Cross is square on plan, and has two compartments of high vaulting, as well as vaulting in the aisles. The eastern compartment has five cells, a half rib, springing from the eastern wall to the intersection of the groins, dividing what would otherwise be a single cell into two smaller ones, the crowns of which are necessarily oblique, as in sexpartite vaulting. The other compartment is quadripartite, and measures roughly 4.80 × 6.80 metres. The ribs are all pointed, and spring from the same level, so that the conoids widen as they rise against the clerestory wall. The crowns of the groin ribs rise higher than the others, but the vault surfaces are, for the most part, hardly at all concave, the crowns of the cells being in nearly straight, though inclined,

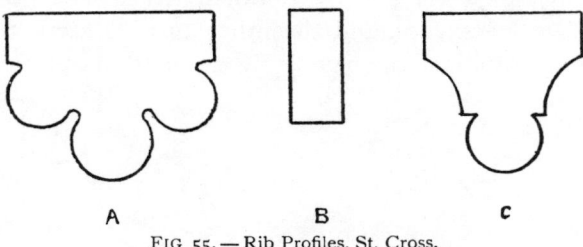

FIG 55.—Rib Profiles, St. Cross.

lines. There is, however, as in most other cases, considerable irregularity. The crowns of the oblique cells of the eastern compartment are apparently a little arched, while the lateral cells of the same compartment seem to curve downward a little. These vaults are of cut stones, well faced and jointed, and the courses are parallel at the crown. The rib profiles are of common early French Gothic forms, with one rib in the western compartment which is a variant of those in the aisles of Canterbury. Profile A (Fig. 55) is that of the groin ribs of the eastern compartment, B is that of the longitudinal ribs,

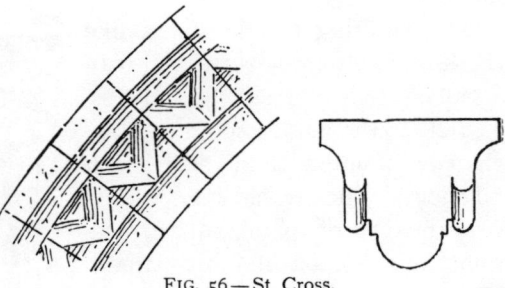

FIG. 56—St. Cross.

C is one groin rib of the western compartment, while its companion (Fig. 56) has the Canterbury form. This vaulting thus exhibits a combination of French Gothic and Anglo-Norman characteristics. It is French in its squared masonry and in most of its rib profiles, and Anglo-Norman in having the longitudinal rib spring from the same level with the other ribs. The supporting members are not well adjusted to those of the

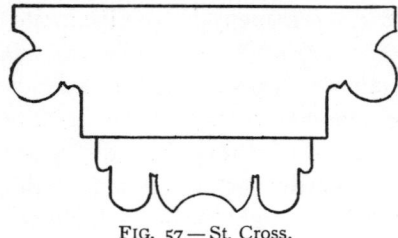

FIG. 57—St. Cross.

vaults, as will be seen from the sections (Figs. 57 and 58) of the transverse rib and the pier shafts respectively. Of the seven members of the shaft group three (*a*) fall under the sub-order of the double transverse rib, two (*b*) support the first order, and the other two (*c*) carry the groin ribs, the longitudinal rib having no support of its own. The

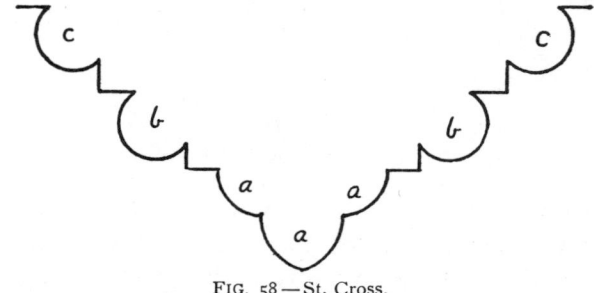

FIG. 58—St. Cross.

whole group starts from a corbel set about one metre above the impost of the ground story arcade, and thus there is no continuous support from the pavement.

The vaulting of the aisles, like the high vaulting, is furnished with a full system of ribs, but the ribs, as well as the vault itself, are more sharply pointed, and are much heavier. The transverse rib is very heavy, of plain square section, and is considerably stilted. The crowns of these cells appear nearly level, the masonry is again of well cut stones laid, for the most part, in nearly straight courses, and in order to get them so the groin ribs are in some places pieced out as in the west bays of Worcester, but even more extensively. This

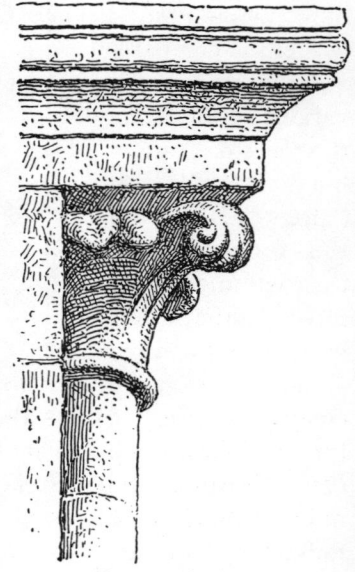

FIG. 59—St. Cross.

aisle vaulting is thus more Anglo-Norman than French. Direct French influence is, however, apparent in the supporting members. The shafts resemble those of St. Denis, though they are banded as at Sens; while the capitals (Fig. 59) and bases (Fig. 60) are of pure early French Gothic design, and appear like French workmanship.

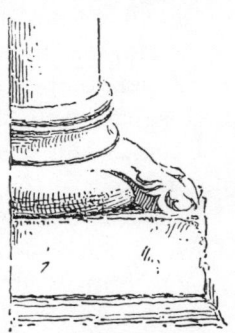

FIG. 60 — St. Cross.

The pointed arch occurs in the nave also, but this part is more distinctly Anglo-Norman, and resembles, in its lower system, the nave of Malmesbury, though it is less advanced than Malmesbury in retaining the low segmental groin rib.

The choir of St. Mary's church, New Shoreham, is a pointed Norman work up to the triforium string, above which it has been rebuilt in the Early English style. While it includes nothing of purely French character, it shows, I think, strong French influence modifying the Norman art in nearly every part. It may be remarked in passing that this choir affords one of those exceptional, and unaccountable, instances (of which St. Pierre of Chartres is another) of a system in which one side is designed differently from the other.[1] On the north side the piers are substantially like those of Malmesbury and the nave of St. Cross — consisting of massive cylindrical columns (Fig. 61)

FIG. 61 — New Shoreham.

---

[1] The same thing occurs later, though with less marked difference, in the nave of Worcester Cathedral. But at Worcester the opposite sides are not quite contemporaneous.

alternating with octagonal ones, while on the south side they are on plan squares set diagonally, and scalloped into a semblance of small shafts, crowned with capitals having square abaci answering to the orders of the great archivolts. Against each of these scalloped piers a group of three slender vaulting shafts on a square member rises from the pavement to carry the high vaulting, while a similar group on the opposite side supports the vaulting of the aisle (Fig. 62).

The details of these piers respectively are worthy of notice as showing Anglo-Norman characteristics on the one hand, and Anglo-Norman strongly modified by French influence on the other.

FIG. 62 — New Shoreham.

The profile of the abacus of the round pier (Fig. 61) has already much likeness to the distinctive Early English profiling of abaci, and the rude foliation carved on the bell has the filleted treatment that is peculiar to Early English foliation.[1] The arch profiles are also quite Early English in form. In the scalloped pier (Fig. 62) the top member of the abacus is square, as in French abaci, and the profiling below it is more French than Anglo-Norman. The leafage of the bell is French in composition, but the execution manifests, I think, the hand of the Anglo-Norman.

The aisle vaulting and its supports show a corresponding combination of French and Anglo-Norman characteristics. The forms and proportions of the ribs are like those of French aisle vaulting, but the masonry of the filling, though in courses parallel at the crown in some parts, follows an oblique direction, meeting at an angle in others. The capitals of the aisle responds

[1] Cf. my *Development and Character of Gothic Architecture*, second edition, p. 406.

PLATE VII

Glastonbury Abbey.

have octagonal abaci, with French profiling, but the bases have round plinths.

The great church of Glastonbury, begun after 1184, when an earlier church on the same site was destroyed by fire, exhibits an apparently later phase of pointed Norman design. Unfortunately little remains of this important monument. Only the eastern crossing piers, with parts of the east side of the transept, and of the aisle walls of the choir (Plate VII), survive. But these contain members, and parts of members, that appear to explain the whole system. They show that it was vaulted throughout, and although the actual remains of vaulting are slight, there is enough to give a very clear idea of what it was. The high vaults approached more nearly in form to French Gothic vaults than any that we have before met with in England. The longitudinal ribs are very much stilted, as we see from the stilting shafts still in place. Stumps of the groin ribs still remain also, and it is worthy of notice that the capitals of their supporting shafts are set obliquely in conformity with the direction of these ribs. The rib profiles (Fig. 63) are French, but the fragments of filling which remain are of ragstone. The bay scheme of the transept is peculiar in having a great pointed arch with its impost at the level of the triforium string.

FIG. 63—Glastonbury.

This arch is of three orders, of which the middle one only rests on capitals, while the first order is continuous from the pavement, and the sub-order is a return of the triforium string. This great arch embraces three small cusped arches, of equal height, on slender shafts, and the whole forms an unusual triforium scheme—the main idea of which is, however, foreshadowed in the Norman nave of Oxford Cathedral. The clerestory here has the passageway, and the external openings, as well as those of the inner plane, are pointed. The association of continuous imposts with shafted imposts is a noticeable feature here, and in much other Anglo-Norman work. It is marked in the west bays of Worcester (which strongly resembles Glastonbury) and reappears in the Perpendicular style. It is worthy of notice also, that while the actual construction remains ponderous, the shafting of the vaults and archivolts has the extreme slenderness that we have remarked in the west bays of Worcester. This is especially true of the shafting of the crossing piers, which exceed in attenuation any that we have before met with. The capitals are not quite characteristically French, though they have square abaci with mouldings that are more French than Anglo-Norman. They are of Corinthianesque outline, but differ from typical French Gothic capitals in a peculiar elongation of the bell, with small diameter at the necking and very protruding foliation.[1]

The neighbouring Cathedral of Wells is said to have been set out after Glastonbury was commenced,[2] and it appears to have been built by the same school of workmen. The earliest parts now extant are the western bays of the choir, and it may be doubted whether any other parts go back to the twelfth century. However that may be, the nave, apart from the high vaulting, is ponderous pointed Norman work without any organic system. The high vaulting has a good deal of true Gothic form, with the stilted longitudinal rib, and rib profiles as in Fig. 64, which are almost identical with those of Glastonbury. This vaulting cannot, I think, be earlier than the thirteenth century, and its likeness to the vaulting of Salisbury suggests that it may be contemporaneous. Externally there is nothing to distinguish the building structurally from a round arched Norman one. The clerestory wall is broken only by flat Norman buttresses, which have no power to resist vault thrusts. There are, indeed, rude flying buttresses under the aisle roof, as at Durham; but the thick walls hardly need reënforcement, and if they did, no reënforcement would be effective at this low level.

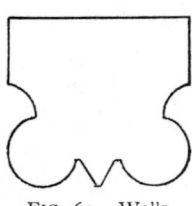

FIG. 64—Wells.

The pointed arch prevails in Wells in the external openings as well as in those of the interior, and the details show marked French influence without, save in the profiles, being distinctly French. The capitals resemble those of Glastonbury, but have more French character, especially in their foliation, although

---

[1] Early French Gothic capitals differ, of course, a good deal in their proportions and in some cases, as in St. Frambourg of Senlis, vaulting capitals that bear some resemblance in outline to those of Glastonbury occur. But an eye habituated to French Gothic will perceive a marked difference from French work in the Glastonbury capitals.

[2] Cf. Willis's *Architectural History of Glastonbury Abbey*, p. 35.

the pronounced salience of the leafage is like that of Glastonbury. The base profiles (Fig. 65) are distinctly French, and the plinths are angular on plan. The nave of Wells, though not large in scale, has much dignity and some beautiful features. The fine north porch — which, from its skeleton sub-arches of the vault lunette, its interpenetrating mouldings, and the generally florid character of the composition, cannot, I think, be of earlier date than the thirteenth century — has a great deal of beauty based on French features, more or less recast by Anglo-Norman taste and workmanship.

The three west bays of the north side of the choir of Ripon Minster have more likeness, in general composition, to contemporaneous continental art than most other architectural works in England have. This may be due to the fact that they were built under Archbishop Roger (1154–1181), who had come from Pont-l'Evêque in Calvados. An eye familiar with the pointed architecture of the twelfth century in Normandy will notice here a strong influence from that

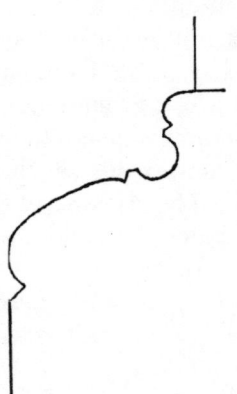

FIG. 65 — Wells.

source. This is manifest in the acute pointing of the arches, and in the comparative lightness of construction — the great archivolts, for instance, having but two orders, as at Coutance, Eu, Dol, and Fécamp. In other respects these bays of Ripon choir follow the general Anglo-Norman style, having the heavily walled clerestory with the passageway, and round arched external openings. As in the west bays of Worcester nave, there are five vaulting shafts in each pier group, but here they start from the capitals of the ground story, instead of rising from the pavement, and all of them are crowned with capitals at the level of the clerestory string. Thus the vaulting, for which these shafts provide completely, would appear not to have been intended to have the longitudinal ribs stilted. But the intention of vaulting, to which the system points, appears to have been abandoned when the springing level was reached, and a clerestory was built which is incompatible with any vaulting, though a wooden imitation of vaulting has been built up against it in modern times. The outer wall of this clerestory is in unmodified Norman Romanesque form, with a single round-headed window, while the inner plane has three shafted arches — the middle one round arched and the others acutely pointed. Between the bays thus composed there is a smaller blind pointed arch in the wall solid over each pier, making the clerestory arcade continuous from end to end of the choir. Except for the blind arches between the bays, the scheme of the clerestory is a variant of that of the triforium, where the middle arch embraces a pair of shafted arches, and the lateral arches are blind.

The ground story pier is composed of eight round members of three magnitudes, but these members have no logical relationship to the members of the superstructure.

The vaulting of the aisles is shaped to acutely pointed ribs to which the supporting shafts are logically adjusted.

In the transept the system of the choir undergoes some changes. The number of high vaulting shafts is reduced to three, and all start from the pavement, giving a very French Gothic appearance to the structural system as a whole.

The vaulting of the aisle of this transept has the novel feature of a ridge rib in both the longitudinal and transverse directions. These ribs are very small, and of simple round section — like the rolls of the groin ribs.

The twelfth century nave of Ripon appears to have been without aisles, and from fragments of the original architectural scheme remaining at the east and west ends it would seem that it had a great arcaded passageway in the thickness of the wall, starting from a level considerably above the pavement, below which the wall presents an unbroken surface. The first and third bays of the arcade at the west end remain intact, and between them is a portion of a wider bay, the lower part of which has been subsequently pierced with an arched opening. The arch of this wider bay is round, while those of the narrow ones are pointed. The bays are separated by single shafts resting on corbels at the level of the string-course. The round arch of the wider bay embraces four shafted arches, of which the middle two are taller than the others, in conformity with the space under the great arch, while under the arch of each narrow bay are two shafted arches. All of these sub-arches are pointed. Above this is another passageway, like that of a clerestory,

PLATE VIII

Temple Church, London.

with a round arched opening flanked by two smaller pointed openings in the wide bay, while in each narrow bay is a row of three pointed openings of equal height. The scheme shows that there was no vaulting, and while it has much beauty as an ornamented composition, it embodies no organic principles of construction.

An exceptional instance of a pointed Norman building on a circular plan is the Temple Church, London (Plate VIII). Like the earlier round arched church of St. Sepulchre at Cambridge, it has a concentric aisle giving rise to a triforium and clerestory. But instead of the ponderous character of the older monument the inner system of the Temple Church exhibits a degree of lightness, of real construction, exceeding that of any Anglo-Norman work of the twelfth century that we have thus far noticed. The central area appears to have been originally covered with pointed vaulting on groin ribs, like that of the early French Gothic apses, save that the wall ribs, still in place, are not stilted. With this exception it is like two such apses set together so as to cover a circular area. Of this vaulting only the ribs remain, the cells being now formed of wood.[1] There are six cells, and the ribs are carried on very slender shafts of Purbeck rising from the capitals of the ground-story piers. The piers are each composed of four detached, but closely grouped, shafts of Purbeck of two magnitudes, — the larger ones supporting the main archivolts, and the smaller ones carrying the vaulting shafts of the nave, and the ribs of the aisle vaulting. The great archivolts are pointed, and each of a single order profiled as in Figure 66. The triforium stage has in each bay a continuous arcade of six pointed arches, formed by intersecting round arches on slender shafts — the two middle ones being open, and the others blind. The shafts of this triforium, with their capitals and bases, are of great elegance, and of thoroughly French form.

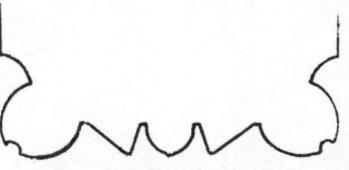

FIG. 66 — Temple Church.

The external walls are of heavier Norman construction, pierced with round arched windows, one in each bay of both aisles and

---

[1] This is my conjecture from the work as it now stands. I know nothing of the early history of the building.

clerestory. The masonry is, in every part of the old work, smooth-faced and finely jointed; but the building has been deplorably worked over by the modern restorer. The piers and responds, with their capitals and bases, appear to be all new, and have, of course, the mechanically perfect character of modern work. Besides this, the marble has been excessively polished.

The vaulting of the aisles, which appears to be mainly intact, is of peculiar interest, and consists of six compartments of quadripartite vaulting alternating with as many triangular compartments (Fig. 67). All the vault ribs are pointed, and the

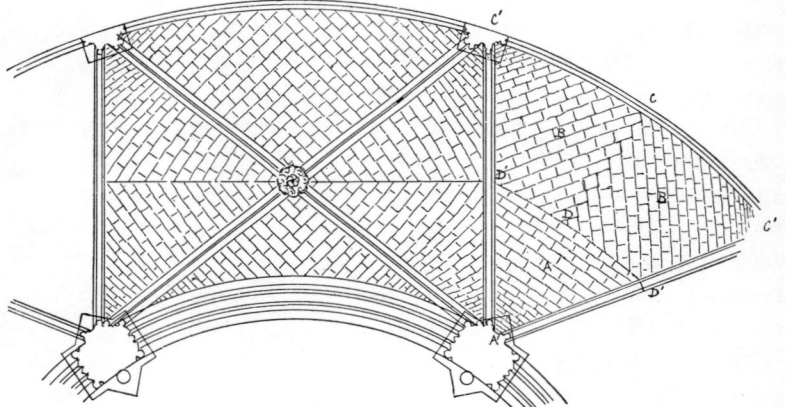

FIG. 67 — Temple Church.

crowns of the groin ribs are higher than the others. The courses of masonry in the cells are for the most part oblique on plan, but in lines nearly straight from rib to rib. They vary a little, however, both in direction and width, and taper considerably in places, forming, of necessity, somewhat warped surfaces, as in most other mediæval vaulting. The cells of the quadripartite compartments are pointed to a well defined line at the crown — a common characteristic of pointed Norman vaulting. The triangular compartments are different, and follow a peculiar form that first appeared, I believe, in the apsidal aisles of the Cathedral of Paris, dating from soon after the year 1163.[1] There can be little doubt that the builders of the vaults of the Temple Church were acquainted with the vaults of Paris, and that they

---

[1] The Cathedral of Paris was begun, as is well known, in 1163.

modelled these triangular compartments after them.[1] But while these vaults follow the French vaults in essential form, they differ from the French models in some details of construction, as Anglo-Norman works based on those of France generally do. The difference appears both in the conformation of the surfaces and in the direction of the courses of masonry. In these triangular compartments there are no salient groins, and therefore no ribs are required other than those on the sides. The surface A (Fig. 67) rises from the point A', in nearly parallel and straight courses, to the line D, in which it meets the surfaces B. The line D is slightly curved on plan so as to be nearly concentric with the circle on which the building is set out. The points D' and C are at the crowns of the bounding ribs, and the courses of masonry forming the surfaces B are oblique, and thus meet at angles on the crown line CD, instead of being parallel as in the French vaulting. They are nearly straight on plan, and level in elevation, whereas in the vaults of Paris they are more or less curved on plan and arched in elevation, so as to form concave surfaces. This oblique direction of the courses became common, though by no means constant, in the pointed vaulting of England, and has been regarded by some writers as a distinctive English characteristic.

It will be seen, I think, from the foregoing examples, that the pointed Norman architecture of England differs not at all in its essential structural character from the round-arched Norman art. It remains an architecture of heavy walls showing no tendency to develop an organic skeleton independent of the walls, and foreshadowing their ultimate elimination, — a tendency which differentiates the transitional Gothic of France from all other architecture. As in the round-arched Norman work, members derived from organic building are more or less freely introduced, but are rarely so used as to form a complete and logical system of functional parts extending through the whole edifice.

The changes thus far introduced were mainly due to such general influences from the Continent as were natural under the conditions that prevailed in the twelfth century. We have next to consider a more complete introduction of the new elements from the Continent in the great work at Canterbury.

[1] The apsidal aisle vaulting of the Cathedral of Paris is described and illustrated in my *Gothic Architecture*, second edition, pp. 168, 169.

## CHAPTER III

#### THE CHOIR OF CANTERBURY

IT is well known how the destruction by fire, in the year 1174, of the greater part of the Norman choir of Canterbury was immediately followed by a rebuilding under the direction of the French architect, William of Sens.[1] In this work we have, for the first time in England, the principles of the early French Gothic art largely embodied in an entire system; and this system is clearly derived from that of the noble cathedral of the architect's native town in the province of Champagne on the confines of the Ile de France.

The architectural relation of Canterbury to Sens has not yet been made the subject of a thorough investigation and fully set forth by a competent and well informed writer. Willis was competent, and knew his Canterbury well, but his knowledge of Sens was slight. The Cathedral of Sens, one of the finest early Gothic monuments of France, was begun about 1140, and appears to have been practically completed before 1170. Its vaulting is sexpartite, and its alternate system of large and small piers is in logical agreement with such vaulting. The main piers, like those of Noyon and Senlis, are compound, and have a full number of vaulting shafts starting from the pavement; while the intermediate piers have, on the ground story, the exceptional form of a pair of cylindrical columns set on a line perpendicular to the long axis of the building. While it is evident that the French architect at Canterbury drew his main inspiration from

---

[1] Cf. *The History of the Burning and Repair of the Church of Canterbury*, by the monk Gervase. Translated and published by Willis in his admirable monograph on Canterbury Cathedral, London, 1845. We are told by Gervase how after the fire which practically destroyed the Norman choir, French and English artificers were summoned, and how "Amongst the other workmen there had come a certain William of Sens, a man active and ready, and a workman most skilful both in wood and stone. Him, therefore, they retained, on account of his lively genius and good reputation, and dismissed the others."

this monument, the new choir which he built is not a close reproduction of it. For not only was close copying foreign to the spirit of the Middle Ages, but the architect had not here a perfectly free hand, and he could not, therefore, follow the French model as closely as he might otherwise have done. Of the ruined Norman Church a good deal remained which the monks of the establishment wished to have preserved in the new fabric.[1] The piers and upper walls appear, for the most part, to have remained standing, but in such damaged condition that they had to be demolished. The aisle walls, however, and the greater part of the walls of the transept, including the chapels of St. Andrew and St. Anselm, remained in good condition, and were preserved in the new work, the general plan of which they determined. The width of the new aisles was fixed by the Norman work, for this work included the crypt, still extant under every part of the existing structure, and the piers of the new choir had to depend for support on the massive piers of this crypt. Willis's plan (Fig. 68) shows, on one side of the axial line, the relation of the new piers to those of the crypt. It will be seen that the spacing is different, the centres of none of the new piers of the choir falling directly over those of the piers below, and some of them overhanging so much that the French architect had to build out additional supports for them, which are now conspicuous features of the crypt.

In his design for the new work the architect, following the scheme of Sens, made his vaulting sexpartite, but in the supports for this vaulting he departed from the system of Sens, and instead of erecting great compound piers in alternation with smaller ones, he made them, on the ground story, all alike in bulk, and in the form of single round columns alternating with octagonal ones (except, of course, the crossing piers), starting his vaulting shafts from the capitals of these piers — as in the cathedrals of Paris and Laon. The pier system is thus not entirely logical, since it does not, on the ground story, express the different functions of the main piers and intermediate piers in the support of sexpartite vaulting. This departure from the logic of the French model may have been made in obedience to local preferences, the monks desiring to preserve as much as possible of the old work; and although the architect was obliged to demolish

---

[1] Willis, *Op. cit.*, p. 36.

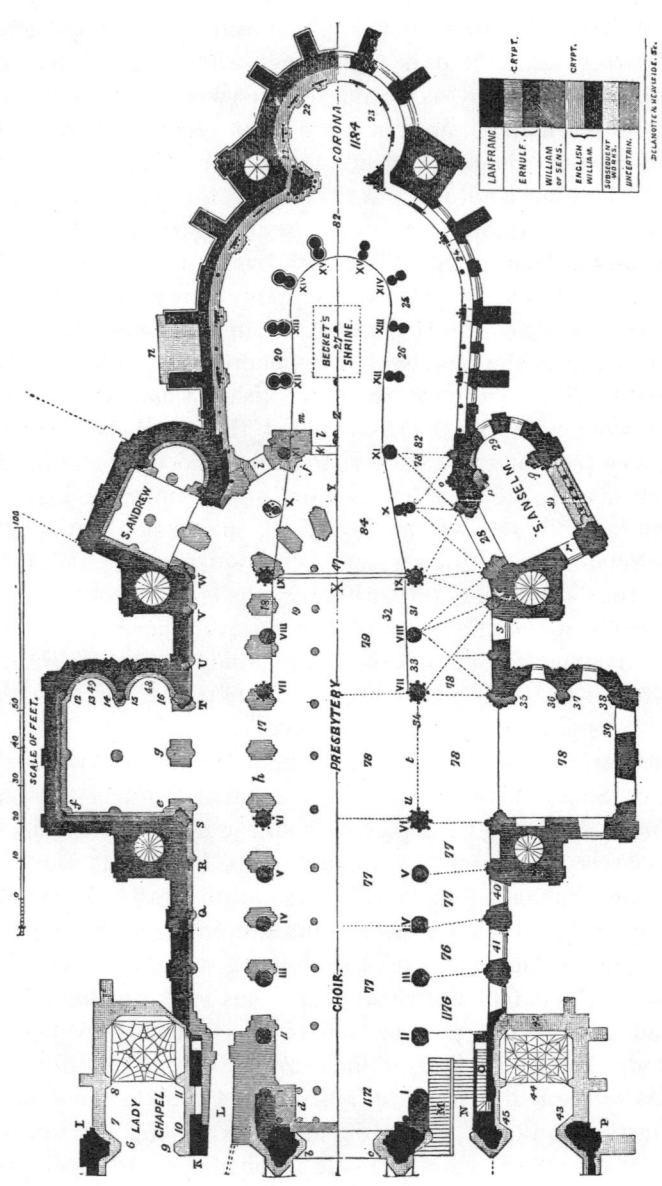

FIG. 68.—Canterbury.

the old piers, on account of their damaged condition, he made the new ones like them in form.  Gervase tells us that "the pillars of the new work were of the same form and diameter as the old, but were about twelve feet higher."

There are other points in which the architect departed, not only from the system of Sens, but from the principles of the early Gothic art as they had by this time been developed in France.  This was largely due to the necessity of adjusting his design to the Norman remains, but beyond this he appears to have been influenced to some extent by the Anglo-Norman modes of building, as a foreign workman in Anglo-Norman employ might naturally be, whether by pressure of local preference, or by voluntary inclination to conform in part to local architectural ideas and habits.  Some of the apparent indications of this I shall endeavour to point out as we proceed in our examination of this remarkable monument.

In studying a vaulted structure of the Middle Ages it is best to begin with the vaulting, because, in a logical vaulted system, the character of the vaulting largely determines that of everything else.  The vaulting of the choir of Canterbury differs from that of Sens in many points.  In Sens the main transverse ribs are heavier than the other ribs, and are of two orders, effectively marking the main divisions of the system.  The groin ribs, which are semicircular, rise a little higher than the transverse ribs, and make the vaults slightly domical.  The intermediate transverse ribs, having a considerably wider span than the main transverse ribs (in consequence of the greater bulk of the main piers, which advances their supporting members farther into the nave, and thus diminishes the spans between them), require to be but slightly pointed in order to bring their crowns up to the level of those of the groin ribs through which they pass.  The longitudinal ribs were originally round arched, with their crowns so low that the lateral cells of the vault were made very domical.[1]  In Canterbury the main transverse ribs and the intermediate transverse ribs do not differ in magnitude.  The groin ribs are semicircular and reach above the main transverse ribs about as much as

[1] The lateral cells of Sens were remodelled toward the close of the thirteenth century, when the clerestory openings were enlarged to their present dimensions. The original forms are clearly indicated by the primitive stilting shafts still in place and by portions of the old longitudinal ribs that remain.  Cf. Viollet le Duc, s.v. *Voute*, p. 508.

in Sens.  The intermediate transverse ribs are also semicircular, or nearly so, and are stilted to raise their crowns to the level of the intersection of the groin ribs.  This vaulting, westward of the eastern transept, consists of two sexpartite compartments and one quadripartite compartment — this last being the westernmost.  The westernmost of the sexpartite compartments is wider than the other, and the lateral cells of this compartment trace round-headed arches against the clerestory wall, and have no longitudinal ribs (Plate IX) — a singular omission for a French architect of the time.  The longitudinal arches of these vaults are higher than those of Sens originally were, so that the vaults are not nearly so domical.  In the narrower eastern compartments the lateral cells have pointed longitudinal arches. All of these longitudinal arches are stilted, but not in quite true French Gothic fashion.  In sexpartite vaulting the stilting produces warped surfaces in the conoids over the main piers only, because these alone have groin ribs.  Here at Canterbury the stilted surfaces of the main conoids are broken to an angle at some distance below the arch impost, so that they come against the clerestory wall in inclined straight lines between the vertical stilting and the imposts, as may be seen on the right-hand side of Plate IX.  Thus the stilting and the arch together have a form very much like that of the elliptical, or oval, arch of the vaulting of Durham (Plate V).

The supporting members consist, in the main piers, of three slender Purbeck shafts resting, as before stated, on the great capitals of the ground story, and, in the intermediate piers, of a single Purbeck shaft.  This single shaft is derived from the intermediate piers of Sens, and is a peculiar feature of that French system.  Thus the scheme of Canterbury is neither so logical nor so effective as that of Sens.  The vaulting members of the main piers of Sens consist of a majestic group of engaged shafts — one for each rib of the vaulting.  They all rise from the pavement, and are of three magnitudes corresponding with the magnitudes of the ribs which they respectively carry, a great shaft supporting the main transverse rib, a smaller one on either side supporting the groin ribs, and a still smaller pair falling under the longitudinal ribs.[1]  In comparison with this the main piers of

[1] These last shafts are not, however, well adjusted to the vaulting.  The longitudinal ribs being stilted they ought to pass up continuously beyond the main im-

Canterbury Choir.

PLATE X

Canterbury Choir.

Canterbury lack the fully functional character, and the emphasis as principal supports, that sexpartite vaulting calls for. And although the system as a whole gains in lightness, it does so at the expense of complete structural propriety. Eastward of the transept the master corrected this, and in the first main pier beyond the crossing (Plate X) he added four shafts to the ground-story column, giving independent support respectively to the main vaulting shafts, the sub-orders of the great archivolts, and to the transverse ribs of the aisle vaulting. This idea was embodied with more structural propriety at the west end of the nave of the Cathedral of Paris,[1] and became the typical form in the fully developed French Gothic, as in the naves of Amiens, Reims, and Beauvais. Here at Canterbury it is very beautiful in design and proportions, and the shafts, being free-standing Purbeck monoliths from base to moulded band, and from band to capital, are more slender than those of the French examples. This, however, is hardly an advantage, for the ground-story pier, in such a system, needs to have an expression of substantial support for the whole superstructure to which these small free-standing Purbeck shafts do not so fully contribute as the more ample shafts of coursed masonry, solidly incorporated with the main body of the pier, do in the French examples. This pier of Canterbury is, nevertheless, a very fine one, and conforms with the continental models in having the capitals of the smaller members proportioned to these members, and thus not so high as the great capital with which they are grouped. The earliest instance in France of this type of pier is, I believe, that of Paris, and it may be doubted whether this was early enough to have served as the model for the Canterbury example. If it was not,

post without capitals at that level. But the wall of the clerestory is a little in retreat of the wall below, and separate stilting shafts are set against this wall and are thus drawn in so that they do not fall directly over the shaft rising from the pavement. And, of course, where the stilting shafts are confined to the clerestory there is no need for more than three shafts rising from the pavement. Such imperfect adjustments are not uncommon in the primitive Gothic art of which Sens is one of the noblest monuments. In such works the builders were feeling their way in new directions, and naturally made some mistakes: but such mistakes were quickly corrected as the style advanced in development. Apart from this defect of adjustment the main piers of Sens are admirably composed and proportioned for their functions — affording complete satisfaction to the eye as logical and beautiful supports for this magnificent early Gothic vaulting.

[1] Cf. my *Development and Character of Gothic Architecture*, p. 127.

then William of Sens would appear to have made an innovation here. The well-known piers (Fig. 69), one on each side of the nave of Laon, which have free-standing shafts grouped with them, may be earlier in date than the western piers of Paris; but they are not composed on the same principle. These shafts are five in number, and four of them stand under the angles of

FIG. 69—Laon.

the great abacus, and are thus less perfectly functional. This pier may have been known to William of Sens, and have suggested his own much finer one. However this may be, these are all French piers, and this of Canterbury is important, as it undoubtedly gave rise to others at Chichester and Lincoln, as we shall see, which in turn influenced subsequent designs.

Although he adopted the single vaulting shafts of the intermediate pier of Sens for his own intermediate pier, the Frenchman did not, in the part west of the transept, reproduce in this pier the coupled round columns of Sens. In the work east of the transept, however, he adopts this form for one pier on either side, but with the addition of a pair of Purbeck shafts to give independent support to the sub-orders of the great archivolts in conformity with the corresponding shafts that were added to the main pier. But the next pier eastward, the last one designed by the Frenchman,[1] is a single round column. The result of these forms, and this arrangement, of the piers eastward of the crossing is that we get in the first double bay here a logical scheme of

[1] Gervase states (Willis, *Op. cit.*, p. 50) that the work of William of Sens included the five piers on each side eastward of the crossing, and the work itself clearly confirms this statement. We gather also from Gervase that the whole system over these piers, up to the vaulting, is the work of the Frenchman; but whether he completed the vaulting as far as the fifth pier, — that is, including the sexpartite compartment over the part that narrows toward the east end, — is not clear.

supports for sexpartite vaulting, which does not occur in any other part of the building, — the great crossing pier and the pier with four shafts being the main piers of this double bay, while the intermediate pier is a plain round column. But the piers of the next double bay, which falls in the narrowing part, are not properly shaped for a sexpartite system, since the intermediate pier is the one with coupled columns and a pair of small shafts (seen to the left in Plate X), while the eastern main pier is a single round column. This last pier ought to be the larger, not only because its function is that of a main pier in an alternate system, but also because it stands on the angle where the narrowing part joins on to Trinity chapel, and thus ought to reënforce this angle. The narrowing part, as will be seen on the plan (Fig. 68), is a consequence of the oblique positions of the chapels of St. Andrew and St. Anselm, which were on the curve of the apse of the Norman choir, and had escaped the fire. The French architect was obliged to fit his new work into the space between them, and he appears to have done what he could to reduce the necessary narrowing to a minimum by making the sides of the central aisle of this part less inclined than the chapels are, thus narrowing the aisles also, as the plan shows.

We may now consider the forms of the ground story, the triforium, and the clerestory, which complete the internal system, and then examine the exterior, observing in these parts, also, to what extent the architect has followed contemporaneous French models, and how far he has departed from them in meeting the conditions imposed by the Norman remains, and possibly by the local tastes.

In the vaulting of the aisles some awkwardnesses occur, owing to the fact that the triforium is not raised quite so high above the great arcade as it is in Sens, and the crowns of the aisle vaults have therefore to be kept low. To effect this the groin ribs are made segmental (as no Frenchman would naturally make them), so that they form angles at the springing (Plate X) as in the Norman vaulting. This low level of the triforium, crowding down the aisle vaulting, is apparently another result of the necessity under which the architect laboured, of adjusting his design to the remains of the old Norman Church.

The clerestory openings of the old work still remain in the walls of the eastern transept, and in developing his own higher structure William of Sens could not make his clerestory openings conform to them. He therefore placed his triforium so as to range on the same level, and raised a new stage on the walls of the old transept, with openings corresponding with those of his new clerestory.[1] The level of the new triforium being thus determined by that of the old Norman clerestory, the vaulting of the aisle could not be raised higher than it is. But it would have been possible to give this vaulting a better form by lowering the level of its springing, and this would, I think, have improved the proportions of the ground-story arcade by shortening the piers, which are now excessively tall in proportion to the total height of the interior. This, however, would have made it impossible to carry out the scheme of the eastern extension, with its elevated pavement, without raising the great arcade of this eastern part, so that it would not range on a level with that of the choir, and that William of Sens had this extension in mind will, I think, appear clearly in the next chapter.

It should be remarked that while the pointed arch prevails in the arcades of the ground story, the arches opening from the aisles into the transept, and the transverse ribs of the aisle vaults, are round. The reason is obvious, since the width of the aisle is greater than the interval between each pair of piers, and thus these arches and ribs have a wider span than the arcade arches have, and could not, therefore, be pointed like the others without raising their crowns too high. In changing, as he did, the spacing of the piers (cf. p. 71) the Frenchman could not change that of the responds, since they were parts of the old work that had to be preserved; and since, in consequence, the new piers do not stand directly opposite the responds, it follows that most of the transverse ribs of the aisle vaulting have an oblique direction, which makes the compartments very much askew, and gives these ribs a segmental form, because it widens their spans while their crowns must remain at the same level that they would reach if they were in planes perpendicular to the aisle wall. In the aisles east of the transept further awkwardnesses arise. Between the narrowing

[1] Cf. Willis, p. 74.

Canterbury Choir.

part and the transept the number of piers does not correspond with that of the responds. There are four responds and only three piers, as shown in Willis's plan (Fig. 68, p. 72). This led the architect to make the vault compartment adjoining the transept quinquepartite by springing the second transverse rib of this compartment from the second pier to the third respond, and then inserting a half rib from the second respond to the intersection of the diagonals, thus making two vault cells on the wall side where there would otherwise have been only one. The next compartment on the south side is on plan an oblong trapezium with its narrow end on the wall side, and the diagonals thus necessarily (since they are straight on plan) intersect considerably to one side, toward the aisle wall. The eastern transverse rib of this compartment, having a shorter span than the other one (which is segmental) is semicircular in elevation, or nearly so; while the next transverse rib, which is in the middle of the inclined part of the aisle, and springs from the pier that has a pair of columns, being shorter in span than any of the others, is pointed. All these irregularities of plan, and variations in the forms of the vault ribs, are consequences of the conditions imposed by the old work.

The triforium arcade (Plate XI) follows that of Sens (Fig. 70) with some variations, and consists of a pair of shafted arches each embracing two smaller ones. But while in Sens all the arches are pointed, in Canterbury the larger ones are round, except in the easternmost bay adjoining the transept. This bay (the one on the right in Plate XI) is narrower than the others, and the form of its triforium arcade is different. Here the arches are pointed, and do not embrace smaller ones. It is not easy to find a reason for the round arch in this triforium, for although with the springing level so high as it is there is not room for them to be pointed, yet there is no apparent structural reason for placing the springing so high. It is much higher in proportion than at Sens, and the effect is inferior to that of Sens. But while there is no structural reason, there is, I think, an æsthetic one in the necessity for some harmony of proportion with the great arcade below. With the tall ground-story piers the shafts of the triforium could not with good effect be shorter than they are. This triforium follows that of Sens also in having the moulding of the abaci of its capitals carried along the wall as a string-course, but in Canterbury this makes a more continuous horizontal line because the high vaulting imposts are here on the same level with those of the triforium, and the vaulting capitals continue the same moulding.  It is worthy of notice, too, that this triforium is open, exposing the timber roof of the aisle to view from the pavement of the choir.  This is, as we have seen, a common Anglo-Norman characteristic, but the triforium

FIG. 70— Triforium of Sens.

of Sens appears to have been originally designed in the same manner, making it a very exceptional instance among French churches.[1]

The clerestory (Plate IX) is radically different from that of Sens, and from the French Gothic clerestory in general.  It follows the Anglo-Norman model with the passageway, and a group of three arched openings in the inner plane.  The true Gothic clerestory has no passageway, though variants of the Anglo-Norman form occur in the Burgundian Gothic, as at Dijon and Auxerre.  In Sens, as in all early French Gothic buildings, the

[1] The triforium of Sens is now screened off by a wall of wood and plaster.

wall survives in the clerestory, but it is a single wall, pierced with a large opening.[1]

The structural system of this choir, made up as it is of the old and new work, will be better understood from the cross-section (Fig. 71). The shallow aisle buttress of the Norman work remains unaltered below, but the French architect has built upon it to the greater height required by his new scheme, and made its top so much deeper that it far overhangs the supporting respond of the aisle, and forms a powerful stay to the thrusts of the vaulting which are brought to bear upon it by means of a transverse arch in the triforium, and a flying buttress over the aisle roof. This buttress system differs materially from that of Sens, and is, I believe, unique in the form of the flying buttress. That of Sens is higher, and has its extrados properly loaded, and brought to the straight sloping line that is common to early French flying buttresses. This unloaded arch of Canterbury is weak in function and in expression, and in consequence of its low position, close to the aisle roof, it is inconspicuous as a feature in the system as a whole. The transverse arch beneath the aisle roof has no counterpart in Sens. It is an Anglo-Norman feature occurring in the triforium of the choir of Durham, and survives, as we shall see, in the choir of Lincoln. The pier buttress is a plain rectangular member reaching to the impost of the clerestory window. At Sens this member reaches to the cornice, and beneath the arch it has the form of a polygonal shaft with a capital, as in some other early French Gothic structures.

A peculiar feature of the choir of Canterbury, not described by Willis, or remarked, so far as I know, by any other writer, is the enclosure of the triforium on the south side by a wall carried up to the height of the internal arcade, and pierced with two pointed openings in each bay. This wall encloses the buttressing arches, but no flying buttresses, and the timber roof over them is nearly flat. In other words, a triforium gallery is developed here, but not on the north side.

The profilings of the vault ribs and archivolts are not of the most characteristic early French Gothic types, which are gen-

---

[1] In the fully developed Gothic of the Ile de France the wall wholly disappears in the clerestory, the entire space between the piers and beneath the arch of the vault being open, as at Amiens.

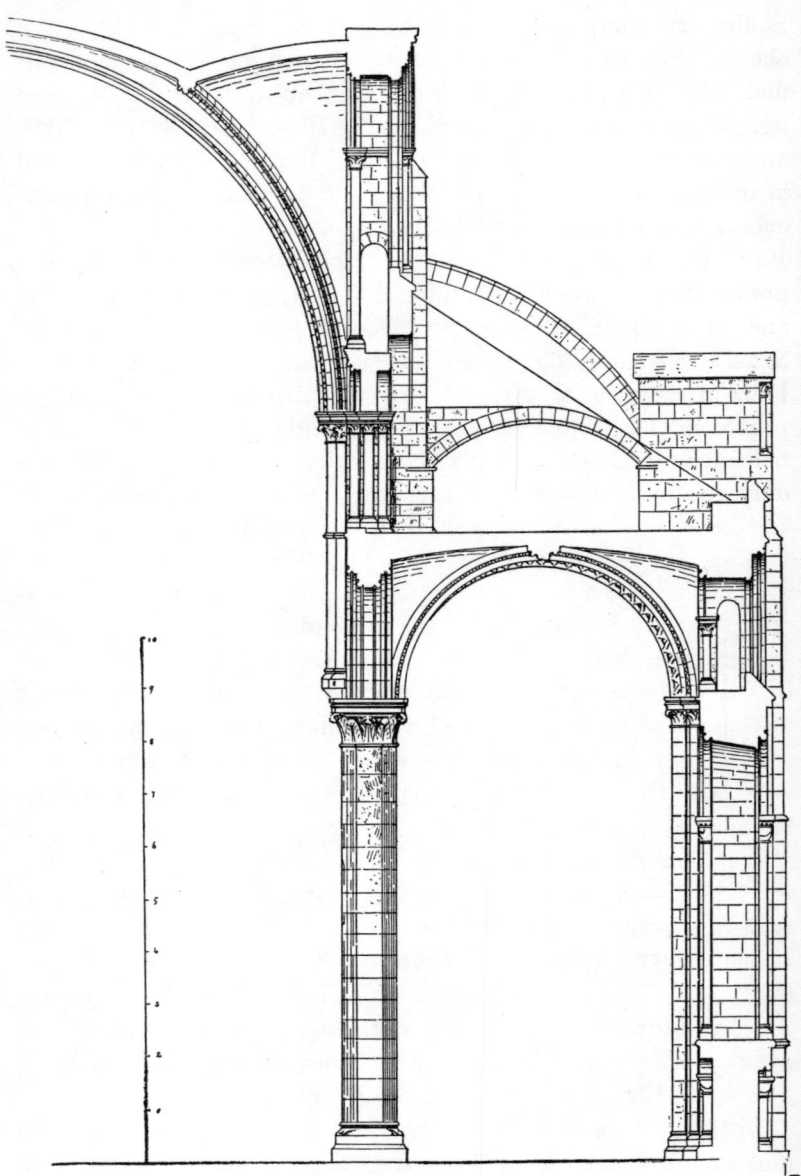

FIG. 71 — Canterbury Choir.

erally square in section, save where in groin ribs a profile more or less like that of A, Fig. 72, is employed, as in the aisles of Senlis. Exceptional forms occur, however, and profiles like B, in the same figure, also from Senlis, and other forms not square in section sometimes occur even in transverse ribs.[1] But the square section predominates, and all rib and archivolt sections in Sens are square (Fig. 73).

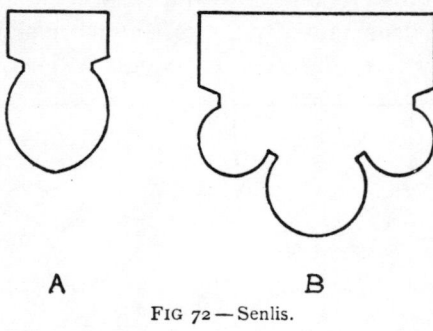

FIG 72 — Senlis.

Here at Canterbury the transverse rib of the high vault has the profile A (Fig. 74), and the groin rib has the profile B.[2] The triforium archivolts, of two orders, have the profile D, and only the archivolts, C, of the great arcade are profiled so as to give a square section. While in general aspect these great archivolts resemble those of the early French Gothic, they exhibit in detail a tendency to greater elaboration such as subsequently became characteristic of the so-called early English style. Instead of the single roll with the sunk fillet, or a cavetto, on the edge, as at Sens, we have in this archivolt of Canterbury, in the first order, above the roll, a billet, a scotia, and a fillet, and on the soffit a fillet, an ogee, and a sunk fillet; and in the sub-order, a dog-tooth, a scotia, and a fillet, above the roll, with a fillet and a cavetto on the soffit —

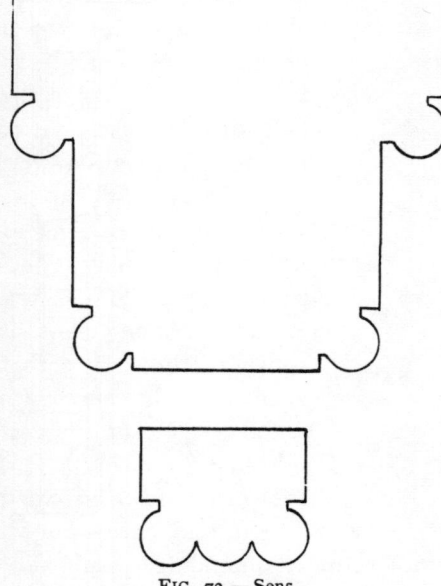

FIG. 73. — Sens.

---

[1] Cf. my *Gothic Architecture*, pp. 332, 333.
[2] These profiles are taken from Willis, and are not exact in all minor details.

the edge of the broad, flat face of the soffit being rounded so as to form with the cavetto a curve of double flexure. These details are not, however, very conspicuous, and the general effect is substantially that of the more simple French archivolts. But where the square section is lost, as in the triforium, a tendency to the Early English character is already noticeable.

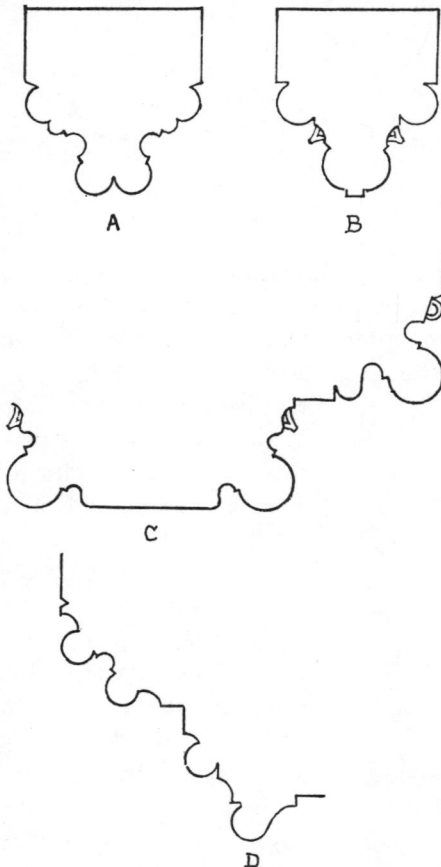
FIG. 74 — Canterbury.

The forms of the capitals and bases in this work of William of Sens (cf. Plate XI) are, for the most part, thoroughly French — the capitals having the square abaci and the French profiling, foliated crockets under the angles, and finely conventionalized leafage, of great beauty of outline and surface, shaping itself to the bell with an expression of living incorporation with it. This type of capital, with many variations of its beautiful foliation, occurs in all parts of the work except in the transept — where the arches that open into the small apscidal recesses on the east side (Fig. 68, p. 72) are sprung from grouped shafts with capitals (Fig. 75), of a different, and entirely new, form, having round abaci, with rounded mouldings, such as a little later become characteristic of the Early English style. It is not easy to account for these capitals. They are apparently contemporaneous with those of the French type, and are, indeed, French crocketed capitals with abaci not well suited to such forms. They are thus not true Early

English capitals, but apparently such capitals in the making, before an appropriate treatment of foliation for the round abacus had been devised — as it was first, I believe, in St. Hugh's transept of Lincoln. What should have led to this innovation, and why a very few only of such capitals should have been inserted among the French ones, it is hard to understand. Whether they were introduced by the Frenchman, or by his successor, the so-called English William, appears equally obscure. Willis says:[1] "The whole of the arcade work and mouldings in the interior of these transepts belongs to William of Sens, with the sole exception of the lower windows, which have been adapted and treated as those of the side aisles." But later he remarks[2] that "as Gervase has distinctly recorded the vaults of these transepts as the last works of the Frenchman, and the finishings of the transepts as the first works of the Englishman, a very probable case is made out in favour of the introduction of the round abacus by him, inasmuch as this is a new feature in the work, and as such, very likely to have been introduced by a new architect." The inconsistency of these statements is obvious, but I think the author is probably right in this last one; for it does not seem likely that William of Sens, with his French tastes and habits of design, would have introduced these capitals — which have no connection with any previous works dear to the hearts of the monks of the establishment, and are not in line with any Anglo-Norman traditions to which he might have wished to conform. It appears to me more likely that a native designer, accustomed to the frequent use of the

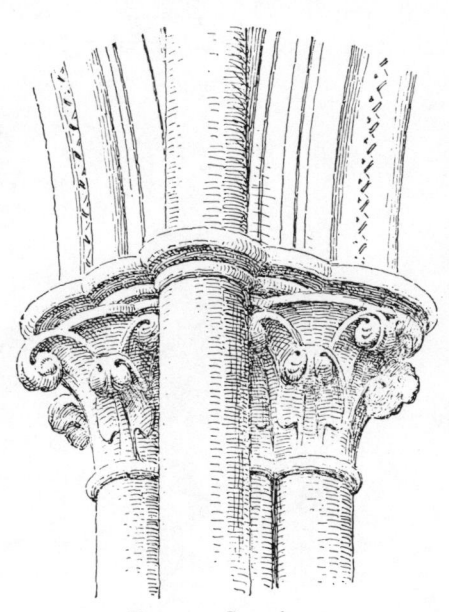

FIG. 75 — Canterbury.

[1] *Op. cit.*, p. 83.   [2] *Ibid.*, p. 94.

round abacus in the great pier capitals of the Norman Romanesque, should have been prompted to make this innovation, especially since the archivolt sections are here not square, and the grouped round abaci fit the compound impost members better than square ones would. This would seem the more probable as the English William employed the round abacus, as we shall see, throughout the eastern crypt where he had a free hand. However this may be, we have apparently in these capitals the initial step in the formation of the distinctive Early English type. It is singular, however, that these new features should have been introduced in this small part of the work, where they do not agree with the rest of the transept, and where, as Willis goes on to say, the architect has adhered to the square abacus of his predecessor everywhere else above the crypt, including Trinity Chapel and the Corona.

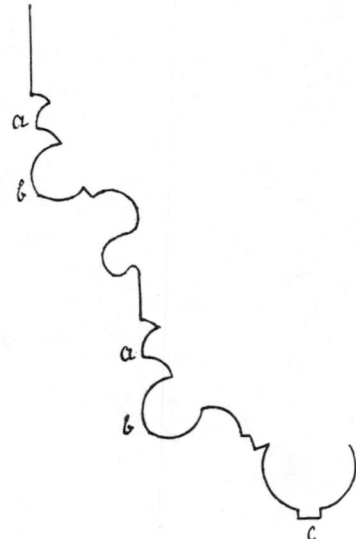

FIG. 76 — Canterbury.

In themselves, although these capitals have much beauty and architectural effectiveness, they are not altogether admirable, because, as before remarked, they are made up of parts that are not mutually related. The crocket is hardly appropriate where the abacus is not square. When the abacus is square the crocket has the effect of giving support to the overhanging angles. But with the round abacus there is nothing to call for this feature.

Together with this new form of capital we have a correspondingly new treatment of the archivolt profiling, and a new form of base, both tending in the direction of the subsequent Early English forms. The archivolt profiles (Fig. 76) are not a very wide departure from those of the choir (Fig. 74, p. 84), in which the mouldings are placed so that the square section is lost. But changes are made in the profiling of these mouldings which give the archivolt as a whole a new character. The members $a$ and $b$ (Fig. 76) have arrises, and the member $c$ has a fillet, the deep and narrow hollows give strong lines of shade, and as these members and intervals are increased in number, an effect is produced which is in marked contrast with the simpler profiling of William of Sens.

The bases, like the capitals, are generally throughout the choir and transept of the French type (Fig. 77), having two tori separated by a scotia and fillets — the lower torus being the larger of the two, and having the *griffe* reaching over the angle of the square plinth. These bases reproduce those of Sens (Plate XV) almost exactly, the only difference being that at Sens the plinth has a second lower member, giving two off-sets instead of one. But in the transept, in connection with the capitals having round abaci just described, a different form of base occurs, as in Fig. 78, from the northwest angle of the north arm. This base is grouped with others of the French form, one of which appears in the illustration.

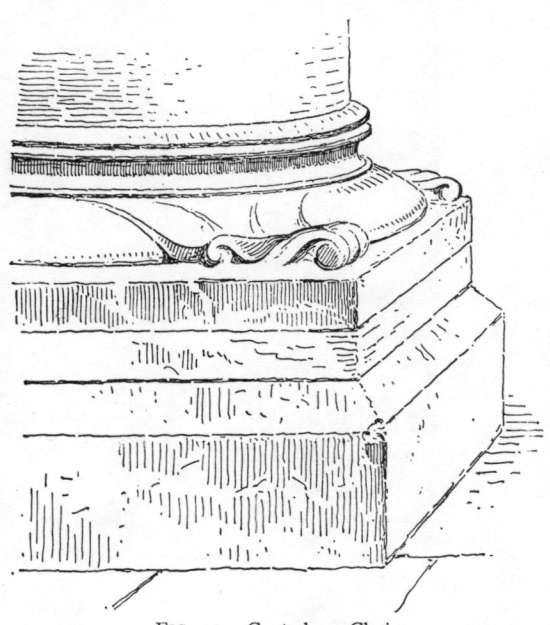

FIG. 77 — Canterbury Choir.

The mouldings immediately beneath the shaft repeat those of the French bases, but the round plinth on which they rest gives no place for the *griffe*, or angle spur, and the composition is thus deprived not only of this beautiful feature, but also of the pleasant contrast which the square plinth affords to the round mouldings. The peculiar ornamentation of this plinth gives it a form that suggests the frustum of a cone, and the supplementary mouldings and plinths, in successively enlarged rings below, give the base, as a whole, a magnitude, in both height and width, out of all proportion to the shaft that is carried.

The choir of Canterbury is thus, in its larger structural features, and in its ornamental details, a work of mixed character. It differs, however, in this respect greatly from the pointed Norman monuments that were considered in the previous chapter. In them the dominating principle is Romanesque, but in this work it is distinctly French Gothic. Cramped and limited by

FIG. 78 — Canterbury, East Transept.

conditions that made entire conformity with the style in which the architect had been bred impossible, we have, nevertheless, in this great work, something wholly new in England. It is no superficial modification of Norman art; but, in the main, a direct importation of a radically different architectural system, quick with new motives. It was inevitable that such a work should strongly influence the local art, and this influence was immediately manifested in the works which followed. But the Anglo-Norman genius was not of a kind to assimilate its essential principles, and thus no profound alteration of the local art resulted. Gothic architecture, in the sense of a radically new and distinctive style of building, was never produced in England. But while the influence of Canterbury did not affect the local art profoundly, it did so superficially to such an extent that the so-called Early English style was, as we shall see, largely a direct result of it.

In the year 1178, as recorded by Gervase, the French architect, having completed the two inclined sides of the Presbytery, was preparing to turn the great vaults of this part, when the scaffolding on which he was gave way, and he fell to the pavement. He continued, however, for a time to direct the works from his bed, and in this way the great vault of the crossing appears to have been completed. But he was at length obliged to give up and return to France — being succeeded by the other William who, Gervase tells us, was an Englishman. The work of this second architect will be considered in the next chapter.

## CHAPTER IV

### TRINITY CHAPEL

OF the eastern extension of Canterbury, which includes Trinity Chapel and the Corona, Willis remarks: "The erection of the new Trinity Chapel, or chapel of Becket, which took place wholly under the direction of the Englishman, must have been intended from the beginning; for the contrivance of narrowing the central alley of the choir, for the purpose of avoiding the old towers, and of adjusting the width to agree with that of the ancient chapel of the Trinity, was due to the French artist, seeing that the inclined part of the choir . . . was carried up to the clerestory before his fall."[1] The tract of Gervase appears to confirm this view, for, after stating what was first done by the English William in completing what had been left unfinished in the upper work by William of Sens, Gervase says: "Moreover, he laid the foundation of the enlargement of the church at the eastern part, because the chapel of St. Thomas was to be built there."[2] This seems clearly to indicate that the building of the chapel of St. Thomas (or the new Trinity Chapel in honour of Becket) had been intended by the Frenchman. And there are many indications in the monument itself that the design for this eastern enlargement had been prepared by William of Sens, and that the English William adhered to this design in all the main features of the work above the crypt, and in the general scheme of the crypt itself. With some minor exceptions the main features, save in the aisles, correspond so closely with those of the choir that they might appear to be the work of the same architect. Yet Willis speaks of the work as showing some originality on the part of the English William. "The greater elevation of the pavement," he says, "wholly alters the proportion of the piers to the arches, and gives a new and original, and at the same time a very elegant, character to this part of the

[1] *Op. cit.*, pp. 91-92.   [2] *Ibid.*, p. 51.

church compared with the work of the Frenchman, of which, at first sight, it seems a mere continuation." But as the raised pavement was planned by the Frenchman, as Gervase implies, and as we shall find other evidence to confirm, it is hard to see how any altered proportions occasioned by it can be thought to show originality on the part of the Englishman. In the aisles, however, some new features occur of which Willis speaks as follows: " However, in the side aisles of the Trinity Chapel, and in the Corona, our English William appears to have freed himself almost as completely from the shackles of imitation as was possible. In the side aisles the mouldings of the ribs still remain the same, but their management in connection with the side walls, and the combination of their slender shafts with those of the twin lancet windows, here for the first time introduced into the building, is very happy." If Willis had known his Sens as well as he knew his Canterbury, I do not think he would have written this. For where the work in these aisles differs from that of the choir aisles it is so much like the corresponding parts of Sens as to point to that monument as the source of the apparent novelties, and thus to the French master as the real author of the new features. This will appear as we proceed in our examination and comparison of the two works.

The plan of the east end of Canterbury corresponds with that of the Cathedral of Sens, as given by Viollet le Duc,[1] in having a circular chapel on the main axis, opening out of the apsidal aisle, without other apsidal chapels. But the original axial chapel of Sens has been demolished, and the present one is a rebuilding in a later style. Thus this part of Viollet le Duc's plan is a conjectural restoration. It is, however, an entirely reasonable one in view of the known relationship between the two monuments, and their likeness in other features to be presently noticed. Moreover, the Canterbury Corona, though exceptional both in plan[2] and elevation, is altogether French in style, and substantially like the work of William of Sens in the choir and transept. It would therefore seem most probable that it formed a part of the Frenchman's scheme. But there is a passage in Gervase which may appear to imply that it was

[1] *Dictionnaire*, etc., vol. 2, p. 348.
[2] Circular apsidal chapels are not unknown in other twelfth century French Gothic monuments, and are found in St. Remi of Reims.

an independent addition by the English William. The passage reads as follows: "But the master (the Englishman) had begun a tower at the eastern part outside the circuit of the wall, as it were, the lower vault of which was completed before the winter."[1] That by what is here called a tower is meant the Corona, is clear from its position, and from another passage in the narrative where the whole eastern enclosure is described as follows: "The outer wall, which extends from the aforesaid towers" (*i.e.* the towers of St. Andrew and St. Anslem) "first proceeds in a straight line, is then bent into a curve, and thus in the round tower the wall on each side comes together in one, and is there ended."[2] The wall bent into a curve is, of course, the apse, and thus the round tower is obviously the Corona, which does, indeed, rise like a tower against the apsidal aisle. But Gervase does not affirm the tower to be an independent work of the Englishman, and its character shows plainly that it is not. That the English William, in the whole eastern extension, worked on lines that had been laid down by the first architect there can, I think, be no reasonable question.

His first work, after completing what had remained unfinished of the parts on which the French master was engaged before his fall, was, of course, the eastern crypt on which both Trinity Chapel and the Corona are built. In this noble crypt (Plate XII), while following the general scheme prepared by his predecessor, he had a free hand as to details, and the style has little resemblance to that of William of Sens. It is equally unlike the adjoining Norman crypt, though it has some Norman features. In plan (Fig. 68, p. 72) it has a short nave with aisles, an apse, an apsidal aisle, and a circular chapel on the main axis, opening out of the apsidal aisle, which is the basement of the Corona (the tower of Gervase, the vault of which, he tells us, was completed before the winter of the sixth year). The nave is subdivided lengthwise by three small supports which hold up the pavement of Trinity Chapel. That the crypt was not only planned, but its execution actually commenced, by William of Sens, is shown, I think, by the first of these supports at the junction of the old crypt and the new. The illustration (Plate XIII) shows this member as seen from the east looking back into the apsidal aisle of the Norman crypt. It is

[1] Willis, *Op. cit.*, p. 56.  [2] *Ibid.*, p. 61.

PLATE XII

Eastern Crypt of Canterbury.

a thoroughly French design, with a square abacus to the compound capital, and square plinth with angle spurs to the base of its coupled columns, all corresponding in style with the work of William of Sens in the choir and transept. Moreover, it stands directly under the point in the upper work where the French artist left off, and between the piers which Gervase tells us were the last executed by him. We could hardly require clearer evidence that this eastern crypt was the Frenchman's project, and, since this pier is of the same height as those of William the Englishman, it appears clear also that he determined the level of the pavement of Trinity Chapel. All the other supports are different (Plate XII), the capitals having round abaci, and the bases round plinths. The great piers are of the Norman cylindrical form, and resemble those of Malmesbury, save that they are in pairs instead of being single, — a scheme presumably suggested by the coupled columns of the Frenchman; while the smaller columns, which are single, are noticeable as having capitals that anticipate the moulded variety of the Early English style.

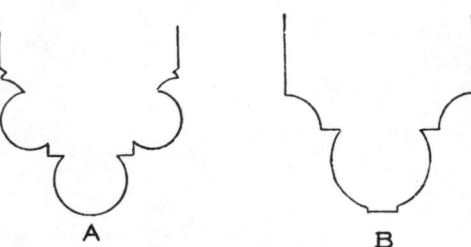

FIG. 79 — Canterbury.

The smaller subdividing columns give to the straight part of the nave four measurably square vault compartments, instead of two oblong ones which would be formed without the longitudinal subdivision; but as the crypt widens eastward its sides are not parallel, and thus the vault compartments are not perfectly rectangular. The vaulting has the French conformation with domical form and concave surfaces, and its well-cut masonry is in courses parallel at the crown. It is thus far removed in character from Anglo-Norman pointed vaulting, like that of the contemporaneous Temple Church, considered in a preceding chapter. The ribs over the shorter spans are pointed, and have the profile shown at B, Fig. 79.

On account of the longitudinal subdivision, the apse could not be vaulted in the usual manner, with ribs in the form of half arches abutting on the crown of a transverse rib spanning the whole width of the nave; for instead of such a rib there are two smaller ones springing from the central column, and each spanning half the width of the nave. The radiating ribs of the apse are therefore complete arches and spring from the same column. The triangular compartments thus formed are vaulted on the principle of those of the Temple Church already described, but they differ in having round wall arches, concave surfaces, and masonry in courses parallel at the crown. In other words,

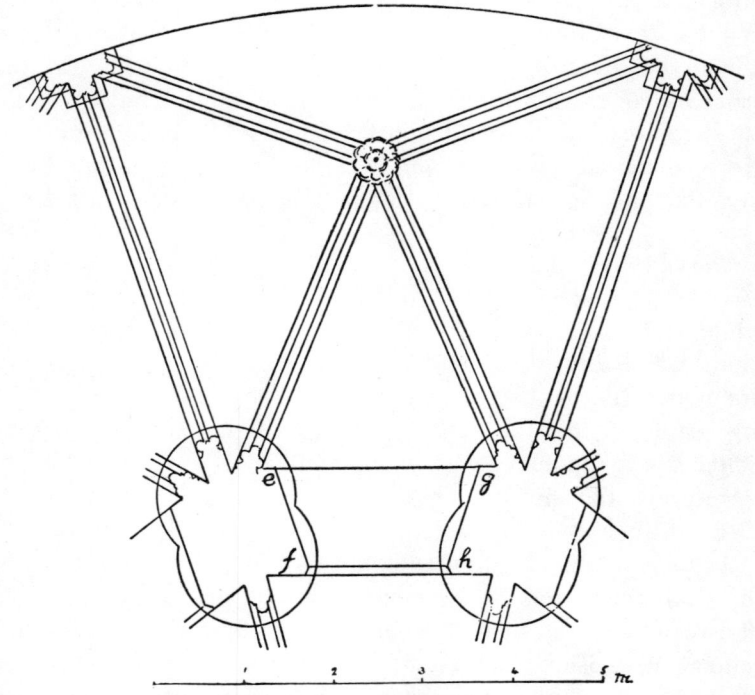

FIG. 80 — Eastern Crypt, Canterbury.

they have, like the vaults of the straight part, the French conformation, and are executed in the French manner.

The apsidal aisle of this crypt has some features that are worthy of notice. The plan (Fig. 80) and the cross-section (Fig. 81) of one compartment will explain these. It will be seen (Fig. 80) that the groin ribs, though broken on plan so that their opposite sides meet at an angle, do not intersect in the middle of the vault, but in a point considerably beyond the centre toward the outer wall. By this arrangement all the half ribs be-

French Pier of Canterbury Crypt.

come of nearly equal length, and the crowns of the cells are more nearly perpendicular to the transverse ribs than they would be if the point of intersection were in the middle of the axial line. But what is thus gained in regularity in the forms of the cells is lost in the general aspect of the vault by the one-sided position of its crown. The apsidal aisle vaulting of Sens has the same peculiarity (Fig. 82), and its reproduction here may be taken, I think, among the many other indications that this eastern ex-

FIG. 81 — Eastern Crypt, Canterbury.

tension of Canterbury was all planned, in its larger features, by the French architect. And this is further apparent in the profiling — the transverse ribs having the profile A (Fig. 83) which is almost exactly the same as that of the groin ribs B of the aisle of Sens, while the groin ribs have the profile C, which is only a variant of that of the sub-order D of the great archivolts of Sens, with a roll added to the soffit.

The coupled columns of the great piers are mutually engaged so that they stand free for only about three-quarters of their diameters. This brings the round abaci of their capitals into the same relation (Fig. 80) and gives a surface for the archivolt and vault ribs that would fall within an oblong rectangle. As

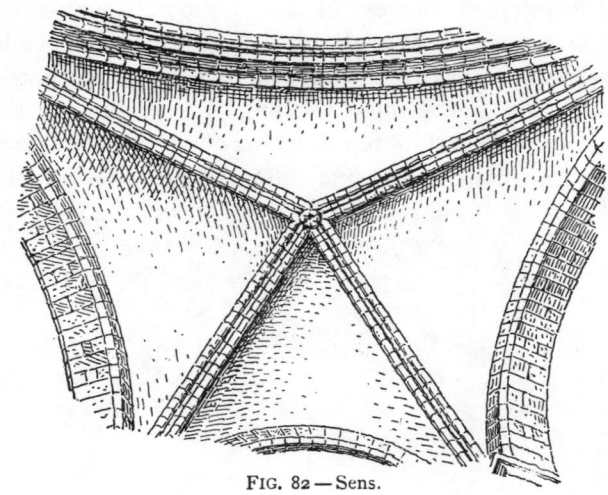

FIG. 82 — Sens.

the soffits of the great archivolts at the springing are nearly parallel with what would be the long sides of such rectangles,

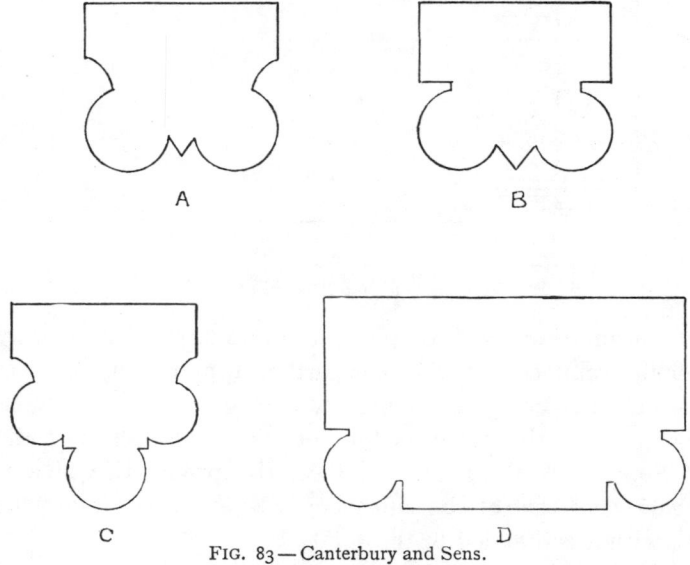

FIG. 83 — Canterbury and Sens.

they are also parallel with the radii of the apse on which the coupled columns are set, and thus their opposite sides, *ef* and *gh* are not parallel — the span *eg* being greater than the span *fh*, which warps the soffit so that the point *b* (Fig. 81) is higher than the point *a*, and makes the crown line *ab* slope steeply. In other words, the idea of avoiding, or of minimizing, the distortion of the soffit over such a span by giving the capital a wedge shape, as in the adjoining Norman crypt, is not carried out here. The archivolts are not, however, in this case, curved on plan. They are in planes, giving a polygonal form to this part of the apse, although the stylobate of the arcade, and the outer wall of the aisle, are curved. This apse is set out on a curve of more than half a circle, and the easternmost pair of transverse ribs of the nave are on the chord of the arc. This brings the middle column westward of the true centre, makes the radiating ribs of unequal length, and deflects them a little from the direction of the transverse ribs of the aisle (tending toward the true centre) with which they would naturally be in line if they converged on the true centre.

The great archivolts are both stilted and pointed, but not enough to make them equal in height to the round archivolts of the nave, and no structural motive governs the stilting and pointing, since their crowns are still far below the level of the vaulting. They thus have no function as vault ribs.

Coming now to the upper work of English William we find in Trinity Chapel and the Corona a very different, and more elegant, style of architecture. In the crypt the architect was largely untrammelled by the need for conformity with the work of his predecessor; but in the superstructure it was not so. Here, as the Frenchman's pupil and continuator, every consideration of harmony and propriety would lead him to adhere, in the main, to the work of the choir and transept. Accordingly, the style of Trinity Chapel is that of William of Sens, except for a few minor details to be presently noticed.

As in the crypt, the apse of Trinity Chapel is set out (Fig. 84) on an arc of more than half a circle, and on the crown of the easternmost transverse rib, spanning the chord of this arc, the ribs of the five-celled vault of the apse abut in the usual manner of early French apsidal vaulting. The point of intersection being thus, as before, westward of the centre, the ribs are again necessarily of unequal length. To give them abutment the adjoining rectangular vault is made tripartite, thus directing its groin ribs to the point where the ribs of the apse meet. The horseshoe form of the apse on plan is a characteristic of Sens, of Paris, and of other French monuments, and the same adjustment of the ribs of the apse to those of the adjoining rectangular vaults occurs in Noyon and Paris.

The narrowing of the central aisle of the choir by the French master made that of Trinity Chapel correspondingly narrow, so

FIG. 84 — Plan of Trinity Chapel, Canterbury.

that at its west end it measures in width, from centre to centre of its piers, only 8.60 metres, but like the crypt it widens eastward, and measures, at its junction with the apse, 9.33 metres. It may have been to gain additional space in the sanctuary that the apse was set out on so large a segment. The narrow proportions of this eastern work gives its vaulting a different form from that of the choir — the springing being at the same level with that of the choir vaults, while the crown is brought up to the same height. This may account for the peculiarity noticeable in the transverse ribs, and the ribs of the apse, which are in curves struck from centres above the springing level — giving a pointed horseshoe shape to the arches. This occurs also in the easternmost transverse ribs of the oblique part of the choir where the narrowing spans give rise to it. It is not a pleasant feature, and might have been avoided by stilting. It is most marked in the ribs of the apse, and it will be seen that, in a vault so high in proportion to its span, curves struck from the springing level (since they would have to be arcs of larger circles in order to pass through both the points of springing and the crown of the vault) would bring the groins farther inward, and shut off from view considerably more of the clerestory lights.

The cells of the apse vaults are in French Gothic form, the crowns of the wall arches being on about the same level as the point on which the ribs converge, giving sharp groins and winding surfaces. But the relation of the vault to the enclosure is not like that of French vaulting. The cells differ, however, one from another — the one on the main axis alone being shaped to the pointed archivolt of the clerestory opening in the French Gothic manner. The adjoining cells are narrower and are pointed against the wall, but they are not concentric with the clerestory archivolts — which are more acutely pointed. The other two cells, adjoining the straight part, are wider and round arched, and thus do not at all conform with the respective clerestory archivolts.

There are but two rectangular compartments of vaulting in the central aisle of Trinity Chapel, of which the one adjoining the apse is tripartite, as I have already said, and the other is quadripartite — like the westernmost one in the choir of the Frenchman. The longitudinal arches of these compartments are round, and have no ribs, while the profiling of the transverse ribs and groin ribs is like that of William of Sens. There are but two piers on each side by the English William (the westernmost pair being the last work of the Frenchman), and these, from the impost of the great arcade upward, are like those of the choir. For although there is no sexpartite vaulting in Trinity Chapel, the vaulting scheme is such as to require the same number and arrangement of vaulting shafts. Since the westernmost of these piers by the English architect stand between the two rectangular compartments, it has a transverse rib and two groin ribs to carry, and is therefore provided with three vaulting shafts, while the eastern pair, standing on the line of junction with the apse, have (since the eastern rectangular compartment is tripartite) only the transverse rib that divides the vault of the apse from the rectangular one to carry, and thus, like the intermediate piers of the choir, require each only one vaulting shaft. On the ground story these piers consist of coupled round columns, like the intermediate piers of Sens, a variant of which was introduced by the Frenchman in the oblique part of the choir. In that pier, as we have seen (cf. Plate X), small supplementary shafts are inserted to carry the sub-order of the great archivolt, and these shafts are crowned with small capitals incorporated with the larger ones. Here in Trinity Chapel the small shafts are omitted, and the capitals are corbelled for the support of the sub-order.

The great archivolts of the English William are not pointed like those of the Frenchman, and they exhibit some awkwardness of form and execution in marked contrast with the choir arcades. The two orders, for instance, of which they are composed, are not concentric one with the other — the sub-order interpenetrating at the springing so as to bring it within the edge of the narrow abacus. The western bay is considerably wider than the other, and the sub-order of the archivolt of this bay has to be a segment of less than half a circle, so that it starts from the capital at an angle; while in the first order of the same archivolt the angle is avoided by bending the arch to a smaller curve at the springing, thus making it three centred. The greater width of this western bay is apparently due to the chapels of St. Andrew and St. Anselm, the small apses of which extend so far eastward (Fig. 68, p. 72) that the spaces between them and the English William's first buttresses would be practically filled up if they were set farther westward than they now are. As it is, this wide western bay of Trinity Chapel is much narrower on the outside than the others.

The triforium is an amplification of the scheme of the first bay west of the transept in the choir of William of Sens, where a pair of pointed arches (cf. Plate XI) without subdivision takes the place of the round arches, each embracing two smaller pointed ones, that occur everywhere else in the choir. But in reproducing this simpler arcade of the Frenchman, the English William has given, in each bay of the straight part, a series of four arches instead of only two. In the narrower bays of the apse, however, he has them in pairs precisely like those of the choir.[1]

That the system of Trinity Chapel as a whole is a close copy of that of the choir, with but slight variation of some minor details, will be seen on comparing the cross-section (Fig. 85) with that of the choir (Fig. 71, p. 82). Its quadripartite vaulting follows that of the westernmost bay of the choir, with no changes in either the profiling, or the magnitudes, of the ribs. The piers, with their vaulting shafts are the same above the imposts of the great arcade, while on the ground story they reproduce, as before observed, the coupled round columns that were introduced by the Frenchman in the middle pier of the oblique part. The flying buttresses and the abutting arches in the triforium are exact copies of those of the Frenchman; but the outer abutments, being wholly new work, naturally differ from those of the choir in which the Norman work was largely retained. The English architect properly built them out far beyond the aisle enclosure, but in doing this, he merely followed the established French Gothic form, which, if he did not derive it from William of Sens, shows that he was acquainted with French models. For this buttress is thoroughly French in character, and is, I believe, the first of its kind built on English soil. The clerestory follows that of the choir in having the Anglo-Norman passageway, but the triforium also has a passageway — which is not an Anglo-Norman, but a French Gothic, feature.

Coming now to the aisles of Trinity Chapel, we find new features of considerable interest and significance, especially in the aisle of the apse. The plan (Fig. 86) of one compartment of this aisle shows that, as in the corresponding compartment of the crypt, the point of intersection of the groin ribs is beyond the centre of the axial line.[2] The transverse ribs are round arched, or nearly so (as they are also in Sens), the wall arch is

---

[1] It is singular that Willis (p. 94), speaking of the triforium of Trinity Chapel, remarks that it "differs from that of the choir," and implies that it was a new departure on the part of the English William, saying that "the effect is richer." He overlooks the fact that it is modelled on the triforium of the easternmost bay of the choir by the French architect, as stated in the text.

[2] As before remarked, this is a peculiarity of the vaulting of the apsidal aisle of Sens. But the vaults of Sens differ one from another in this respect. In only one of them, namely the one on the main axis of the church, is the point of intersection so far from the middle as it is in these vaults of Canterbury.

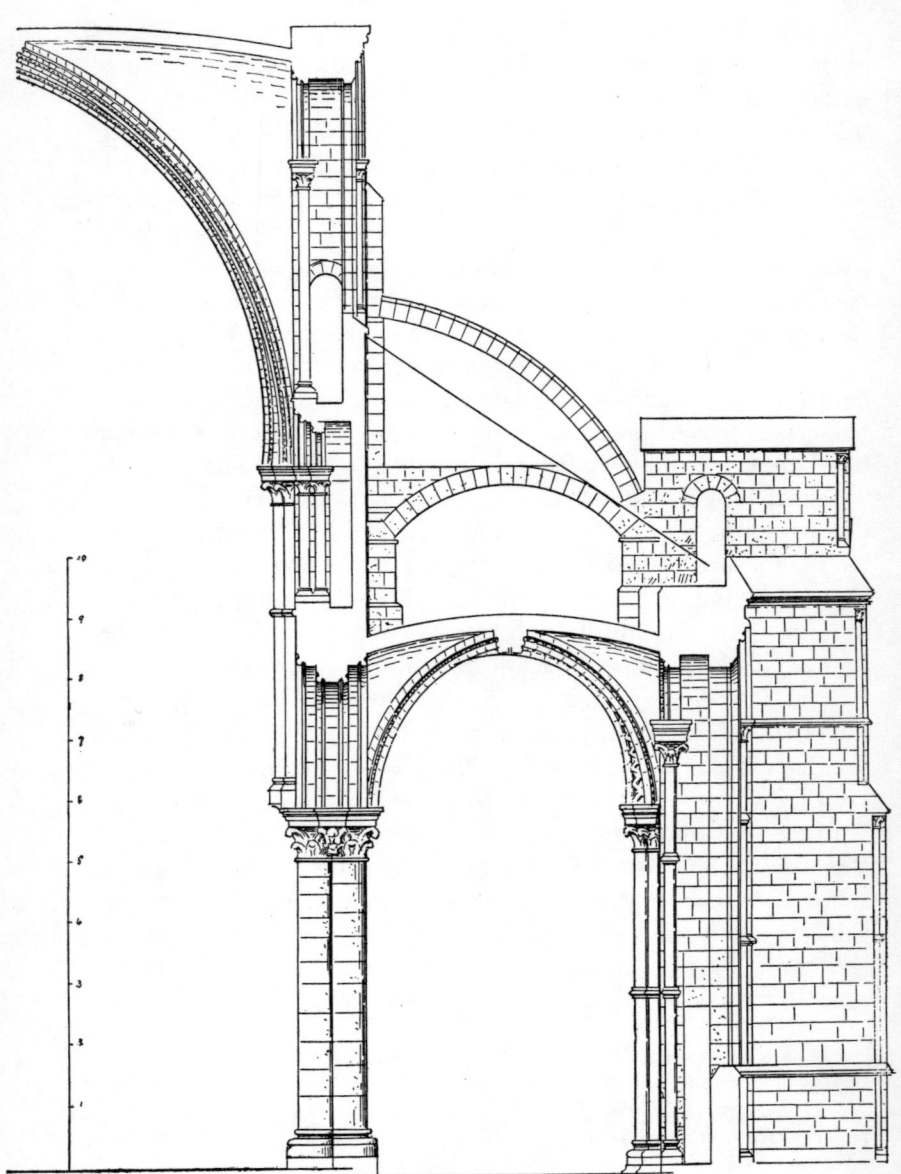

FIG. 85 — Trinity Chapel, Canterbury.

Apsidal Aisle of Trinity Chapel.

round, with the crown flattened, making it roughly three centred, to keep it nearly on a level with the intersection of the groins (Plate XIV), the pier arch, having a very narrow span, is both stilted and pointed, yet it still falls below the levels of other arches; and the groin ribs are segmental curves struck from centres below the springing level. Notwithstanding the depressed form of the wall arch, its greater span still carries it

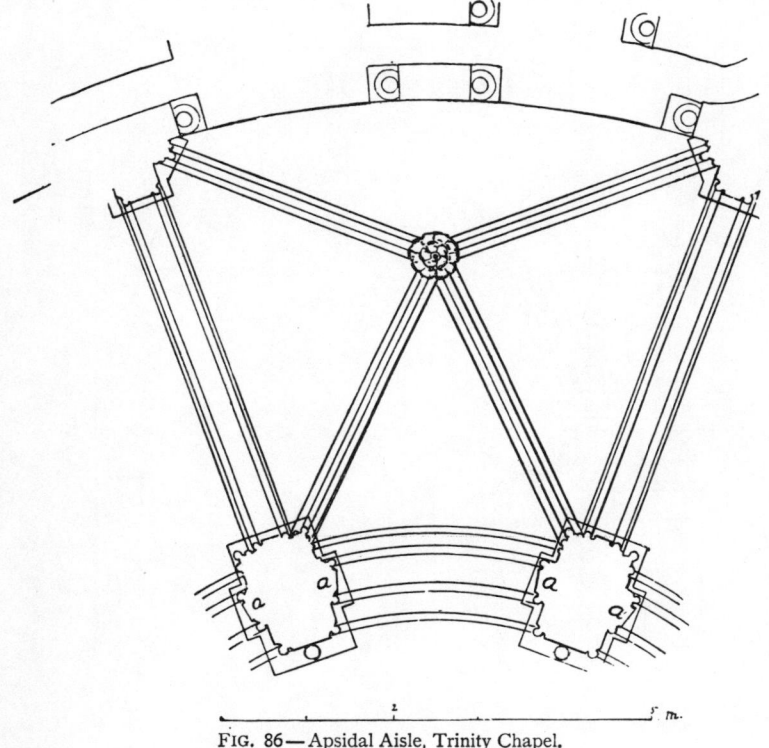

FIG. 86.—Apsidal Aisle, Trinity Chapel.

higher than the others, and the crown of the vault has in consequence a downward slope in the transverse direction (Fig. 87). In Sens (Plate XV) these awkwardnesses are avoided by springing the ribs from different levels according to their spans. In this transitional Gothic vaulting of Sens the possibilities of the pointed arch were not yet fully realized, and only the pier arch (over the narrowest span, and not seen in the illustration) is pointed. A great deal of Romanesque character thus survives in the vaults of this aisle — which may in part account for some of the backward forms in the corresponding vaults of Canterbury. There is, however, a good deal of difference between the two. The vaults of Sens, like most early French Gothic vaults, are very domical, and while the ribs are nearly all round arched, the rib system is complete — a wall rib being included, while in Canterbury this important member is wanting.

FIG. 87 — Apsidal Aisle, Trinity Chapel.

The treatment of the wall side of the apsidal aisle of Canterbury is so closely similar to that of the corresponding part of Sens as to afford, I think, convincing proof of its derivation from that source. It will be seen (Plate XV) that in Sens there are two windows in the bay, and that the archivolts of these windows are carried by slender shafts, each banded with a ring of mouldings. This band is reproduced in the English William's aisle with modifications of detail, indeed, but with substantial

PLATE XV

Apsidal Aisle of Sens.

conformity (Plate XIV). A novel feature of this aisle is the wall passage but slightly raised above the level of the pavement. Such a feature in this position is, of course, without utility, and it is incompatible with the compact skeleton construction of true Gothic architecture.

The piers (Fig. 87) are, as in the straight part, all coupled round columns, and the abaci of their twin capitals are of the same oblong rectangular form on plan. These abaci being set with their axes coinciding with the radii of the apse, would cause the soffits of the archivolts, if set even with them, to be much twisted. To minimize this the sub-orders of the archivolts are set obliquely (*a*, Fig. 86), but not enough so to bring their opposite sides parallel, and thus they are still considerably warped, with a marked inclination at the crown, as shown at *a* in the section, Fig. 87. At Sens the abaci of the two piers of the apse, which have coupled columns,

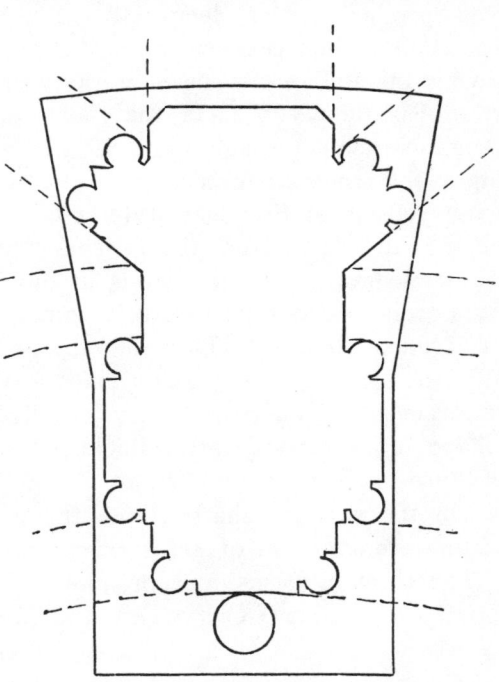

FIG. 88 — Sens.

differ curiously one from the other. Only one of them is an oblong rectangle on plan as at Canterbury. The other has a shape (Fig. 88) in which the half toward the aisle has oblique sides coinciding with the radii of the apse, or nearly so, while the side on the curve is correspondingly curved, the capital under this part being shaped to fit the abacus. But this, as will be seen from the plan, does not obviate the twisting of the archivolt soffit, since this is placed on the rectangular part, and is set even with its edge. The widening of the abacus on the aisle side merely gives room for the groin ribs of the aisle vaulting.

Coming back to Canterbury, it is worthy of notice that in the triforium of the apse the abaci of the small capitals are wedge-shaped on plan, and are curved on both the inside and the outside, in conformity with the curve of the apse. The vaulting of the circular corona is of thoroughly French Gothic character, the crowns of the wall arches reaching up to about the same height as the point on which the groin ribs meet, thus producing very deep cells. The masonry of this vaulting is in arched courses parallel at the crown of each cell, giving the hollowed surfaces of the French vaults. The clerestory has, however, as in the choir and Trinity Chapel, the Anglo-Norman passageway; but the archivolt of the opening in the inner plane is at the same time the end rib of the vault cell, as in French Gothic construction. A slender Purbeck shaft, rising from the pavement and banded at the triforium ledge and at two points in the ground story, supports each groin rib, and the triforium arcade is a repetition of that of Trinity Chapel — which follows, as we have seen, that of William of Sens in the easternmost bay of the choir west of the transept. The ground story has, like the aisles of Trinity Chapel, a passageway in the thickness of the wall, jamb shafts of Purbeck being set on the angles of the wall strips, against which the vaulting shafts stand, the whole forming an architectural composition of great elegance.

The capitals, bases, and profiling, of both the corona and Trinity Chapel, are everywhere the same as in the work of

FIG. 89 — Aisle of Trinity Chapel.

William of Sens, save the bases of the great piers and those of the vaulting shafts, of Trinity Chapel. The first of these have a round plinth under each column with a rectangular plinth under the pair. This deprives the base of the pleasant contrast afforded by the round mouldings in connection with the square member, and eliminates the beautiful angle spur which gives such expression of firm foothold to the French bases (Fig. 89) of the aisle. The profiling of the great base (Fig. 90) is primarily French, with a tendency to that depth of the scotia, and roundness of the tori, that subsequently marked the more complicated Early English profiling. The small bases of the vaulting shafts have round plinths resting directly on the abaci of the great capitals of the ground-story piers. The thoroughly French character of the smaller bases in all other parts of the English William's work is shown in the typical example (Fig. 89) — which might, with almost perfect propriety, stand in the triforium of the Cathedral of Paris. I say *almost* perfect propriety, because none of the profiling of Trinity Chapel has the subtlety of the finest French work. In this respect the profiling of English William differs from that of William of Sens, and is inferior to it, as a comparison of the small bases in the choir and transept with those of this eastern extension will show. For instance, in the work of William of Sens, as in all finest French work, there is a subtle flattening of the torus, like that which we find in the ovolo of Greek Doric capitals, which is not found in the bases of Trinity Chapel.

Such is the work of English William which many writers have affirmed to be an independent English product differing in character from the work of the French master who built the choir and transept.

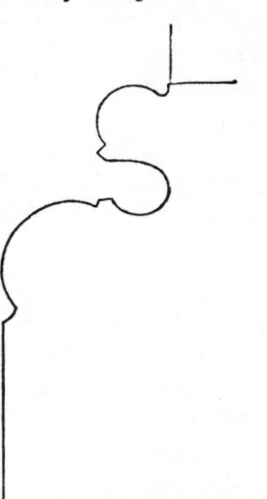

FIG. 90 — Trinity Chapel.

Thus Mr. Parker, in his *Introduction to the Study of Gothic Architecture*, p. 93, says: "The progressive change in the character of the work is very remarkable. At first it is almost pure Norman (sic), though late, this is the work of the first year, 1175, and before its completion in 1184, it has gradually changed into almost pure Early English." And more recently Mr. E. S. Prior, in *The Cathedral Builders in England*, a book that contains much that is good, says, p. 47: "The architecture of Canterbury as we see it shows us exactly what is French, and what is not — and the latter to be no copying of the French, but an English style, a grown-up Gothic by the side of its French brother." By what is here called an

English style is meant the work of English William in Trinity Chapel and the corona. And further on, after saying that in the choir "the mason-craft is French in its setting out and in the leading lines of its construction. French, too, in the detail of the carved capitals . . . for their forms are of the local style of the Ile-de-France," he adds: "But with it and around it at Canterbury, then succeeding it and blotting out its character, was the English work of the southeastern masons, who, despite the French master, were the predominant builders at Canterbury." From what we have seen, however, it must be apparent how mistaken are these affirmations that there is any change of style wrought in the eastern extension of this monument. It conforms so closely with that of the French master that Willis, who knew it thoroughly, remarks: "it is very difficult to separate the original work of William the Englishman from that of his predecessor."[1] There could, of course, be no such difficulty if the work of the one master differed from that of the other as these writers affirm. There is no such difference. Standing at the west end of the choir and looking eastward there is no break in the continuity of style. The vaulting has precisely the same character throughout, and the system of supports is the same from end to end. It is only in the round plinths to a few of the bases in Trinity Chapel, and in such lack of refinements in profiling as I have indicated, that any difference occurs. The whole of the twelfth century work, after 1174, is transitional French Gothic, with such modifications as the conditions imposed, and with the minor exceptions that we have noticed, and is radically different in character from anything that had before appeared in England.

[1] *Op. cit.*, p. 91.

# CHAPTER V

### BEGINNINGS OF EARLY ENGLISH

SUCH changes in the forms of bases, capitals, and mouldings as we have found in a few exceptional instances in the transept, in the eastern crypt, and in Trinity Chapel at Canterbury, were destined to be carried farther, to become more general, and to be associated with corresponding changes and readjustments in the larger features of Anglo-Norman architecture, until was produced what is known as the Early English style — the more distinct beginnings of which we have now to consider.

The first building after Canterbury in which these changes more extensively appear is the neighbouring Cathedral of Chichester. Chichester, like Canterbury, was a Norman structure dating from the close of the eleventh century and the beginning of the century following; and like Canterbury, also, it was damaged by fire and repaired in a new style. This fire occurred in the year 1186, but the injury it occasioned was not so great, and did little more, save to the extreme east end, than to destroy the timber roof of the unvaulted nave and the vaulting of the aisles. The Norman nave had been one of the most admirable in England as its structural system was entirely logical, having no vaulting shafts whatever, since there was no vaulting to call for them. The most important work of repair consisted in substituting stone vaulting for the wooden ceiling, and in the almost entirely new construction of two bays at the east end — which was made rectangular, whereas before it had been apsidal.[1] To support the vaulting, shafts were introduced starting from the pavement, and flying buttresses were added both within the triforium and over the aisle roof. The vaulting shafts and other shafts are of Purbeck marble, a material that appears to have been first used by William of Sens in the great work

---

[1] Cf. the historical plan given by Willis in his *Architectural History of Chichester Cathedral*, Chichester, 1861.

at Canterbury, as other suitable material (such as the French quarries afforded) was not obtainable in England. In addition to this the piers, and the walls of the clerestory, were refaced, the first orders of the great archivolts were also refaced, and new profiles given them, while Purbeck shafts were inserted to carry them. The arcades of the clerestory were rebuilt and provided with Purbeck shafting, with elegant capitals and bases, and string-courses of Purbeck were added to the triforium and clerestory. Thus a light skeleton of structural members was engrafted on the walls of the massive Norman fabric. This skeleton has, indeed, little congruity with the old structure, but it has a structural suggestiveness, and gives a new expression to the whole.

In this work of repair the influence of Canterbury is very marked, and beyond question, yet almost every feature has a different character from that of the Canterbury work, and bears an Anglo-Norman impress.

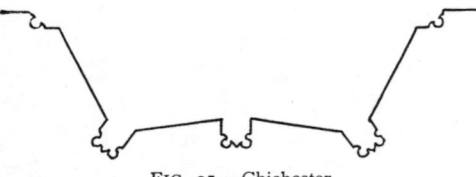

FIG. 91—Chichester.

The vaulting of the nave is quadripartite, and has a full system of ribs, of which the transverse and longitudinal ribs are pointed, and the groin ribs are semicircular. The longitudinal rib is not stilted, however, and the vaulting conoid is, therefore, in horizontal section at the haunch, shaped as in Fig. 91, instead of having the triangular form of French Gothic vaulting,[1] as at Canterbury. But the presence of the longitudinal rib makes the rib system complete, which it is not, as we have seen, at Canterbury.[2] The vaults are obtusely pointed, and the ribs all reach to nearly the same level. The compartments are therefore not domical, but the masonry is in slightly arched courses which are parallel at the crown, as in

---

[1] Cf. my *Gothic Architecture*, second edition, pp. 130 *et seq.*

[2] The reader unfamiliar with French Gothic construction may here question the need for the longitudinal rib, since in most cases where they do not occur the vaults are still intact. So long as walls remain a vault may secure enough without this rib; but in developed French Gothic the wall is eliminated, and the longitudinal rib then becomes an essential member of the skeleton system. In transitional stages of Gothic Art the skeleton system is gradually perfecting within the walled enclosure.

French vaulting. The eastern rib of the easternmost compartment, which is against the end wall, is semicircular, and is in fact little more than a moulding. The transverse ribs have the profile A (Fig. 92), and the groin ribs of the easternmost bay the profile B, with a tooth ornament on the soffit between the rolls. It will be seen that these are variants of the Canterbury profiles. The vaulting shafts have the pointed section (Fig. 93), a form that is frequent in the Romanesque, and primitive Gothic, art of the Ile de France — as in St. Étienne of Beauvais. They are very slender, are continuous from the pavement (save in the eastern bays), and are banded at the ground-story impost, and by the triforium string.

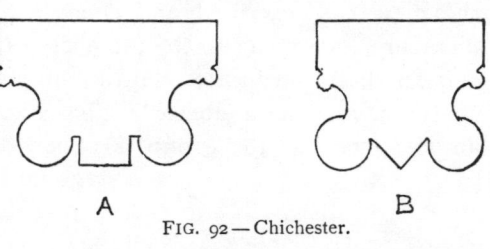

FIG. 92—Chichester.

In the new work at the east end the pier which divides the two bays (figured in my *Gothic Architecture*, p. 199, Second Edition) is a variant of the Canterbury pier with four supplementary shafts (Plate X) in the oblique part of the choir. Here at Chichester the ground story is lower than at Canterbury, and the pier is correspondingly shorter. The central column is cylindrical, and the shafts stand free at a considerable distance from it. Of the compound capital the member that crowns the great cylinder has a round abacus, while those of the smaller shafts have the square abaci with the corners cut off of Canterbury. The abacus profiling is French, but the foliation of the capitals, while in the form of crockets, as at Canterbury, has peculiarities which characterize the so-called stiff-leaved foliage of the Early English style, the most noticeable of which is the mid-rib of fillet-like section (cf. my *Gothic Architecture*, p. 406, Second Edition). The bases of these piers have round plinths, and are variants of those of the small colonnettes of the eastern crypt of Canterbury, with more finely cut, and more distinctly French, profiling. The

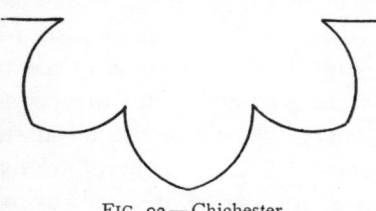

FIG. 93—Chichester.

vaulting shafts of this pier are not brought down to the pavement, but rest on foliated corbels set directly above the great capital. This is a first step in the direction of that corbelling of vaulting shafts that became characteristic, as we shall see, of the Early English systems. The next pier westward is an original Norman one with its eastern side rebuilt in the style of the new work; but it is differently composed from the pier just described, and consists of three orders of square members, answering to the members of the great archivolt, with smaller shafts set in the reëntrant angles. The capitals of these shafts have square abaci, the bases have square plinths with angle spurs, and the group is raised on a high plinth of semi-octagonal form. It is thus, as a whole, a French composition, though the foliation of the capitals exhibits a mixture of French and Anglo-Norman peculiarities. It has crockets, which are French, and stiff-leaved details, which are Anglo-Norman.

FIG. 94 — Chichester.

In the remaining bays of the eastern arm, as far as the transept, the new shafts, which replace the Norman ones to carry the first order of the great archivolts, have capitals in the French style, and these shafts are not banded. But the corresponding shafts of the nave, west of the transept, have capitals with the upper member of the abacus rounded. The bases of these shafts are profiled like those of Canterbury, and have square plinths, but no angle spurs. Of the four small shafts in each bay of the clerestory, two have capitals with round abaci, and bases with round plinths, and two have capitals with square abaci and bases with square plinths. The capitals with round abaci have crockets, and are like those of the eastern apses of the east transept of Canterbury. In the responds of the aisles, however, are capitals having round abaci without crockets (Fig. 94), which are, I suppose, among the earliest examples of the beautiful Early English type that was perfected in St. Hugh's transept at Lincoln. This appropriate treatment of foliation in connection with the round abacus, with leaves tending in one direction round the bell finds a rude foreshadowing in the capital of one of the great round piers of the Pointed Norman Choir of St. Mary's New Shoreham (Fig. 61, p. 61). The grouped capitals of the high vaulting shafts have the French crockets, but each group is covered by a single round abacus. Thus while at Chichester the survival of so much of the old Norman work precluded, in the rebuilding, any extensive following of the structural system of Canterbury, in many of the details of the new work the direct influence of Canterbury is naturally very marked.

The first great new work after Canterbury was that of Lincoln Cathedral. Lincoln, like Canterbury and Chichester, was formerly a Norman structure of the eleventh century. It is said to have been damaged by an earthquake in 1185, and shortly after this, as is well known, the famous St. Hugh of Avalon became bishop of the diocese, and immediately set about rebuilding the east end of the church in a new style. The work appears to have been begun about 1192, and included a choir, an eastern transept, an apse, and part of a western transept. This work was, as we shall see, profoundly influenced by Canterbury, although the style of its details is nowhere purely French, but manifests, on the contrary, some of the finest Early English features in their primitive form.

The plan (Fig. 95) bears a striking resemblance to that of Canterbury (Fig. 68, p. 72) in having two transepts,[1] in the small apses on the east side of the eastern transept, and in the peculiar shape of its former apse — which suggests an influence from the oblique part of Canterbury choir. The double transept arose in Canterbury as a result of Ernulf and Conrad's addition to the nave and transept of Lanfranc, and the scheme thus fortuitously developed was repeated at Lincoln in the original setting out of St. Hugh's rebuilding.[2] The apse of this remarkable work was demolished in the thirteenth century in order to build the present square-ended eastern extension known as the Angel Choir, so that we are deprived of the opportunity

---

[1] Only one of these is shown in the cut.
[2] The double transept was a feature of the great Abbey Church of Cluny, and the idea of adding the second transept at Canterbury may have been derived from that source. In England, after Lincoln, the double transept occurs in Beverley and Salisbury.

of studying a great apse as designed and constructed in the twelfth century, in a pointed style, by Anglo-Norman builders. But the eastern transept and the choir remain in substantial integrity, save for some mutilations of the ground story, especially in the choir, and some minor alterations in the south transept. Beginning with the eastern transept, as presumably the earliest surviving part of the work, we find a system

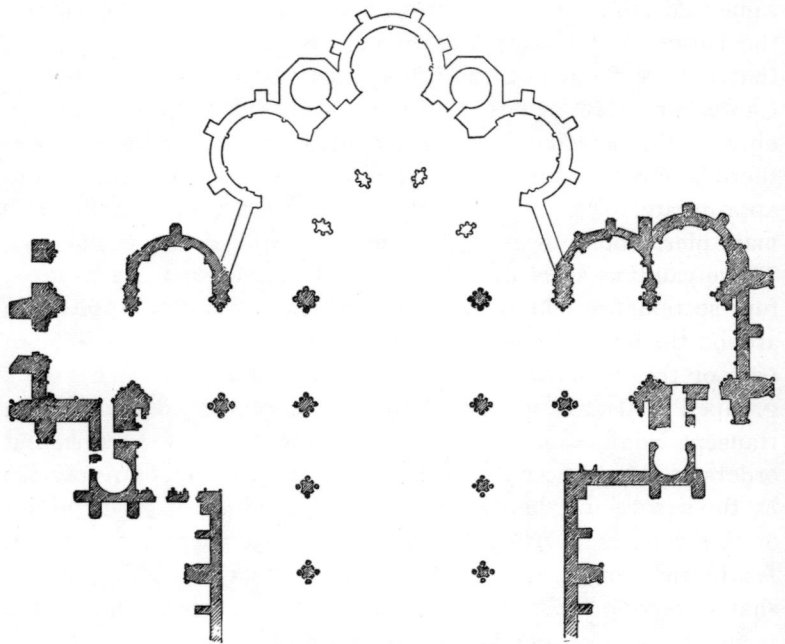

FIG. 95 — Lincoln Choir and East Transept.

of great interest and beauty, and also, in part, of logical design. The vaulting has the sexpartite form that was introduced by the French architect at Canterbury, and, as at Canterbury, it springs from a level below that of the clerestory string, but unlike the vaulting of Canterbury each compartment covers only one bay of the system, the intermediate transverse rib springing from a corbel in the triforium spandrel, instead of a shaft rising from below.[1] On the east side the piers have each

---

[1] This peculiarly illogical adjustment of sexpartite vaulting to a uniform system finds, so far as I know, only one counterpart on the Continent, that of the small church at Nesle in the Ile de France. Viollet le Duc (*Dictionnaire*, etc., IX, p. 250) justifies it on the ground that in so small a building an intermediate pier

three vaulting shafts rising from the pavement (an improvement on the system of Canterbury, since it gives independent support from the pavement for each rib) to which the main transverse ribs, and the groin ribs, are well adjusted; but on the opposite side one shaft only is given to these ribs. This illogical use of a single shaft for a group of high vaulting ribs, which was repeated in the choir, looks like an instance of the same indiscriminate imitation that is so frequently met with in the earlier Norman art. There can, I think, be little doubt that the single shaft here is derived from the single shaft of Canterbury. But the single shaft of William of Sens occurs only in the intermediate piers of his alternate system where there is only one rib to carry, and where it is therefore entirely appropriate. To use it, as St. Hugh's architect has done, in a main pier, from which three ribs necessarily spring, is illogical. These vaulting shafts are of Purbeck marble, and are each in four sections banded at the joints, as at Canterbury. The piers are, on the ground story, amplifications of those in the inclined part of the choir of Canterbury, which have each four shafts grouped with the main column (Plate X). Here in Lincoln transept additional shafts are introduced to carry the first orders of the great archivolts, which at Canterbury are carried by the square abacus of the great capital. Of these piers, those on the west side, having the single vaulting shaft, are peculiar. As in the compound pier of the east end of Chichester the shafts are widely detached, and in the interval, on each cardinal face of the octagonal main column, a series of crockets is worked. This novelty is not, however, I think, altogether admirable. The face of an important bearing member is not the place for salient ornament, and builders having true regard for the proper function, and functional expression, of a compound pier would not so widely separate the subordinate shafts, but would either engage them, like the Romanesque and French Gothic builders, or set them close to the main column, as William of Sens has done at Canterbury.

To come back to the vaulting, the forms of the longitudinal arches, which are here provided with ribs, are radically different from those of Canterbury. They not only spring from the same

would be useless and cumbrous. But in that case it would appear better to avoid the sexpartite form of vaulting.

level as the transverse and groin ribs, but are cusped (Fig. 96). Thus the vaulting conoid is widened against the clerestory wall, instead of narrowing to concentrate the vault thrust — as they do when stilted in the French Gothic manner. In this, and in the conformation of the upper parts of the cells, which are sharply pointed, this vaulting shows the hand of the Anglo-Norman.

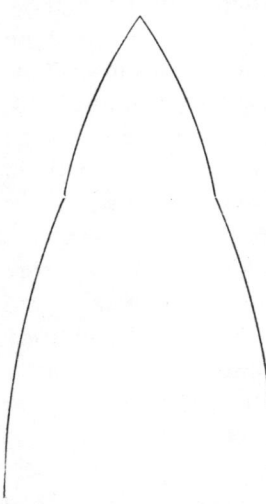

FIG. 96 — Lincoln, East Transept.

The rib and archivolt profiles follow those of Canterbury with slight variations. The capitals and bases have round abaci and round plinths throughout this work, and in the profiling of these members some of the distinctive Early English forms are developed, as in the abaci of the capitals of the wall arcade and in the bases of the crocketed piers, where there are three tori with narrow, water-holding scotias, as in Fig. 97.

In the triforium of the north arm, on the east side, are a few capitals of the finest foliated Early English type — the first really beautiful ones, I believe, in which the foliation is consistently adapted to the round abacus.[1] The foliated capitals with round abaci at Canterbury and Chichester retain the crocket (save a few in the aisles of Chichester) which properly belongs to the French capital with the square abacus, its expressive function being to support the projecting angles of the abacus, but with the round abacus the crocket has (as I have said, p. 84) no such propriety, and accordingly the designer of this Lincoln capital has omitted it, devising a new scheme of leafage admirably adapted to this form of abacus. This leafage, while quite different from the

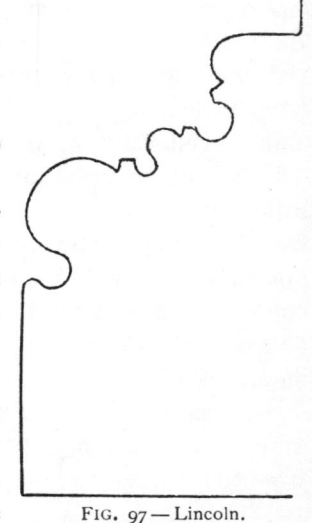

FIG. 97 — Lincoln.

[1] One of these capitals is figured in my *Gothic Architecture*, Second Edition, p. 339.

French types, is at once finely expressive of the living qualities of nature nobly conventionalized for architectural effect. Rising out of the lower surface of the bell, the broad trefoils spring as with a common impulse, and, moving in one direction around its upper part, clasp the lower member of the abacus in a manner that pleasantly binds the two parts together without confusing them. The fillet-like form of the midribs, above noticed in the capitals of Chichester, have value here in giving contrast to the rounded surfaces that make up all other parts of the composition. The moderation of curvature, and of salience, in this leafage, and its severe simplicity, give an architectural value that is most admirable. It has the merit of a distinctive type appropriate to its place and function, and may, I think, rank with the finest artistic products of any time or country. But there are few capitals of this beautiful type in the twelfth-century work at Lincoln. One, however, in the wall arcade of the choir appears to me even finer in its mere leafage, but the capital as a whole is not so well formed. This leafage (Plate XVI) is arranged in the same rhythmical order, but with a finer subordinate freedom in the parts, with an exquisite expression of nervous life and movement, and with remarkable subtlety of line and surface. In most of the others the crocket survives, and has a peculiar Anglo-Norman character in which the salience of the leafage becomes excessive, and the curvature extravagant. There are, however, some others of great beauty, though they have less ornamental restraint and architectural propriety. One of these (Fig. 98) crowns the vaulting shaft of the northwest angle of this transept.

The general internal aspect of this transept is very beautiful. Before the reconstruction of the lower parts of the crossing piers, and the end of the south arm, and before the introduction of the florid wooden beams, now fixed between the crossing piers — which disfigure the system and obstruct the view from end to end — this interior must have been exceedingly fine. As it is there is nothing to compare with it, save the choir, in any other part of the Cathedral.

Externally, where it has not been worked over, this transept is very pure and beautiful in style. There are no flying buttresses, and the plain pier buttresses, and buttresses of the aisles, show clearly the inspiration of the east end of Canterbury. The clerestory is an almost exact reproduction of the English William's clerestory, and the walls of the small apses are carried up above the vaulting, and pierced with small pointed openings to light the triforium, precisely as was done on a larger scale by William of Sens on the south side of Canterbury choir. No finer art than this has been produced in England, and in some

FIG. 98 — Lincoln, East Transept.

of its features we have what is best in the Early English style substantially developed.

Coming now to the choir of this twelfth-century work, we find a fuller system which includes external flying buttresses. But, like almost all other noble works of the Middle Ages, it has been deplorably mutilated and disfigured, as well as encumbered by the extravagantly florid stalls in an inharmonious and debased style of a later period. An analysis of this work will show that it, like the transept, is based on the work at Canterbury, though the system undergoes many modifications, and the ornamental details are almost wholly Anglo-Norman, and quite unlike those of Canterbury. The question whether St. Hugh's architect with a French name was a Frenchman is of little importance — since the monument itself shows plainly that the primary source of inspiration was French, mainly, though not exclusively, through Canterbury.

The vaulting of the choir has, as is well known, a singular character, and is not at all like any French vaulting.[1] There are four compartments, of which only three are of the original

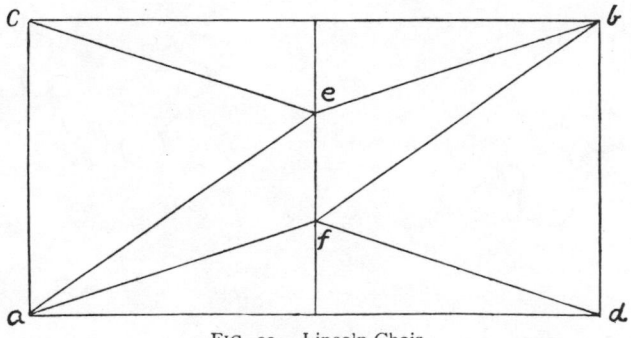

FIG. 99 — Lincoln Choir.

construction, the westernmost one having been rebuilt in the sexpartite form after the fall of the central tower in 1239. These three compartments, and the one over the eastern crossing, are each divided into eight cells by a peculiar arrangement of structural ribs, including a longitudinal ridge rib, a member that has no structural necessity. The arrangement will be understood by the plan (Fig. 99), where it will be seen that instead of two groin ribs intersecting at the centre of the compartment, there are three, two of which spring from the points $a$ and $b$, diverging as they rise, so that their opposite branches meet at the crown of the vault in points which divide the longitudinal ridge rib into three nearly equal parts; and the half ribs from $c$ and $d$ meet the others in the points $e$ and $f$. This is a tortuous and unsightly way of doing what could be better done

---

[1] The date of this vaulting has been questioned, but I see no reason to doubt that it belongs to the original construction.

in a simple and straightforward manner.[1]  The longitudinal rib, which is but a narrow moulding, is again cusped as in the transept, and springs from the same level as the greater ribs. The transverse ribs are profiled as at A, Fig. 100,[2] and the groin ribs have the profile B.  All the ribs, at each point of springing, are gathered upon the capital of a single vaulting shaft, and in order that they may do so, they are made to interpenetrate so that only the larger mouldings remain at the springing.  It is worthy of notice, too, that the unequal number of ribs in the conoids — four groin ribs springing from one point and only two from another alternately — gives the

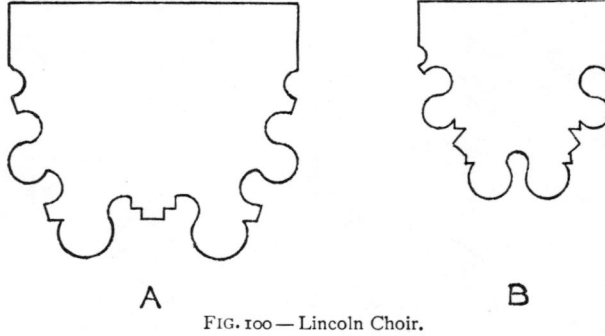

FIG. 100 — Lincoln Choir.

vaulting shafts unequal burdens, though they are of equal magnitude.

Apart from the peculiarities of the vaulting the system of this choir (Fig. 101) has many fine points.  It was, however, sadly mutilated in the fourteenth century by the cutting off of the vaulting shafts, which formerly rose from the pavement, in order to make room for the existing stalls.  On the ground story the pier (Figs. 101 and 102) is finely composed and well adapted to its function.  A comparison of this pier with the compound pier (Plate X) of William of Sens in the oblique-sided part of Canterbury choir shows that there can be little

---

[1] Mr. E. S. Prior in *A History of Gothic Art in England*, p. 95, London, 1900, remarks on this vaulting of St. Hugh's choir as follows: " Clearly the purpose of the architect is here shown straining after the English idea of a continual coherence of vault surfaces."  But what is meant by continual coherence of vault surface, and how is any coherence of surface attained by this unnatural disposition of ribs?

[2] The profiles were taken by eye from a distance, and may not be strictly accurate, but they are, I believe, substantially correct.

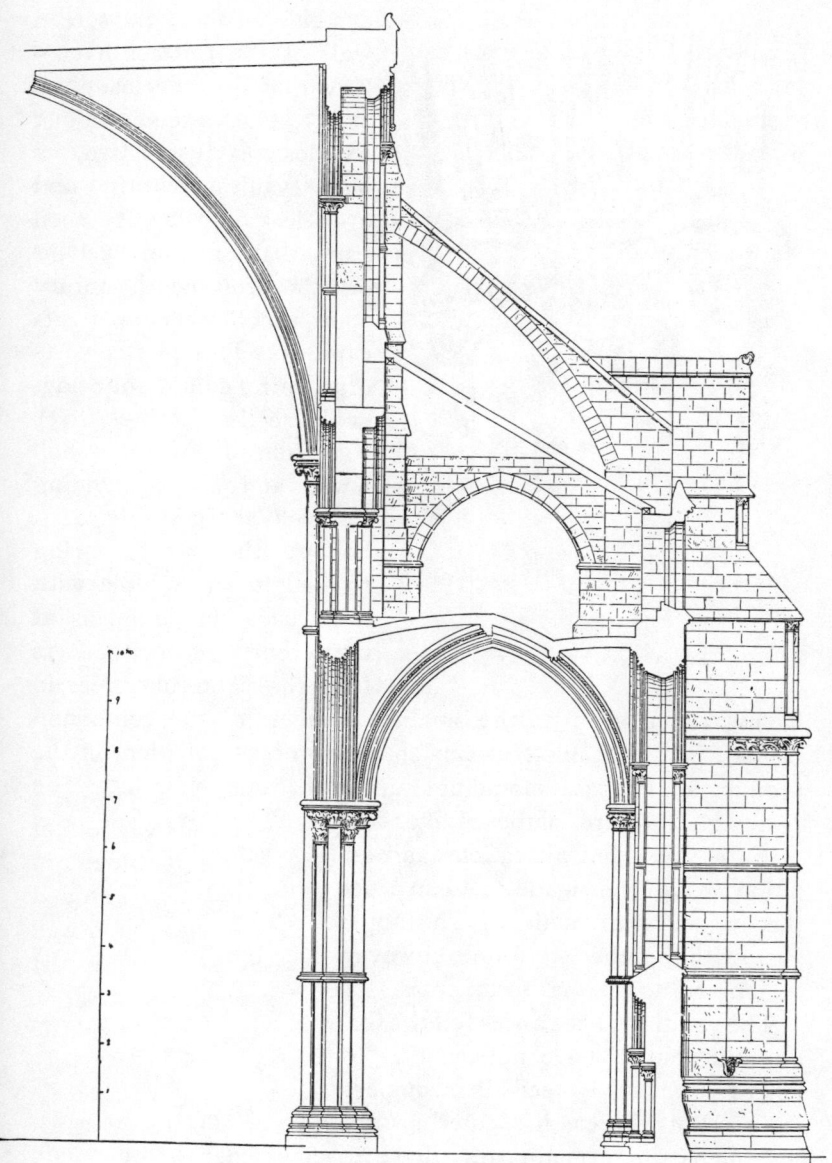

FIG. 101 — Lincoln Choir.

question of its direct derivation from that source. The illustration (Fig. 102) is taken from the north aisle, and shows all that can be seen above the screen wall of the thirteenth century that now encloses the choir. On the choir side it has lost, as just stated, its main vaulting shaft, and even less of it can be seen from that side on account of the fourteenth-century stalls which reach up to its capitals. This pier consists of a central column of octagonal section (Fig. 103), with four of its sides hollowed and a free-standing Purbeck shaft set in each hollow, the whole being banded in the middle with a Purbeck moulding, as at Canterbury. But it differs from the Canterbury pier in having round abaci to the smaller members of the compound capital, in the Anglo-Norman character of its foliation, in the profiling of its base mouldings and in its round plinths. The crossing piers were composed like those of Canterbury, but alterations and additions have been made in them since the original construction. The upper part of the southwestern one, however, remains in its original form.

FIG. 102 — Lincoln Choir.

The vaulting of the aisles follows that of Canterbury, above noticed (p. 79), where there are five cells in a compartment. But whereas in Canterbury the quinquepartite form appears to have arisen by chance from a lack of correspondence between the number of piers in the new work and of responds in the old, they are here so planned of deliberate purpose, probably in imitation of Canterbury. In fact, each bay

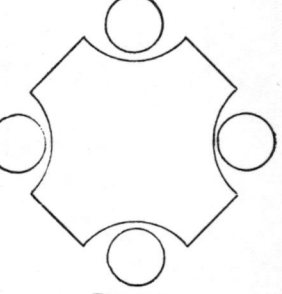
FIG. 103.

PLATE XVI

Capital of Lincoln Choir Aisle.

of this Lincoln choir aisle has features that appear to have been borrowed from two different parts of the Canterbury work. The quinquepartite vaults of Canterbury occur in the choir east of the transept, and there is but one such vault on each side. These cover compartments lying between the transept and the chapels of St. Andrew and St. Anselm, respectively, as shown in Willis's plan (Fig. 68, p. 72). In each of these compartments there is room for but one window opening because a part of the wall is covered by one of the small apses of the transept. But in the aisles of Trinity Chapel there are, as we have seen, two windows in each aisle bay. The Lincoln builder, following this scheme, has given two windows to each bay and then, following William of Sens, he has sprung a half rib from the shaft, between the windows, and made his vault quinquepartite — which the English William, in the aisles of Trinity Chapel, has not done. Another feature that this aisle vaulting has in common with Canterbury is the segmental form of the groin rib, making it spring from the capital at an angle. In the work of the Frenchman at Canterbury this appears to have been due to the crowded space fixed by the old work. In the work of the English William it was determined by the need for conformity of level with the vaulting of the choir aisle. But here in Lincoln the architect was not handicapped by any such conditions, and its use by him may be due in part to imitation of Canterbury, and in part to the force of Anglo-Norman custom — since it is, as we have seen, almost constant in the round-arched Norman, and the pointed Norman, vaulting of England.

The responds (Fig. 101) are clearly reminiscent of those of Trinity Chapel, Canterbury, and consist of five banded Purbeck shafts — one for each rib in the vaulting. But these members are not all well adjusted to the vault ribs, as they are in Canterbury. In some cases the rib does not fall directly upon the shaft, but is so far to one side that a considerable part of the capital is uncovered, and the member thus appears largely useless. The shaft that supports the intermediate half rib rests on a foliated corbel at the level of the window-sills, and its base mouldings, as well as the corbel itself, are excessively developed.[1]

[1] This shaft and its corbel do not show in Fig. 101, because the section of this part of the aisle is taken through one of the two windows, and not through the middle of the vault compartment.

The aisle wall is treated differently from that of Canterbury, though it follows Canterbury in the twin window openings. A double arcade, of great elegance, is carried under the window openings, and the wall above this is solid, and of almost Norman thickness. The effect of massiveness is, however, relieved by elegant banded Purbeck jamb shafts flanking the windows.

This arcade has some details that seem to show direct French influence, enough to suggest that French carvers were employed in their execution. The capital (Fig. 104), from the arcade of the south aisle, has not only the French form of crocket (like the capitals with round abaci in the transept of Canterbury), but crockets that in design and execution have a perfectly French character—which consists in a peculiar subtlety of outline and surface modelling, and in the rounding of salient members in the finely conventionalized leafage. In contrast to these the other capitals (Fig. 105) have the Anglo-Norman characteristics of design and execution, in which the details of the leafage become more angular in section, and the French refinements of line and surface are wanting. The Anglo-Norman capital is, however, I think, the finer of the two in general outline — the bell being better proportioned to the abacus, and the crockets conforming more closely with the shape of the bell. The capital of French workmanship wants the square abacus, and a different adjustment of the crockets, such as the square abacus would require,

FIG. 104 — Lincoln Choir Aisle.

PLATE XVII

Lincoln Choir.

to make it right. In striving to conform his crocket scheme to the round abacus, the designer has lost the beauty of the French type without attaining that of the pure Anglo-Norman type. But while the Anglo-Norman capital is in general form the better of the two, it is not, I think, nearly so fine as the pure Early English capital, referred to on p. 116, of the transept.

The general scheme of the triforium (Plate XVII) follows that of the choir of Canterbury, but the arches here at Lincoln are all pointed, and there are many other points of difference in proportions and details. In order to point the larger arches, as well as the smaller ones, their springing is placed lower than at Canterbury, shortening the supporting shafts, and improving the effect of the arcade as a whole. Moreover, a third order is introduced, which gives a redundance to the composition that became a characteristic of the Early English style, and this redundance is increased, at the expense of logical design, by the introduction of functionless shafts set between those that carry the several orders

FIG. 105 — Lincoln Choir Aisle.

of the archivolts, as well as by hood moulds — superfluous members for an interior — springing from foliated corbels. The profiling of these archivolts (Fig. 106) is substantially the same as that of the triforium of Canterbury.

The clerestory (Fig. 101 and Plate XVII) has the Norman passageway, and is a development of that of Canterbury (Fig. 71, p. 82, and Plate IX) with three openings in the outer wall, and five in the inner plane, of which the smaller ones are very diminutive. The arches are acutely pointed, and those of the inner plane are carried on groups of slender

Purbeck shafts. The supports of the middle arch consist each of three shafts incorporated with a rectangular member, while the taller ones on either side have only two shafts each, and those of the diminutive arches but one on each side. As the five arches have each but one order, the lack of logic in this scheme will be obvious. The taller shafts are banded in the middle, and are steadied by bonding stones reaching across the passageway from the outer wall; and it is worthy

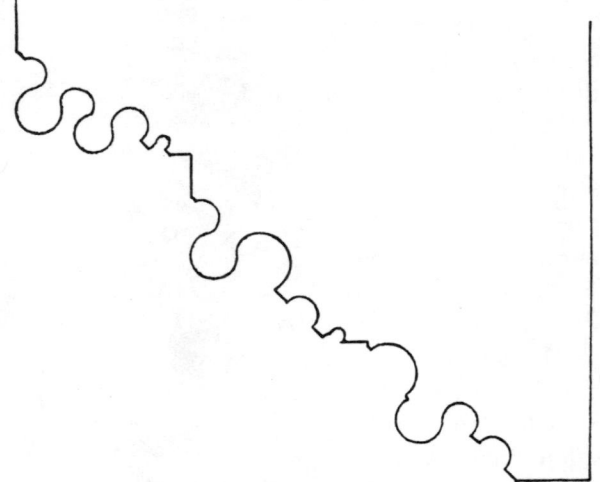

FIG. 106 — Triforium Archivolt, Lincoln.

of notice that the cusped arch of the vault, that we found in the transept, reappears here.

A comparison of the section (Fig. 101, p. 121) with those of the choir and Trinity Chapel of Canterbury (Figs. 71 and 85, pp. 82, 102), will show a striking resemblance which points clearly, I think, to direct, though modified, imitation. The transverse abutting arch in the triforium is precisely like that of Canterbury, save that here it is pointed. The carrying up of the aisle wall, so as to raise the height of the triforium on that side, and the piercing of this wall[1] with small openings,[1] is an imitation of the work of William of Sens on the south side of the Canterbury choir. The pier buttress and the great outer buttress are clearly modelled on those of Trinity Chapel, and both were new features in

[1] This pierced wall of the triforium comes, of course, in both cases from the gallery over the aisle of many Norman and other Romanesque churches.

England, earlier buttresses having the flat Norman form.[1] The flying buttress differs from that of Canterbury in having the arch properly loaded, but it is otherwise substantially the same, having the low segmental curve in which Canterbury is peculiar, and being placed comparatively low down near the aisle roof.

Of the outside of this choir little can be seen in the general view, since only two bays stand free of the eastern and western transepts. In fact the whole of this earliest and finest pointed work of Lincoln, including the eastern transept, is so engulfed in the later works east and west, so masked internally, and so mutilated in many parts, that few beholders are able to form a correct idea of its appearance in its original integrity. Notwithstanding the structural inconsistencies and ornamental redundancies that have been noticed, it is a very noble work. It is fine in proportions, broad and quiet in effect, and beautiful in details. The distinctive characteristics of the Early English style are here so far advanced, and so far prevail throughout, as to give a new aspect to the monument. The structural system, however, derives too much from Canterbury to be properly called Early English — for in the true Early English style vaulting shafts rising from the pavement disappear, and the flying buttress also is wanting. The Early English features are superficial, and apparent at a glance, while the essential structural system is little noticed by the casual eye. Thus has arisen the mistaken idea that we have in this choir a radically new departure in architectural design. The Canterbury system is not reproduced in Lincoln so as to be at once obvious, any more than the system of Sens is thus reproduced in Canterbury. This choir and transept have not yet been faithfully studied and described, as to their essential structural features, in the light of a full knowledge of Canterbury on the one hand, and of the Continental Gothic art of the twelfth century on the other. Opinions have been hastily formed, and confidently expressed, which the facts do not justify. Even so learned a writer as the late Mr. Freeman, in his zeal for the credit of native artistic achievement, has been led to conclusions that will, I think, in the light of the foregoing analysis and comparison, be seen to be quite unfounded.

---

[1] The nearly contemporaneous outer buttresses of Chichester have, indeed, the French form, but they also were probably derived from Canterbury.

To say, as he has said, that "what Diocletian did at Spalato for the round arch, St. Hugh did at Lincoln for the pointed arch," and that "St. Hugh was strictly the first to design a building in which the pointed arch should be allowed full play,"[1] is to say what is untrue. For at the time when St. Hugh's choir was begun the great cathedrals of Paris and Laon were nearing completion, and in both of them not only does the pointed arch prevail throughout, but the marvellous Gothic structural skeleton is fully, and magnificently, developed. Mr. Freeman, however, was a historian, and had not a constructor's knowledge of architecture. It is more surprising to find the great French architect, and illuminating writer on architecture, Viollet le Duc, affirming[2] that there is no French influence manifested at Lincoln. For Viollet le Duc did not, like Freeman, write of architecture without a competent constructor's knowledge of mediæval building. But the French master's inspection of Lincoln appears to have been hasty, and his remarks apply mainly to ornamental details which, as we have seen, are indeed unlike those of the French Gothic art. He speaks, it is true, of the "system of architecture," but he makes no analysis of the structural forms and adjustments, and his statement that the outside of the choir is "thoroughly English, or Norman if you will," is surprisingly short-sighted. But (strangely for him) he does not here appear to mean by the "system of architecture" the more essential forms and adjustments, but confines his remarks to "arches acutely pointed, blank windows in the clerestory, . . . a low triforium; each bay of the aisles divided into two by a small buttress; shafts banded," etc. But while this twelfth-century work of Lincoln is not, as we have seen, exactly like any French work, or even exactly like that of Canterbury, the system is clearly derived from that of Canterbury, and has more French Gothic character than any other building in England, except Westminster Abbey. As I have said, no account of the monument, based on a proper analysis of its essential structural system, and on adequate acquaintance with the earlier Gothic systems of the Continent, as well as with Canterbury, has hitherto been given. But in lieu of this writers have gone on repeating

---

[1] *Norman Conquest*, vol. 5, p. 641.

[2] In the much quoted letter contributed to the *Gentleman's Magazine* for May, 1861

PLATE XVIII

Presbytery of Rochester.

the short-sighted remarks of Viollet le Duc, and those of Freeman and Parker, and many others, so that a true understanding of the real character of this great work has been rendered impossible for those who look for help to the literature of the subject. How what there is of French Gothic character in St. Hugh's choir was gradually eliminated, and the Anglo-Norman characteristics reëstablished, as the Early English style developed, will appear as we go on.

The next important work in which the Early English style is seen advancing is the east end of Rochester, begun about the year 1200.[1] The Norman structure of the eleventh and twelfth centuries had been damaged by fire in 1179, and some rebuilding appears to have been done soon after, but this was demolished in the early years of the thirteenth century, and the now existing east end and transept were built. The influence of Canterbury is here obvious at a glance, although the system, save that of the vaulting, is very different. This work consists (Fig. 107) of a rectangular Presbytery without aisles, and a transept with an eastern aisle. A crypt extends under the whole of both Presbytery and transept, and the supporting colonnettes of this crypt resemble those of the English William's crypt of Canterbury, though their moulded capitals are more advanced toward Early English character. The vaulting, however, has no likeness to that of the Canterbury crypt. It is of purely Anglo-Norman form, with low segmental groin ribs, pointed transverse and longitudinal ribs, level crowns, and surfaces hardly at all concave, though necessarily warped in their shaping to the ribs.

The Presbytery (Plate XVIII) is enclosed by walls of Norman massiveness which are divided into two stages of openings. The openings of the lower stage are deeply recessed internally beneath a tall arcade in the thickness of the wall, supported on salient rectangular piers with Purbeck shafts. The upper stage is treated like a clerestory, in the form of that of Canterbury. Three compartments of vaulting cover this part, of which the western one is quadripartite, and the other two are sexpartite. All of these compartments are oblong with their long axes run-

---

[1] Cf. the admirable monograph by Mr. W. H. St. John Hope, M.A., *The Architectural History of the Cathedral Church and Monastery of St. Andrew at Rochester*, London, 1900.

ning transversely, and are of unequal width in consequence of irregular spacing of their supports. The crowns of the transverse and groin ribs are on about the same level, and the cells are sharply pointed with their crowns in straight lines. There are no longitudinal ribs, but the wall arches are stilted — warping the surfaces of the lateral cells. Thus while, as to the sexpartite form, modelled on the vaulting of Canterbury, this vaulting of

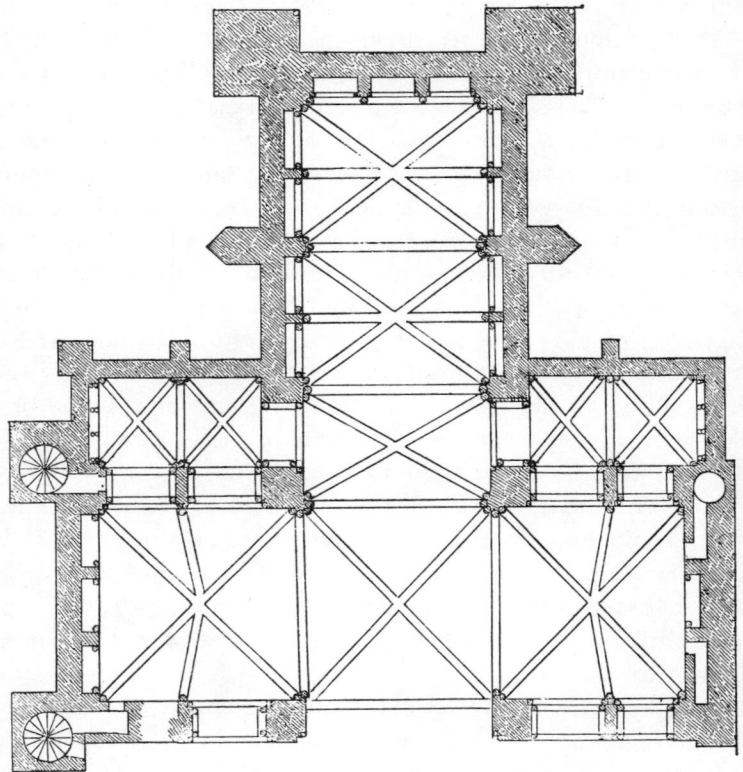

FIG. 107 — Eastern Transept and Presbytery of Rochester.

Rochester is Anglo-Norman in its general conformation. The supports follow those of Canterbury in having three Purbeck shafts for each main pier, and a single one for each intermediate pier — thus forming a logical alternate system corresponding with the vault ribs. But unlike Canterbury the shafts here are all brought down to the pavement, giving a continuity to the system that is more like the developed French Gothic. Notwithstanding this, however, the structure consists mainly of the ponderous walls to which the internal skeleton is applied very much as in the nave of Chichester. There is a vast difference between this and an organic skeleton constituting the structure itself according to the French Gothic idea. A single sexpartite vault, nearly square on plan, covers each arm of the transept; but as the bays on each side are unequal in width, so that the supports of the intermediate transverse rib cannot be in the middle, the opposite branches of this rib have to take an oblique direction in order to meet at the centre of the vault (cf. the plan, Fig. 107). The same irregularity is noticeable in some of the sexpartite vaults of Canterbury.

The survival of Norman tradition in the design and construction of this east end of Rochester is strikingly manifest in the exterior which is substantially a reproduction of the neighbouring castle keep — the great square angle buttresses answering to the square angle turrets of the keep, and the smaller mid wall buttresses having their counterparts also in the Norman castle.

Thus in such monuments as Chichester, Lincoln, and Rochester we see the Anglo-Norman genius variously modifying the achitectural forms that had been introduced at Canterbury, working them thus modified, without strict regard for functional propriety, into the local Norman fabric, and so evolving the so-called Early English style. At Chichester the new elements are engrafted on the old Norman structure; at Lincoln the whole fabric is new, and an unwonted lightness of construction is attained under the inspiration of Canterbury, but the ornamental details are so entirely transformed that the general aspect of the monument differs widely from that of Canterbury; while at Rochester the heavy-walled Norman construction reappears, with a modified Canterbury vaulting system worked into it, and with the moulded capital prevailing throughout. We may next consider the more fully developed Early English style in some of the works which immediately followed.

## CHAPTER VI

### THE EARLY ENGLISH STYLE

THE works considered in the foregoing chapter show the old Norman system and the newly engrafted French details undergoing various changes and readjustments, both structural and ornamental, which give the buildings a new aspect. The Early English style is taking form in such buildings, but its distinctive character is not yet fully reached. This condition survives to some extent in the nave of Lincoln, which we have next to examine, though on the whole it belongs in the category of Early English works.

The precise date of this nave is unknown, but it cannot have been begun before the death of St. Hugh (A.D. 1200). Its style, however, would appear to show that it must have been commenced soon after that time. The vaulting is about 2.50 metres higher than that of the choir, improving the proportions, which are, I think, exceptionally fine. In this vaulting (Plate XIX) the Anglo-Norman proclivities in construction appear in the introduction of ribs without structural necessity, and in the relations of their curves, giving new forms to the vaults. In addition to a longitudinal ridge rib — an instance of which we have already noticed in the choir — this vaulting has in each compartment six other superfluous ribs, namely, four tiercerons ($cc'$ on the plan, Fig. 108) and two liernes ($d$ on the same plan). None of these members have any necessary structural function, but their curves are such as to produce obtuse groins midway between the springing and the crown, as will be seen in the horizontal section of the conoid (Fig. 109) taken at this level. Here $a$ is the transverse rib and $b$ the normal groin rib. The ribs $cc'$ are tiercerons so placed that the lines $ac$, $cb$, and $bc$ meet at angles and thus create groins, and where there are groins, ribs have function, of course, in fortifying them. But such superfluous ribs and factitious groins have no justification in principles of straight-

PLATE XIX

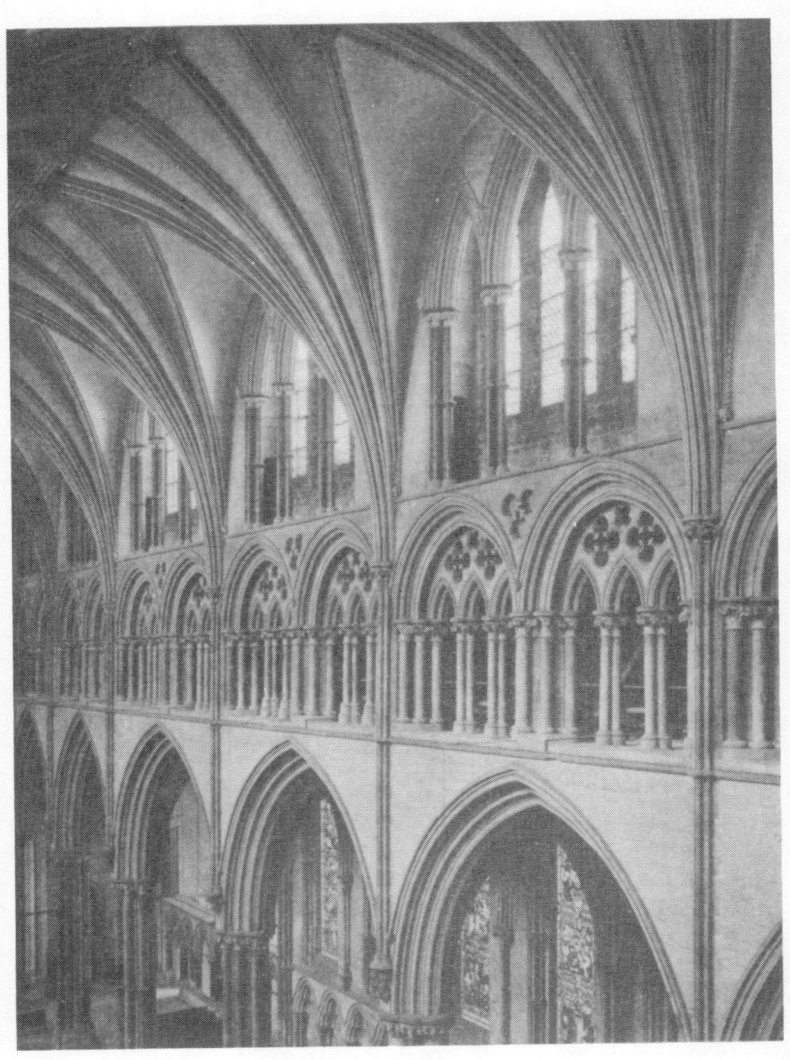

Lincoln Nave.

forward construction. Tiercerons not being in vertical planes, their opposite branches meet on plan at an angle, and require abutment. The tiercerons *c* meet on the longitudinal ridge rib which gives them abutment, but to abut the tiercerons *c'* liernes, or short transverse ridge ribs, *d* are inserted. There is nothing

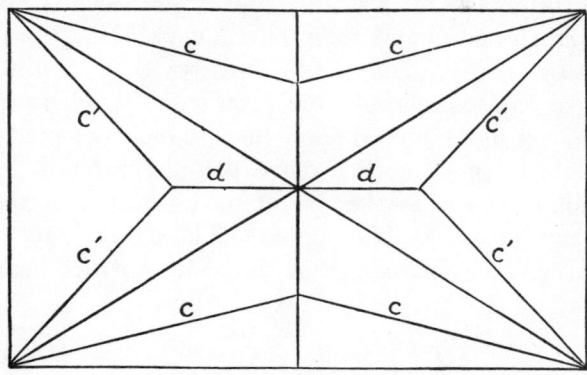

FIG. 108 — Lincoln Nave.

in this vaulting that can be properly called a longitudinal rib, but in place of such a rib there is a narrow moulding with a tooth ornament. This longitudinal arch is not pointed, but has an approximately semielliptical form, like that of the Norman vaulting of the nave of Durham. In consequence of this the conoid widens against the clerestory wall from the springing upwards, after the usual manner of English vaulting, and its outline in section on the inner side, between the tiercerons *c'*, is, in consequence of the curves of the principal ribs, a curve foreshadowing that of the fan vaulting of the subsequent perpendicular style.

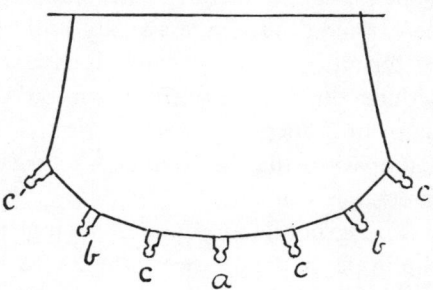

FIG. 109 — Lincoln Nave.

The surfaces are in most parts slightly concave, at the crown of the vault very distinctly so, since the ridge rib and the liernes are arched from one to another of the other ribs.

The composition and adjustment of the supports is already characteristic of the Early English style in which the pier, as a logical and continuous compound member, reaching from the pavement to the external cornice, does not exist. In the old Norman art, notwithstanding its structural inconsistencies, the continuity of the vaulting members, from the pavement upward, was generally preserved. But among the singular departures from the principles of organic construction in which the Early English craftsmen outdid their Norman predecessors, was that of breaking this continuity. We first saw this done in the rebuilding of the east end of Chichester (p. 112), where the vaulting shafts are disconnected from the ground-story pier, and are made to start from a corbel above the pier capital. This disconnection is carried further in the nave of Lincoln, the corbel being placed considerably higher. There are three vaulting shafts, instead of only one, as in the choir, but no more logical

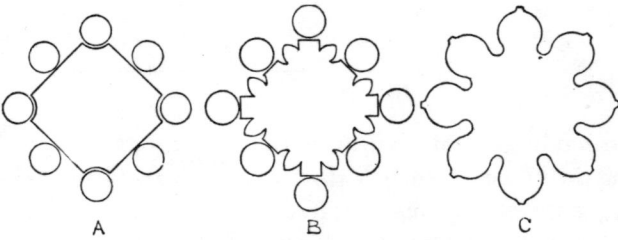

FIG. 110—Lincoln Nave.

relationship subsists between them and the vaulting members than we found in the choir, since there are here seven ribs to be carried. We have already noticed, in the west bays of Worcester and the reconstructed nave of Chichester, a tendency to reduce the vaulting shafts in bulk excessively. Here in the nave of Lincoln this is carried farther still, and the extreme attenuation that became characteristic of Early English design is established.

The ground-story piers, having no organic connection with the upper system, are of the same general character from end to end, but there are in the series several variants of the general type, as at A, B, and C (Fig. 110)—the members corresponding to the arch orders of the great arcades, except in form B, where the small almond-shaped members of the main column correspond to nothing above, their diminutive capitals dying away in the foliation of the larger ones. In A and B the shafts stand free, and are each of two monolithic lengths of Purbeck banded at the junction, while in C the pier is shaped into a semblance of shafts, as in the nave of Kirkstall (cf. p. 47). In themselves these piers have, I think, much beauty of proportion and elegance of form.

The clerestory and triforium are variants of those of the choir. In the clerestory the diminutive arches of the inner wall plane of the choir are omitted, and in the triforium each great arch embraces three subordinate ones, instead of only two, as in the choir; the piercings of the tympanums are multiplied, and trefoiled panels are worked in the spandrels between each pair of arches. Thus an increase of ornamentation is noticeable as the style progresses, and it is in this largely that the later pointed architecture of England, as well as that of the Continent, differs from the earlier. This ornamental elaboration is shown further in the introduction of a third order in the great archivolts, — the choir, like that of Canterbury, having only two,[1] — together with a closer grouping of the mouldings, and the absence of broad, flat surfaces on the soffits. Thus the Early English archivolts exhibit an increasing multiplicity of members, with increasing depth of intervening hollows. At the same time the orders became more rounded in section, in better conformity with the round abacus that had become a constant feature of the style.

The aisle vaulting of this nave follows that of the choir in its five-celled form (the choir vaults, as we have seen, following Canterbury), but it is better proportioned in height above the springing, so that the groin ribs have their curves struck from the impost level, and thus rise without forming angles at the springing. This vaulting has a tierceron and lierne in each longitudinal cell, and the half transverse rib is struck from a centre above the springing level, and thus has a horseshoe shape, like the ribs of the high vaulting of the east end of Canterbury, already noticed.

The cross-section reproduces that of the choir (cf. Fig. 101, p. 121) with some change of proportions, but with substantial exactness, save for the curtailments of the vaulting system already noticed, to which may be added the reduction of

---

[1] Three or more orders in the great archivolts are frequent in the later Norman churches, as in the choir of New Shoreham, where there are three, and in the west bays of Worcester, where there are four.

the pier buttress to insignificant proportions. This member is, in fact, practically suppressed; but to eliminate so important a part of an organic system is like eliminating a bone from the skeleton of an animal. Apart from these changes — which break up the organic character of the structure — the section is essentially identical with that of the choir, and as the choir derives from Canterbury it will be seen how mistaken is the common affirmation that in the nave of Lincoln we have an independent English art. The far-reaching influence of Canterbury in the formation of the Early English style out of the Norman Romanesque has not hitherto been recognized. It is, however, apparent from first to last, as we shall see. But it should be noticed that in what it embodies of French Gothic principles of construction the influence of Canterbury was slight after the building of St. Hugh's choir.

FIG. 111 — Lincoln Nave.

The profiling throughout the nave is nearly the same as in the choir, but there is a marked loss of vital quality, especially in the outlines of capitals and bases. This lack of vital beauty is particularly noticeable in the foliation of capitals, which becomes excessive in convolution, and in the multiplication of the peculiar Anglo-Norman leaf ribs of angular section,[1] while the surfaces lack fineness of flexure, and the total effect becomes hard and linear. A comparison of Plate XVI, from the arcade of the choir aisle, with Fig. 111, from the triforium of the nave, will show this difference.

The monument in which the Early English style is commonly held to attain its fullest development, and its most distinctive character, is the Cathedral of Salisbury, begun in the year 1220. As the system of Canterbury is traceable in Lincoln, so the

[1] Cf. my *Gothic Architecture*, p. 406.

scheme of Lincoln is traceable in Salisbury. The plan follows that of Lincoln, save that the east end is rectangular, instead of apsidal as Lincoln then was, and that the chapels are omitted from the east side of the eastern transept, the square chambers from the west side, and the eastern aisle from the western transept. In both plans the western transept has three bays beyond the aisles in each arm, and the eastern transept two, and in both two bays of the choir fall between the two transepts.

In elevation the system — except in the vaulting — goes far beyond that of Lincoln nave in departure from any suggestion of French Gothic construction. The organic skeleton so extensively, though imperfectly, developed in the Lincoln choir, and still in part suggested, though not carried out, in the nave, is quite eliminated here at Salisbury, and the essentially Norman wall construction is hardly disguised by the Early English overlay of Purbeck shafting and multiplied mouldings.

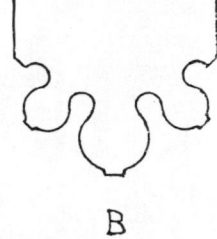

FIG. 112 — Salisbury Nave.

But while in Salisbury the distinctive features of the Early English style are largely developed, they do not extend to the vaulting — which has little Early English character, but is fashioned substantially on the French Gothic model, having the longitudinal rib stilted so as to narrow the conoid against the wall, and including no superfluous ribs. There are, however, no stilting shafts, the longitudinal ribs being embedded in the vault at the springing, and the masonry is not in parallel courses at the crown. The profiling of the ribs is shown in Fig. 112, where A is the transverse rib, and B the groin rib.

No likeness to French Gothic is found in any other part of the monument. Not only does the pier as a continuous member not exist at all, but there is no sort of division into bays — the ground story and triforium having unbroken arcades from end to end of the nave. The vaulting springs (Fig. 113) from diminutive remnants of shafts, three in each group, resting on corbels in the triforium spandrels, and are thus insignificant both in function and expression. The great piers each consist of four mutually engaged cylindrical columns of Purbeck built in courses, with four slender, free-standing Purbeck shafts, each of two lengths, banded at the junction by metal rings keyed into the

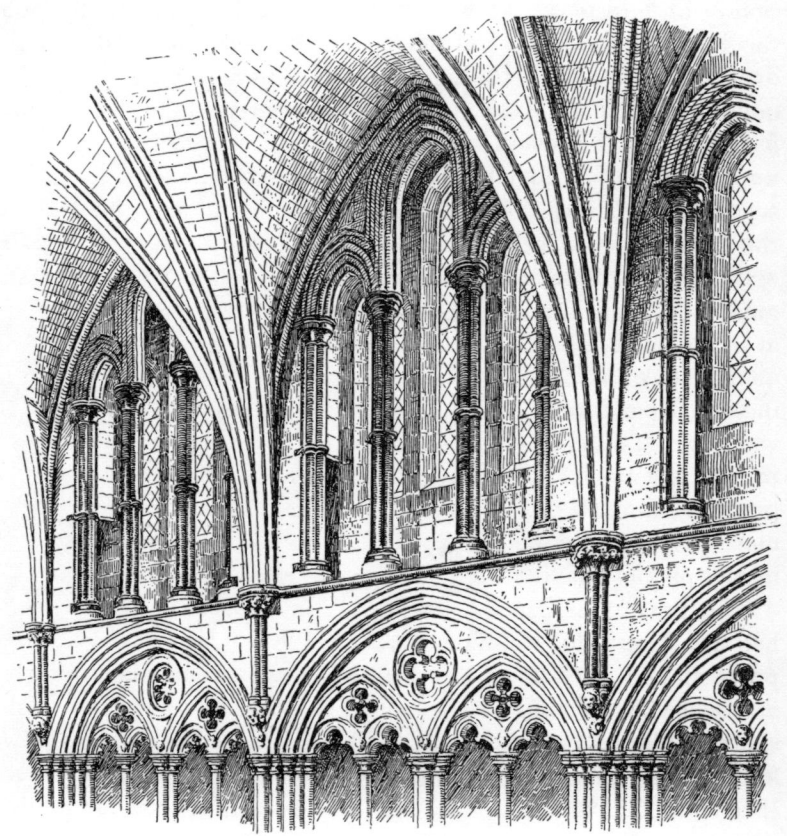

FIG. 113 — Salisbury.

main columns. These piers stand on a raised stylobate, and have bases with round plinths with mouldings profiled, as in Fig. 114. This profile marks a noticeable decline in the character of base mouldings — some of the steps of which it will be worth while to notice. Starting with the pure French bases of the great piers of Canterbury choir (Fig. 77, p. 87), where the lower torus is flattened with subtle beauty of surface, as in the ovolo of the finest Greek capitals, the tori become rounded in the bases of Trinity Chapel (Fig. 90, p. 107), while the reverse curve of the scotia, the contrasting fillets, and the fine proportions make this still a very beautiful base of strictly French character. Then in St. Hugh's choir of Lincoln (Fig. 97, p. 116) the Anglo-Norman proclivity for redundance in profiling leads to the addition of an intermediate torus and a second scotia, while beneath the great lower torus a third scotia is cut — all the scotias being deeply hollowed. In the nave of Lincoln the middle torus is omitted, but much of the beauty of the earlier profiles is lost by the elimination of the fillet from the upper torus, by the contraction of the scotia to an insignificant cavetto, by the substitution of an arris for the fillet of the lower torus, and by an extravagantly deep cavetto and scalloped slant at the bottom. But in the Salisbury base all beauty of associated curves, contrasting fillets, and regulated proportions is wanting. This dull series of segmental rounds is a poor substitute for the early profiling, and the eye searches for the most part in vain for beauty of details in any part of this interior.

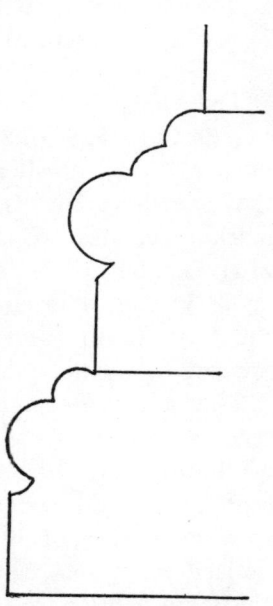

FIG. 114 — Salisbury.

The great pier capitals are, however, better. The smaller members are well proportioned both to the main capital, and to the shafts which they crown, while their profiling is composed of rounds and hollows well proportioned in relation to each other. The top member is finely undercut, and the rounds are broken by fillets.

The great archivolts are profiled much like those of Lincoln nave save that each of the three orders of which they are composed has a rounded section. Their mouldings are so nearly equal in magnitude, so equally spaced, and each order is shaped in section to so large an arc, that together they have almost the effect of one great order.

The triforium scheme is a variant of that of Lincoln nave, the two compound openings being here embraced by a larger arch. To get this combination into the space, the arches are struck from centres far below the springing, making marked angles with their supports. The quatrefoil piercings of the tympanums, and the blind quatrefoils of the wall spandrels, follow also, with variations, those of Lincoln. But the smaller arches of the sub-orders differ from those of Lincoln, being round in some of the bays and cusped in all. Each order of the arches has a colonnette of Purbeck, which gives, on the side facing the nave, nine of them in each main group, three in each middle group, and one between each pair of the smaller arches. In the absence of vaulting shafts the main supports of this triforium thus present to the eye merely a group of Purbeck shafts set close together.

The clerestory follows that of Lincoln with little variation, save in the arches of the inner plane, the middle one of which is much stilted, and all are obtusely pointed, whereas in Lincoln they are sharp lancets. In point of elegance there is, I think, a marked decline in English clerestories after the building of St. Hugh's choir. The general proportions of the clerestory of that choir (which, in its elongated middle shafts corresponding with the form of the arch of the vault, follows Canterbury) are, it appears to me, unequalled in any subsequent English work.

The crossing piers are furnished with Purbeck shafts reaching from the pavement, and answering to the orders of the crossing arches. Thus they are variants of the crossing piers of Canterbury and Lincoln, where the shafts are, as we have seen, of two superimposed orders. We have already noticed a similar composition at Rochester, except that the shafts there are banded at several different levels. Thus it will be seen how the idea of the Canterbury pier persists in these, as well as in other, subsequent works.

The aisle vaulting is quadripartite on a full system of ribs, and the responds are single, slender, free-standing Purbeck shafts resting, like the great piers, on a raised stylobate. The aisle walls, which are heavy and of full thickness all the way up, are pierced with two pointed and deeply splayed openings in each bay. It will be seen that such walls and openings are essentially the same as those of the most primitive Norman Romanesque building, although the slender jamb shafts and moulded scoinson arches with which they are furnished give a superficial effect of lightness suggestive of Gothic design. A narrow Purbeck string-course marks the level of the window-sills, and below this the wall of each bay is unbroken.

The interior of Salisbury is exceptional among mediæval monuments in being almost wholly in one style throughout. Few buildings of the Middle Ages on so large a scale were brought to completion at one epoch, and few have suffered so little from material alterations.[1] The most noticeable discord is that of the later vaulting over the crossing of the greater transept. The network of liernes in this compartment breaks the unity of the finest feature of the building,

Externally no flying buttresses appear; even vigorous wall buttresses are wanting in the clerestory. Only flat pilaster strips, substantially like those of Durham, are set against the wall, which, in its Norman massiveness, requires no buttressing of a Gothic kind. Well-developed buttresses, however, like those of Lincoln, fortify the walls of the aisles. Salisbury is thus in reality a ponderous walled structure on essentially Norman principles, with an appearance of lightness got by a free use of slender Purbeck shafting, and by a multiplicity of mouldings.

These last remarks apply, however, only to the enclosing walls and to the system of the nave exclusive of the vaulting. The internal supports of the choir, transepts, and Lady Chapel are of exaggerated attenuation — far exceeding in this respect any French Gothic works of the first half of the thirteenth century. Of French Gothic art in its integrity excessive lightness of construction is not, as I have before said, a characteristic. But these extremely slender, detached Purbeck shafts of Salisbury give to the eye almost a sense of insecurity. But enclosed as they are within walls of Norman massiveness, and steadied in places by iron tie rods, they are, indeed, quite safe.

The nearly contemporaneous choir of Beverley Minster exhibits another phase of the Early English style. The vaulting of Beverley, though, like that of Salisbury, unencumbered by superfluous ribs, has the Anglo-Norman form of conoid resulting from the absence of stilting of the longitudinal rib. The supporting shafts are again of Purbeck, and rise from corbels just

---

[1] While it has not been materially altered, the interior of Salisbury has been deplorably renewed, scraped, and polished.

above the ground-story imposts. They consist in each group of a single shaft reaching to the triforium string, surmounted by three shafts reaching to the vaulting impost. The magnitudes of these shafts make them conspicuous, and, in connection with the taller proportions of the system, give, at first glance, a suggestion of organic character, which does not really exist, any more than in other compositions of the Early English style. Among structural inconsistencies such as we have remarked in other buildings, may be noticed the five ribs of the vaulting gathered on three shafts, the capitals of which are covered with a single abacus.

The influence of Lincoln is marked in many parts of the system, notwithstanding that the proportions and general effect are different. Beverley is exceptional among English churches in its proportionate height, and in this it is more like the French churches.[1] In its obtuse pointing, and its rib profiling, the vaulting of this choir resembles that of Canterbury, but in the level of its springing it is quite different, and different also from Lincoln and Salisbury. In the buildings thus far considered a steady increase in the height of springing is noticeable. In Canterbury the vaults spring from the level of the triforium imposts, in Lincoln choir and nave the springing is about midway between the triforium imposts and the clerestory string, in Salisbury it is at the level of the clerestory string, and here at Beverley it is raised to the clerestory impost. The ground-story pier is modelled on those piers of the nave of Lincoln which are shaped to a semblance of shafting, and the orders and profiling of the great archivolts follow those of Lincoln closely. The triforium follows the French Gothic in being walled in, and its arcade is a reproduction, with variations of detail, of the double-wall arcade of the aisle of St. Hugh's choir, but it lacks the beauty of that superb model. The variations impair the elegance of the composition both in proportions and in details. The excessive lowering of the arcade of the inner plane, for instance, gives a stumpy form to the supporting colonnettes, and the substitution of triple shafts for single ones hardly improves the outer series, while the use of moulded capitals gives a dry and monotonous effect to the total scheme. The clerestory is a

[1] Proportions differ greatly in both English and French churches, but in general, as is well known, English churches are relatively low, and French ones high.

PLATE XX

Worcester Choir.

variant of that of St. Hugh's choir of Lincoln, having, in the inner plane, five arches of graduated magnitudes following in outline the arch of the vault. The arches are carried on single Purbeck shafts, an improvement on the Lincoln scheme, since the arches in both cases are of one order. In the outer plane there is but one opening, but this is flanked on the outside by blind arches, making a triple group. This choir has flying buttresses springing near the aisle roof, as at Lincoln and Canterbury, and a vigorous wall buttress reaches to a corbel table under the main cornice.

The purest example of Early English architecture is, I think, the east end of Worcester Cathedral (Plate XX), begun in the year 1224.[1] Here, and not at Salisbury, the Early English style appears to me to stand forth in its most distinctive, its most beautiful, and its most monumental form. It has neither the dryness of Salisbury, nor the inconsistency of vaulting on the foreign Gothic model. The scheme still follows that of Lincoln, and in its walled structural character it differs not at all from a Norman Romanesque building, but its pointed arches and rich ornamental details differentiate it, as far as such features can, from the old Norman style.

Worcester has suffered greatly and continuously, from the fourteenth century to the present time, from alterations and so-called restorations; and of late much new work in imitation of old has been built into its beautiful east end — making it, to a greater extent than most other mediæval monuments, a corrupt document, which needs to be studied with caution. In addition to actual renewals much of what remains of the genuine old work has been, as at Salisbury, so scraped and polished that it has as a whole the appearance of a new work.

The vaulting, which springs from the level of the clerestory string, has a longitudinal ridge rib, but no other superfluous members. This ridge rib is in a horizontal right line, instead of being arched from rib to rib, as at Lincoln. The longitudinal rib is not stilted, but interpenetrates at the springing with the transverse and groin ribs, so that all are gathered into small compass on the capital of a single Purbeck shaft. This shaft is supported, at the level of the triforium string, on the capital of a

[1] Cf. Willis, *The Architectural History of the Cathedral and Monastery at Worcester*, p. 2, London, 1863.

smaller shaft that rises from another corbel placed considerably above the ground-story impost. The vaulting system is thus a combination of the systems of the choir and nave of Lincoln, with the omission of all superfluous ribs except the longitudinal ridge rib, and of that of the choir of Beverley, which it partly follows in the fashion of its vaulting shafts.

The ground-story pier is a variant of the pier with Purbeck shafting of the Lincoln nave, having on plan the form of a square set diagonally. Two of these piers (the second on each side east of the eastern transept) are logically composed in conformity with the archivolts. The others have an additional shaft without function between each pair of functional ones. We have noticed such shafts in the triforium of St. Hugh's choir at Lincoln, and again in some of the piers of Lincoln nave.[1] Both the piers and the archivolts of the Early English work of Worcester are heavy. The great wall thickness of the Norman west bays is not, indeed, maintained throughout the subsequent works, but the heavy wall idea persists even in this most characteristic monument of the Early English style. It is necessarily so, since no adequate structural framework is provided for the support of the vaulting.

As to the secondary features of the interior, the arcade of the inner plane of the clerestory is supported on single shafts, as at Beverley, and the triforium has a walled passageway with a continuous blind arcade against the wall.[2] The open arcade is a variant of that of Lincoln choir with all French characteristics of profiling eliminated, while sculptures in high relief are introduced in the tympanums. The moulded capital is used exclusively in the blind arcade, and for the middle shafts of the open arcade, but all other capitals of this interior are richly foliated.

The two stages of lancet openings that now pierce the wall of the east end are the work of a modern architect, and follow, with

---

[1] Such superfluous shafts are found in some instances in subordinate parts of the later, and more florid, thirteenth-century Gothic of France, as in the western portals of Amiens, where the integrity of the early time was beginning to yield to ornamental redundance at the expense of logical composition. But these useless members will not, I believe, be found in the main structural parts of a Gothic edifice of the Ile de France at any time.

[2] In this feature the Early English of Worcester is not characteristic. As I have elsewhere remarked, the open triforium, with the timber roof exposed to view, prevails in Anglo-Norman building.

ornamental additions, the original openings that survive in the transept.[1] The primitive group of lancet openings was replaced, at an unknown time, by a great opening in the perpendicular style. I know not on what authority the modern architect has based his scheme of restoration, but it is more florid in ornamentation than the surviving old work in the transept, and too much so to accord with the monumental simplicity of the pure Early English style. Its academic sculpture is foreign to the spirit of the Middle Ages, and misleading to the student of mediæval art.

The aisle vaulting has the longitudinal ridge rib, but no other unnecessary members; and on the wall side these ribs are gathered on the single abacus of responds consisting of three small, and closely grouped, shafts, banded by a string at the level of the window-sills.

The openings of the aisles are in groups of three in each bay, and are in two planes with a passageway like that of the clerestory. The inner groups are original, but the outer ones are modern — modelled on one, of primitive workmanship, that appears to have been left when the others were reconstructed in the Perpendicular style. Beneath these openings a blind arcade, resembling the outer plane of the double arcade of St. Hugh's choir aisle, is carried along the wall, and around the entire east end and the eastern transept. Some fine examples of thirteenth-century sculpture adorn the spandrels of this arcade. Of the original capitals here many have been replaced by the restorer, but the old ones that remain are of great beauty, and refined workmanship.

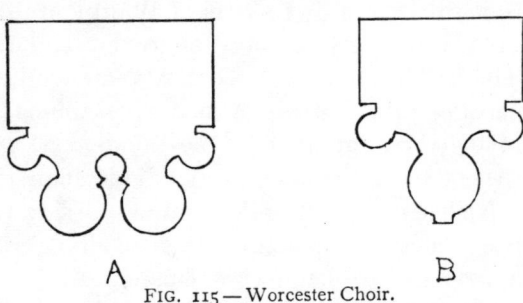

FIG. 115 — Worcester Choir.

They are, however, all of the crocketed form, and thus not of distinctly Early English type.

The scheme of the choir is a continuation of that of the east end with some variations of proportion and details. The profiling of the vault ribs, in which A (Fig. 115) is the transverse rib

[1] Cf. Willis, *Op. cit.*, p. 22.

and B the groin rib, is worthy of notice as showing the persistence of the Canterbury influence through Lincoln, Salisbury, and other early monuments.

On the outside no flying buttresses belonging to the original work occur. Only flat Norman pilaster strips mark in the clerestory the divisions of the interior. As in Wells and Salisbury the whole external character and expression of this clerestory is essentially Norman. Notwithstanding the heavy wall construction, it has been found necessary to insert several flying buttresses, and on the north side of the choir, where the aisle wall has pushed out greatly, one of massive proportions has been built from the ground to meet the middle aisle respond, with another over the aisle roof.[1] These buttresses are in the style of the fourteenth century.

The idea of Lincoln nave is again discernible in what remains of the scheme of the transept of York Minster (circa 1230-1241), though there are marked points of difference in proportions and details, and the vaulting, for which the system provides, is wanting. The vaulting shafts, the level of the supporting corbels, the composition of the ground-story piers, and the profiling of the archivolts, all substantially agree with the corresponding features of the nave of Lincoln; but the triforium openings are variants of those of the nave of Salisbury.

A similar scheme occurs in the remains of Whitby choir, though the vaulting shafts of Whitby are carried up to the top of the wall, as in most of round arched Norman churches. The building was, therefore, not intended to be vaulted, and accordingly the clerestory has a continuous arcade with arches of equal height, though the middle one in each bay, opposite the external opening, is of wider span than the others. On this clerestory of Whitby that of York transept appears to have been modelled when the idea of vaulting, with which the builders appear to have begun, was abandoned.

Thus in all of these buildings in which the Early English style culminates, the features of Lincoln nave are distinctly, though variously, traceable — these features themselves being, as we have seen, largely modifications and variations, in Anglo-Norman hands, of the French features of Canterbury.

---

[1] The flying buttress from the ground is found elsewhere in England, as in the Chapter House of Lincoln.

The internal scheme of Lincoln was in a few cases modified so as to give an appearance in the interior of only two stories, as in Pershore Abbey, where the arcade of the inner plane of the clerestory is brought down to the triforium string — the clerestory string being eliminated, and the passage brought down to the triforium. This is an indirect and factitious mode of design which violates true principles of architectural expression. For the building, having aisles, has also a triforium just as much as Lincoln and Salisbury have. To eliminate this division in the architectural scheme of the interior is to falsify its expression. For the rest, the system of Pershore has much beauty. Advanced, however, in Early English character as it is, the persistence of a primitive form in the vaulting is noticeable. The longitudinal rib is so obtusely pointed, and is stilted with such a slant, that it is much like the corresponding arch in the nave of Lincoln which, as we have seen, resembles that of Durham. This vaulting has tiercerons and liernes in the lateral cells, and the curve of the tierceron nearest the wall is such as to give a pronounced ploughshare form to the vault surface, notwithstanding that the conoid is considerably widened against the wall by the inclined stilting.

It is not worth while to prolong this examination of particular systems of the Early English style. We have seen enough to enable us to understand their distinctive character, and to see that while differing in details they agree in principle, and are, as we shall see more fully further on, essentially different from the French Gothic systems. There are, in fact, few other buildings in which the Early English architecture extends through the greater part of the edifice.

It remains only to consider briefly some of the larger features of the exterior, the finest of which are, I think, east ends and transepts. Of west ends few, if any, were built on a large scale in the purest style. As with the French Gothic, the great west ends of Early English churches are generally later and more florid than the naves they enclose, and are composed with little conformity to the cross-sections of these naves. But in transepts, like those of Lincoln, Salisbury, Beverley, and Worcester, the Early English art attains its most admirable character. The sheer rise of wall and buttress, the conformity of outline with internal structure of which the exterior is a true expression, the justness of proportions, and the monumental simplicity of the whole, entitle such works to rank among the finest creations of art. But how completely they retain the Norman character, refined and beautified but not essentially altered, may be seen on comparing them with such unmodified Norman transepts as those of New Shoreham or St. Cross at Winchester.

## CHAPTER VII

### THE CHOIR OF WESTMINSTER

AFTER Canterbury, no other work of distinctly French art was built on English soil. But a second strong influence direct from

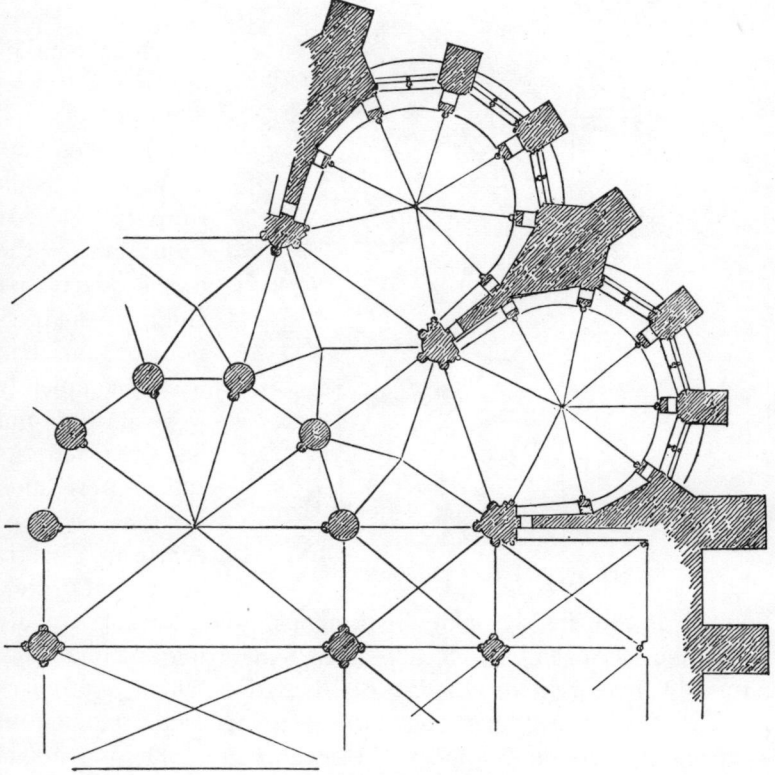

FIG. 116 — Reims.

overseas, and largely shaping an entire monument, came with the building of the choir and transept of Westminster Abbey, begun in the year 1245. This great work, due to the personal enterprise of Henry III, — whose French sympathies, and admiration for French art naturally led him to look to foreign sources for guidance in the design of this royal fane, — is French in plan, proportions, and general outline; and has enough resemblance to French composition in the larger features of its system to give it much the aspect of a true French Gothic monument. A little scrutiny, however, shows that it is not the work of Frenchmen, but of English craftsmen, too strongly imbued with the Anglo-Norman traditions to grasp the French Gothic principles of design and construction.

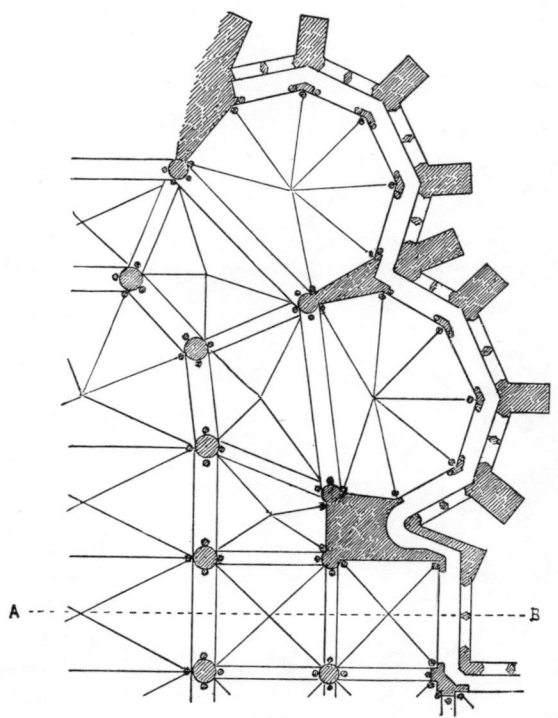

FIG. 117 — Westminster Abbey.

Since the building of the Cathedral of Sens, which had furnished the main inspiration for Canterbury, the evolution of Gothic construction in France had been completely worked out, and had reached its fullest perfection in the nave of Amiens. This magnificent creation, and the nearly contemporaneous, and almost equally admirable, east end of Reims, were inspiring models that naturally gave rise to a spirit of emulation which soon bore fruit in the stupendous choir of Beauvais, and, outside of France, in Cologne Cathedral, in several great monuments in Spain, and here in Westminster Abbey.

The primary source of King Henry's scheme was apparently that part of Reims which was then completed, but this scheme was modified to some extent by the influence of Amiens. The plan of the east end of Reims (Fig. 116) is peculiar among those of

## VII THE CHOIR OF WESTMINSTER

French Gothic churches of the thirteenth century in having an apse of only five sides. The apse of Westminster (Fig. 117) follows this peculiarity. Reims has a single apsidal aisle with two radial chapels on each side of a larger one on the main axis, and Westminster reproduces this arrangement. But in many particulars the apse of Westminster departs from that of Reims and follows Amiens (Fig. 118). The apsidal chapels of Reims are

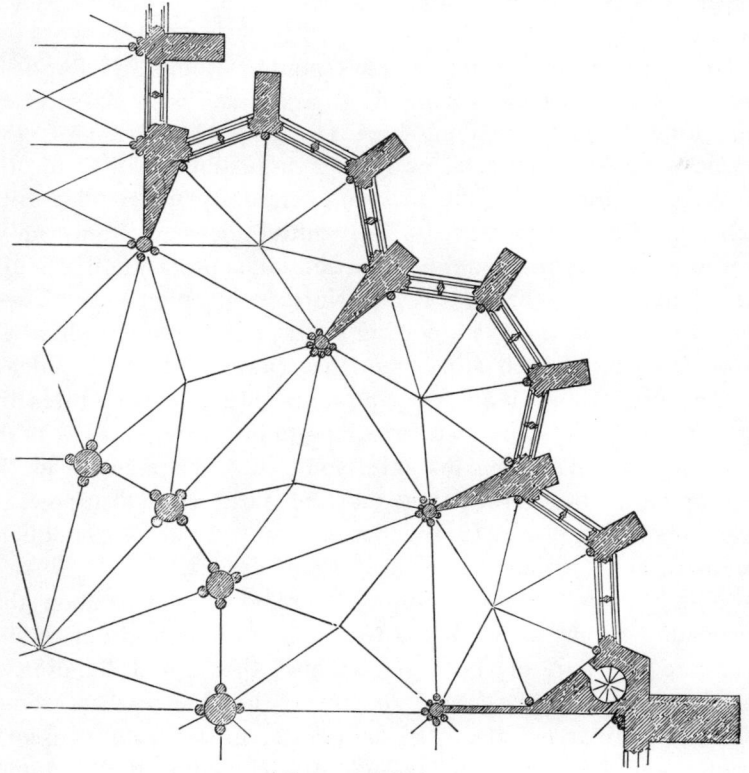

FIG. 118 — Amiens.

on massive foundations circular on plan, and their walls are carried up in the circular form to the level of the window openings. From this level the plan becomes polygonal, and a passageway is carried around the inside, on the thickness of the circular wall. At Amiens the chapels are polygonal on plan from the foundation, and the walls are thin, affording no space for a passageway — a feature not found in a developed French Gothic building, save in the triforium. At Westminster the chapels follow Reims in thickness of wall and in the passageway, but they conform with Amiens in the polygonal plan from the foundation. The choir follows that of Reims in having only three bays,[1] and the transept, as at Reims, has an aisle on both sides, except in the south arm, where a part of the cloister takes the place of a western aisle.[2] In its development north and south, the transept follows the tendency of Anglo-Norman planning — being extended to four bays, instead of only two, as at Reims, or three, as at Amiens.

In elevation the system follows neither Reims nor Amiens, nor any other French model, though, as before remarked, its proportions and leading lines are those of a French Gothic structure. Its members, and their adjustments, are, for the most part, Early English in character, and far removed from those of the Ile de France. The vaulting, however, conforms to the French Gothic model in its essential conformation, though it exhibits some marked Anglo-Norman peculiarities. These are: (1) the lack of supporting shafts for the longitudinal rib which, though much stilted (so that the warped and concave surfaces of the vault are very pronounced), interpenetrates the vault, as at Salisbury; (2) the longitudinal ridge rib; (3) the transverse and groin ribs interpenetrating excessively at the springing in order that they may be gathered on supports of very small magnitude; (4) the masonry courses running obliquely, so as to meet at the crown line in sharp angles.

The vaulting impost follows a method of construction that was adopted in the developed Gothic of France in order to consolidate this part of the system where the lighter building of the thirteenth century rendered the earlier method hazardous. Instead of starting the ribs, as before, in separate voussoirs, and the filling with small stones, the conoid is built up to a considerable height of single blocks, with horizontal beds, shaped to the proper form, with the rib profiles worked upon

---

[1] In an architectural sense the choir of a Gothic church with a transept is that part of the nave, or the central aisle, which falls between the apse and the crossing. The actual choir enclosure may include either more or less than this according to circumstances. The choir enclosure of Westminster is carried far to the west — crossing the transept, and reaching into the western nave.

[2] Professor Lethaby (*Westminster Abbey and the King's Craftsmen*, London: Duckworth & Co., 1906, pp. 120 *et. seq.*) notices some other points of likeness between the east end of Westminster and that of Reims.

them.[1] In following this method the Westminster builder has carried the filling up in horizontal courses to a considerable height above the level where the ribs begin to separate, and to be formed of voussoirs, as will be seen in the section (Fig. 119).

The vault supports consist of three excessively slender shafts of which the middle one is in several monolithic sections of Purbeck, and the others are of coursed masonry. These shafts rest, without bases, on the great capital of the ground-story pier, and only the middle one has a capital — on the mouldings of the under side of which the others intersect. In a normal Gothic system they would, of course, carry the transverse rib and the groin ribs respectively, each rib having its own supporting shaft; but here they cannot do so, for the rib group is so much more bulky than the shaft group that it was impossible to adjust them so as to give each rib its own supporting shaft. We have found this misadjustment common in the Early English style. The non-conformity with French Gothic appears equally in the system of the apse where, although there is only one rib for each impost, a group of three shafts, like those of the choir, is employed.

The ground-story pier is Early English, like that of Salisbury, save that the main column is one great cylinder instead of being composed of four cylinders mutually engaged. The attached shafts, and the great compound capital, are practically identical with those of Salisbury, except that the large and small members of the capital are of equal height, whereas at Salisbury the smaller ones are proportionately lower than the great one.

The cross-section (Fig. 119), which is taken through the line AB of the plan (Fig. 117), shows other points of departure from Gothic, notwithstanding its general likeness, at first glance, to a French system.[2] It will be seen that there is a triforium gallery — a singular survival in mid-thirteenth century of a feature which does not occur in the developed Gothic of France, where the triforium is merely a narrow passage, as at Reims and Amiens. In the larger churches of the early French Gothic the

---

[1] Cf. Voillet le Duc, s.v. *Tas de charge*.

[2] The external system of Westminster has been, as is well known, extensively rebuilt.

FIG. 119—Choir of Westminster Abbey.

gallery over the entire aisle is common,[1] as at Noyon, Senlis, Paris, and Laon ; but in these cases it is vaulted, and thus partakes of the monumental character of the rest of the building. The timber roof is not open to view, as it is in the triforium of Westminster, in any part of a Gothic building of the Ile de France, early or late. Moreover, where this gallery occurs in early French Gothic there is generally an upper triforium. For the vaulting of the gallery has to be covered with a sloping roof giving space for a triforium, like that which occurs at the lower level in cases where there is no vaulted gallery. The system of Westminster is unlike French Gothic in having the great triforium gallery without the upper triforium, or at least a space answering to it. Since its bay scheme, as to the stages into which it is divided, follows the developed French Gothic in which there is no gallery, the builder could not have a sloping roof to form an upper triforium, for this would reach high up against the clerestory openings. He was, therefore, obliged to make his roof nearly flat,[2] an undesirable form in a northern climate, and not characteristic of Gothic design.

The triforium is unusually wide, embracing both the choir aisle and the square compartments and chapels opening out of it. It will be seen in the section that the architect has utilized the space under the roof, and between the great buttress and the enclosing wall, for an outer abutment in the form of a heavily loaded pointed arch, substantially like the primitive abutting arches in the triforiums of Canterbury and Lincoln; but the higher external buttress system is in substantially true Gothic form. A pier buttress rises through the triforium and is reënforced by two superimposed flying buttresses reaching both high enough and low enough to meet the vault thrusts effectively. It appears to have been the intention to carry up a free-standing shaft to the intrados of the lower flying buttress, for a portion of such a shaft is found in the triforium, as shown at *a* in the section (Fig. 119), and in the horizontal section of the pier at this level (Fig. 120), drawn to a larger scale. Such a shaft is common in French Gothic structures, but in France it does not rise from within the triforium ; it starts from the square

---

[1] It is, of course, a survival, through the various forms of Romanesque, of the tribune gallery of the Christian Roman basilica.

[2] This nearly flat roof is represented in Fig. 119 by a single line.

pier buttress just above the triforium roof. At Reims there is an engaged shaft in this position, but at Amiens a free-standing one is added, with an interval for circulation.[1]

The triforium arcade is in two planes, the outer one occupying the place that in a French system would be taken by the thin enclosing wall of the passage. This is due, I suppose, to the great thickness of the wall, which is carried up to the main cornice of the building. Such a wall is opposed to the principles of French Gothic construction, and the double arcade would not occur in a Gothic building of the Ile de France in its integrity, though toward the middle of the thirteenth century (when the Gothic builders were beginning to seek novelties of design at the expense of straightforward building), in order to light the triforium, the lean-to aisle roof was replaced by a gabled one, and the wall of the passage was pierced with openings — as in the choir of Amiens and the nave of St. Denis.[2] This does, indeed, make a double arcade, but the system of construction is essentially different from that of Westminster. The wall of the triforium passage in France, whether perforated or not, carries no superstructure. It stands out from the rest of the building, and is covered by a mere coping, which also roofs the passage and forms a ledge for external circulation. The mullions and tracery of the clerestory opening stand on the triforium arcade, and there is nothing else between the piers — the wall being entirely eliminated.

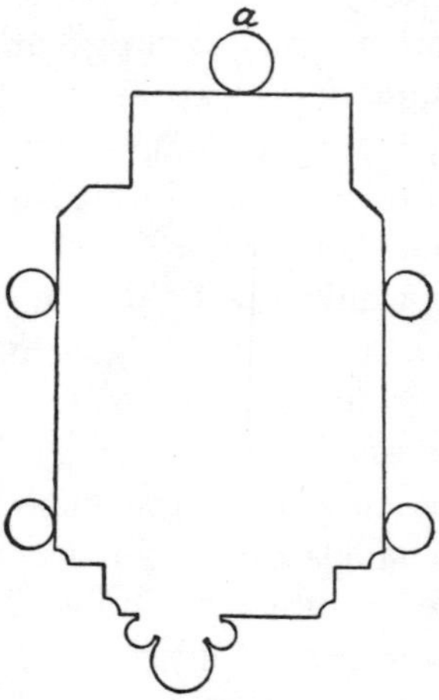

FIG. 120 — Westminster.

The clerestory of Westminster differs essentially from a developed French Gothic clerestory, inasmuch as it has the thick wall already mentioned. The opening is thus a window, whereas in France it is not a window, in a proper sense, but an

---

[1] At Amiens, where the skeleton principle of Gothic architecture is most fully and finely carried out, the pier buttress itself becomes a skeleton. Cf. Voillet le Duc, s.v. *Cathédrale*, p. 329.

[2] Cf. my *Gothic Architecture*, second edition, p. 253.

intercolumniation. The French Gothic clerestory has no passageway, its mullions and tracery are in one plane, and its archivolt is also the longitudinal rib of the vault. But at Westminster a survival of the Norman idea appears in a semblance of two planes of masonry, although there is no passageway. The opening is in two distinct planes, the inner one being undivided and the outer one having the mullion and tracery. It is worthy of notice, too, that the inner archivolt is distinct from the longitudinal rib of the vault, and is not concentric with it. In a French Gothic clerestory the mullions and tracery are, as already remarked, over the inner plane of the triforium passage — the coping of the outer plane forming a ledge for outside circulation; but at Westminster, the mullions and tracery being over the outer plane, a ledge is formed inside (cf. the cross-section, Fig. 119). This ledge cannot, however, be used for circulation since, as we have seen, the wall has no passage.

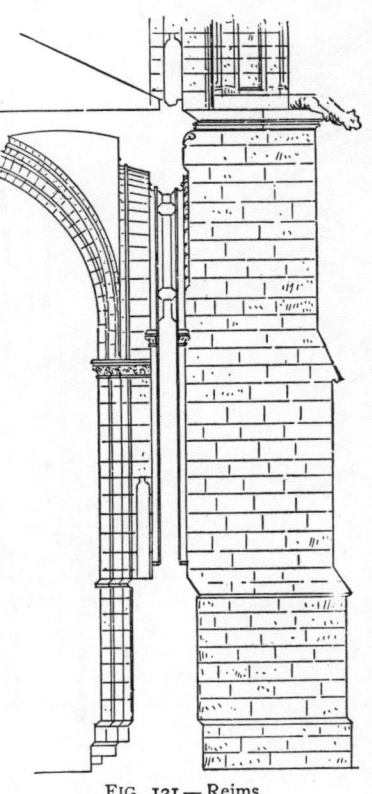

FIG. 121 — Reims.

The ground-story enclosure follows, with variations of details, that of Reims Cathedral — which in this part is peculiar among French Gothic churches. At Reims (Fig. 121) the enclosing wall,[1] like all the rest of the ground story of the monument, is exceptionally massive. The archivolt of the aisle opening is of two orders, of which the first forms the longitudinal rib of the vault. The sub-order, containing the mullions and tracery, is set on the outer face of the wall, leaving a ledge on the inside

---

[1] In French Gothic, while the wall, as to structural function, is practically eliminated, there remain, of course, small areas of wall for enclosure. Cf. my *Gothic Architecture*, pp. 18, 20, 153, 160.

which is utilized for a passage — the buttresses being pierced for circulation. At Westminster (b, Fig. 119) a scoinson arch is added, and a blind arcade skirts the wall beneath.¹

The lack of conformity with French Gothic construction is further shown in the ground-story arcade of the apse, where the arches spring directly from the general impost level of the choir arcade. But in French Gothic these arches would be much stilted, on account of the narrowing of the aisle vaults against the vertical line of the pier, as at Amiens (Fig. 122). At Westminster the vaults are not thus narrowed. With the wall construction that so largely prevails in this monument it matters little from a structural point of view, but such forms would be incompatible with the skeleton construction of French Gothic.

FIG. 122 — Amiens.

The idea of organic skeleton construction (which distinguishes the Gothic of France from all other architecture) finds little embodiment in the choir of Westminster. The pier, as a consistent compound member rising from the pavement through the several stories of the building, does not exist. Standing on the pavement

¹ This scheme is reproduced in the eastern transept, called the Chapel of the Nine Altars, at Durham.

of the transept, and looking into the choir, it will be seen that the vaulting shafts rise against strips of wall,[1] which in the clerestory are wider than in the triforium.  It will be noticed, also, that the vertical axes of these wall strips in the clerestory do not coincide with those of the triforium — the upper walls overhanging on one side more than on the other.  In other words, the spacings are not only unequal in both stories, but those of the one are independent of those of the other.  It thus appears that the French Gothic idea of a coherent organic pier, as the main support of the fabric, was not in the mind of the builder.

Next to the general plan, proportions, and leading divisions of the system the character of the openings contributes more than anything else to such likeness to French Gothic as the choir and transept of Westminster exhibit.  These openings are divided by mullions and tracery such as were developed in the Ile de France early in the thirteenth century, and were introduced in the apsidal chapels of Reims dating from about 1212.[2]  The openings of the ground story and clerestory of Westminster appear to have been modelled directly on these, and consist each of a single mullion surmounted by two skeleton arches and a cusped circle.  And it is worthy of notice that a variant of this composition, in which the skeleton arches, as well as the circle, are cusped, fills the tympanum of each arch of the triforium.  In France the triforium openings are not treated in this way.  No features of Westminster in its integrity could, I suppose, have had more of the French Gothic character than the great wheel windows of the transept, but of these nothing of the original work remains.

The hand of the English craftsman appears almost exclusively in the forms of capitals and the profiling of archivolts — which follow the Early English models, and have no likeness to con-

---

[1] Such strips of wall occur, indeed, in the early Gothic of France, but a logical organic skeleton is associated with them, and this skeleton tends more and more to free itself from the walls until, in the developed style, it does so with practical completeness.

[2] The evolution of this first Gothic tracery is discussed in my *Gothic Architecture*, pp. 155 *et seq.*  I there (footnote, p. 157) call attention to an article by M. Demaison, published in the *Bulletin Archéologique* in the year 1894, in which this form of tracery is said to have appeared first in the Abbey Church of Orbais, begun about A.D. 1200, presumably by the same architect who designed the earlier portions of Reims.

temporaneous French design. The English tradition appears also in the use of internal hoodmoulds. In the Gothic of the Ile de France this feature does not occur internally until the florid impulse sets in about the middle of the thirteenth century.

Thus, while largely emulating French Gothic art, the choir and transept of Westminster Abbey are not by any means of true French Gothic character. Their English builders were men of different genius from their contemporaries of the Ile de France, and could not enter into the spirit of the foreign art.

Presbytery of Lincoln.

## CHAPTER VIII

### THE LATER POINTED ART

THE building of Westminster Abbey bore no fruit comparable in extent to that which had grown out of Canterbury. The example of what French Gothic there was in Canterbury had not, indeed, as we have seen, been followed without important modifications made in accordance with the modes of structure that had been derived from the Norman tradition; and so inbred had this tradition become that even Westminster, as we have also seen, remained largely Anglo-Norman in structural character, notwithstanding the large measure of French influence that had shaped it. Its French plan and proportions, and its great French buttress system, were too foreign to the native building habits to materially affect English art. But some of the ornamental features of the more developed French Gothic embodied in the great work of Henry III appealed to the now growing English taste for richness, and chief among these was the enlarged opening with mullions and tracery.[1] This style of opening was promptly taken over and worked extensively into the English architecture of the latter part of the thirteenth century.

Among the first English works of importance erected after the choir and transept of Westminster was the Presbytery of Lincoln (circa 1256–1280). In this monument (Plate XXI), notwithstanding much that may still be worthy of admiration, the discriminating beholder cannot fail to perceive that the finer inspiration of the early building epoch is no longer manifest. In

---

[1] I do not affirm that this form of opening had not appeared in England before the building of Westminster, though I believe it had not. It certainly is not a characteristic feature of English architecture before the middle of the thirteenth century, but it is characteristic of French Gothic from the beginning of that century, and I think there can be no question that its extensive use in England after 1250 was directly due to the influence of Westminster.

England, as in France, the art declined in monumental sobriety after the early part of the thirteenth century, and became more florid while it lost the early fineness of ornament.

The scheme of this Presbytery is largely a reproduction of that of the nave, with some conspicuous new features to be presently noticed. The vaulting, while based on that of the nave, exhibits some marked points of difference. The rib system is simplified by the omission of the tiercerons and liernes of the lateral cells. The ridge rib is made straight, instead of being arched between the other ribs, from which it follows that the conformation of the vault is materially changed. Moreover the masonry runs in straight courses from rib to rib instead of being arched and thus forming concave cells. The longitudinal rib, which is again little more than a moulding, is pointed instead of having the oval shape of the corresponding rib of the nave. This rib springs from the clerestory ledge, and, as the larger ribs spring from a lower level, is stilted a little. It also interpenetrates the vault at its springing, and thus a slight warping of the surface is produced here. Above this, however, the courses of masonry are almost straight from the groin rib to the longitudinal rib, and are nearly perpendicular to the clerestory wall, but in some parts they incline slightly, though the crowns of the lateral cells are in straight lines sloping a little from the longitudinal rib to the groin ribs. Notwithstanding the slight stilting of the longitudinal rib, which gives a somewhat triangular section just above the springing, the conoid has nothing of the French Gothic form in horizontal section midway between the springing and the crown, but is practically square at that level. As in the nave, the ribs interpenetrate so as to become only a group of mouldings at the impost, and are gathered on the closely grouped capitals of five very small Purbeck shafts. But the adjustment of these mouldings to the supporting members is not such as to give each one a capital of its own — as will be seen from the impost plan (C, Fig. 123). The transverse rib has the profile A, and the groin ribs and tiercerons have the profile B.[1] Of the transverse rib only parts of the filleted rolls, *a*, are free at the impost. Of the tierceron only a small part of the lower

---

[1] These profiles were drawn by eye, and are correct only as to the numbers and arrangements of the parts. The proportions are not exact, and the hollows are, I think, too deep.

roll, *b*, remains — its fillet being brought close to that of the transverse rib. Then the lower member, *c*, of the groin rib is so closely engaged with the tierceron that very little of either is left on the sides where they come together, but the outside of the groin rib stands entirely free against the wall, and of its two filleted rolls, *c* and *c'*, one rests on the abacus of one capital and the other on another, while the transverse rib and the tiercerons are all gathered on the central capital. In other words, portions of

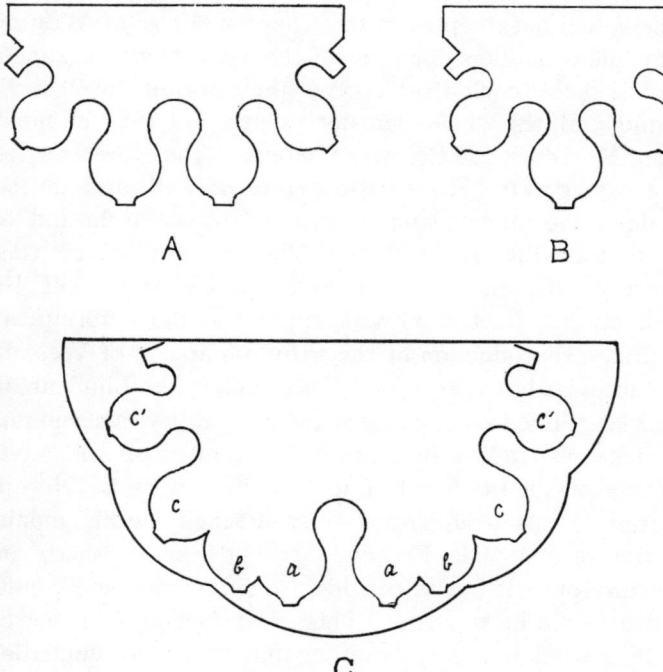

FIG. 123 — Lincoln Presbytery.

the transverse rib and of the tiercerons rest together on one capital while the groin rib alone is spread over two — which is not logical composition.

The proneness of English builders to work away from the organic system (which they had extensively followed in St. Hugh's choir), of which we have already had so many other illustrations, is further shown in the buttress system of this Presbytery where, although the flying buttress reappears (I think under the more or less direct influence of Westminster), it is unaccompanied by any pier buttress whatever, the abutting arch being brought to bear directly against the clerestory wall.

In the aisles and in the clerestory the new features of the enlarged openings with mullions and tracery, that had been introduced at Westminster, appear. In the choir of Westminster these divided openings are more simple, having but one mullion and one circle above, as at Reims; but in the great clerestory of Amiens three mullions, with corresponding additions to the tracery, had been introduced, and these amplified openings of Amiens had been copied in the Chapter House of Westminster. But while these new openings of the Presbytery of Lincoln reproduce the French Gothic type, they do not, like the French openings, fill the whole clerestory space and thus eliminate the wall. Moreover, the clerestory here is of the Norman type, having a passageway between two planes of wall, and the shafted arcade of the inner plane is spanned by an arch, and tracery like that of the outer plane. The introduction of this new feature greatly changed the ornamental character of English architecture. Its tracery was applied to the triforium arcade, which is a reproduction of the triforium arcade of Westminster, with necessarily varied proportions, and to the blind arcades of the aisles. The vast opening of the east end, with seven mullions and a corresponding increase in the number of foliated circles in its tracery, is the finest of its kind in England. No opening so large as this would occur in a French Gothic monument, for the reason that French east ends are apsidal, and no clerestory or aisle space, to which such openings are confined in France, would be so large. This great opening is, however, still largely a window in a wall, rather than an intercolumniation like a French opening, for its archivolt does not coincide with the arch of the vault, as it would in French Gothic construction, nor is it concentric with this arch — it is more acutely pointed, and a crescent of wall solid on each side intervenes between it and the vault rib.

This Presbytery, with its multiplied vault ribs, its rich window tracery, its sculptured spandrels, its elaborately foliated capitals and corbels, and its fretted mouldings, presents an aspect in marked contrast with the monumental simplicity of the choir and eastern transept, and even with the nave, though the nave manifests a tendency in the same direction. This ornament appeals to the eye by profusion rather than by quality. Nothing comparable in character to the finer examples of foliation in St. Hugh's work is found here. There is, nevertheless, much beauty in the carved leafage of the triforium capitals and in those of the vaulting imposts. This leafage, while it exhibits an excess of convolution, and a redundance which in some of the capitals completely masks the bell and gives a bunchy shapelessness to the general outline, has still a good deal of the vital quality of the earlier English leafage; and it is noticeable that the angular section of the leaf ribs, which we have remarked as peculiar to early Anglo-Norman foliate carving, gives place here to a more rounded shaping of some of these details approaching that of French examples. The profiling shows a significant increase in the use of fillets — giving strong accentuation to the lines of the mouldings, and producing an effect that foreshadows the sharp arrises, and linear dryness of the Perpendicular style.

Externally this east end of Lincoln has much of the merit of the earlier English eastern exteriors to which, in its main lines, it conforms, save for the screen gables of the aisle compartments which falsify the expression of those parts, and contribute nothing of value to the composition. A notable feature of this exterior is the south portal, which is more like a French one than any other in England except that of the north transept of Westminster. Like the great portals of Amiens, its deeply splayed jambs and archivolts are brought out flush with the faces of the buttresses that flank it, and with its ornamented gable the likeness to the French model is close. What remained a few years ago of the sculpture of the tympanum and jambs was, I think, the finest mediæval sculpture in England, and if not actually wrought by French carvers, it would at least bear comparison with the best French work.[1]

The nearly contemporaneous nave of Lichfield follows the Lincoln scheme, but with marked points of difference both of proportion and of structure. The triforium is made higher and

---

[1] The so-called restoration to which this sculpture has lately been subjected is deplorable. There is no justification for tampering with the sculpture of ancient monuments. To put modern work where the old is wanting is to make a corrupt document, and thus to put difficulties in the way of the modern student, and to do injustice to the old workman.

the clerestory is considerably lowered, while the level of the vaulting impost is raised to that of the clerestory string. The ravages of modern restoration have left less of the original edifice in this case than in most others, a large part of the vaulting having been destroyed in the eighteenth century and replaced by an imitation in wood and plaster. What remains intact follows the vaulting of Lincoln nave in the number and arrangement of the ribs, save that the transverse rib is omitted. This important omission may not be of serious consequence (as we have seen in the case of Durham). It is, nevertheless, a defect from the point of view of reasonable and straighforward construction. Undoubtedly here, where tiercerons are employed, and set so near together, the function that in normal ribbed vaulting is performed by the transverse rib is sufficiently discharged by them, but to employ two members where there is no need of more than one is not a mark of logical composition. The ribs of this vaulting are so shaped and adjusted as to increase the spread of the conoid against the clerestory wall, and to bring its form, in horizontal section, more nearly to the half circle that characterizes the later fan vaulting of the Perpendicular style.

The vaulting shafts of Lichfield start from the pavement, giving a continuous support that is rare in the English church of the thirteenth century, but the relationship of these shafts to the vault ribs is no more logical than in Lincoln, and no complete organic skeleton is developed in the building, which is carried out with little short of Norman massiveness. With such heavy wall construction there is little need for flying buttresses, yet such buttresses are introduced, meeting the clerestory wall at a level about midway between the springing and the crown of the vaulting.

The aisle openings are variants of those of Lincoln Presbytery, but the clerestory openings are modelled, with variations, on those of the outer wall of the triforium of Westminster, and are each in the form of an equilateral triangle with curved sides and tracery consisting of three cusped circles. This clerestory has no passageway, and its heavy wall gives a deep moulded splay to the opening both inside and out. The triforium arcade has the tracery of the Westminster and Lincoln Presbytery triforiums instead of the pierced tympanums of the early buildings, and variants of the Lincoln foliated panels break the surfaces of the ground-story spandrels. The zigzag leaf ornament of the first order of the Lincoln lower arcade is applied to two orders of the triforium, to the longitudinal rib of the vaulting, and to the clerestory string; while the blind arcades of the aisles have their cusped arches surmounted with crocketed gables.

That the vital beauty, and architectural quality, of the Early English foliation was not long maintained is more apparent here than in the Lincoln Presbytery. While on the ground story there are some capitals of more simple design and graceful leafage, there are many, more especially those of the vaulting imposts, which have lost all beauty and functional expressiveness of form in their excess of involved ornament.

The Norman transept of Hereford Cathedral was rebuilt, as is well known, about 1260, during the Episcopate of Bishop Aquablanca, a foreigner from near Chambéry, who had been appointed by Henry III. While no direct influence from the Continent appears in this work, the influence of Westminster is marked, notwithstand-

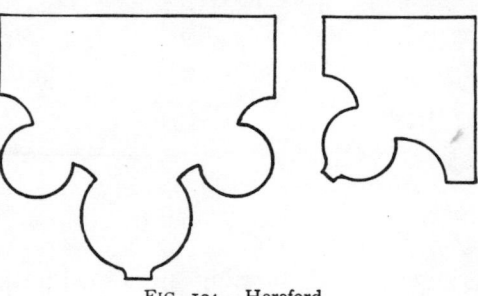

FIG. 124—Hereford.

ing the great difference between the two monuments both in scale and in details. The vaulting of Hereford transept has nothing of the French form that is so marked in Westminster. It is quadripartite in three oblong compartments with transverse ribs, groin ribs, and longitudinal ribs only. The profiling of these ribs (Fig. 124) is distinctly French, but their arrangement is not at all so, since the longitudinal rib springs from the same level as the other ribs, and is so shaped as to widen the conoid greatly against the clerestory wall and give the section shown in Fig. 125 at half the vertical height of the vault.[1] The masonry of the vault shell is in nearly straight and

---

[1] A comparison of this section with that of the vaulting of the nave of St. Leu d'Esserent, figured in my *Gothic Architecture*, p. 133, second edition, will afford an illustration of the most essential difference between French and English high vaulting.

horizontal courses, inclined to the wall from the springing upward, but becoming less so until at the crown those of the opposite sides become parallel. The surfaces are thus greatly warped, but in a direction opposite to that of French Gothic vaulting, and the cells are sharply pointed in the Anglo-Norman manner. The ribs interpenetrate at the springing, and the five are carried on three excessively slender shafts resting on corbels considerably above the impost of the ground-story arcade. What remains of the ribs at the impost is a group of mouldings that fit the triple abacus well, but there can be no logical relationship of the ribs to the shafts since they do not correspond in number. The ribs of the aisle vaults are profiled like those of the high vaulting, but their curves are all struck from centres below the

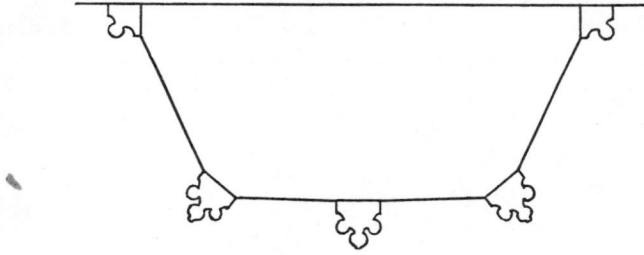

FIG. 125 — Hereford.

springing level, forming angles with their supporting shafts. The keys of the diagonals are a little higher than those of the bounding arches, so that the crowns of the cells, which are sharply pointed, incline upward toward the crown of the vault in nearly straight lines. The arches, both of the arcades and the openings, have their curves struck from points so far below the springing, and with such long radii, that they form angles at the imposts and have but slight curvature. In this they are peculiar, but in their acute pointing, in the tracery and feathering of the tympanums of the triforium, and in the diapering of the triforium spandrels, a resemblance to Westminster is very marked. A further likeness to Westminster is found in the triforium where the aisle wall is carried up and pierced with cusped circular lights, each framed in externally by a semicircular shafted arch, variants of those in the corresponding part of Westminster. The same form of opening is employed in the clerestory, but the arch here is pointed. This clerestory resembles that of Lichfield, and like Lichfield it has no passageway in its heavy wall. These features appear to indicate an influence from Westminster such as the relations of Henry III with the see of Hereford might naturally have given rise to.

The west side of this transept has no aisle, and is properly treated in one stage from the pavement to the vaulting, with a tall opening in each bay having a pair of mullions and simple tracery, as in the apsidal chapels of Amiens, and the Sainte Chapelle of Paris. But it is only in the form of the opening, not in its relation to the building, that resemblance to the French models resides; for these openings do not fill the entire bay and thus eliminate the wall. Large as they are, they still leave considerable wall solid on either side, and over their archivolts, — the French openings being, as we have seen, intercolumniations in the skeleton construction, rather than windows in the proper sense.

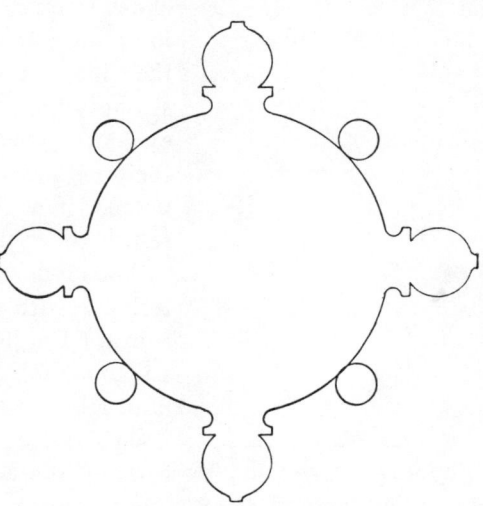

FIG. 126 — Hereford.

Coming back to the east side, the pier is a variant of the Early English type, its section (Fig. 126) showing four small engaged shafts and four slender free-standing shafts of Purbeck — but none of these shafts have any connection with the high vaulting since, as we have seen, the vaulting shafts start from corbels placed at a higher level. The capitals of these shafts are of the moulded type, with round abaci, and the great plinth is a square set diagonally. The base profile (Fig. 127) shows, in its upper part, three rounds together, as at Salisbury. There are no abutting arches in the triforium, and no flying buttresses externally.

One of the most important monuments of pointed architecture in England of the second half of the thirteenth century was the choir and east end of the old St. Paul's Cathedral in London (circa 1255-1283). If the drawings by Ferrey[1] are to be trusted, this composition was almost as French in style as Westminster itself, but like Westminster its French character lay in its proportions and details more than in its structural system, although it was provided with flying buttresses of very true French form, and its square east end was treated like a French transept end. Its vault masonry is represented as consisting, like that of Westminster, of alternate courses of light and dark stone, but, unlike Westminster choir, it appears to have had tiercerons in addition to the structural ribs. That the inspiration of Westminster was strongly felt in St. Paul's there is thus evidence enough in what we know of the monument. It would be strange, indeed, if such influence had not been felt.

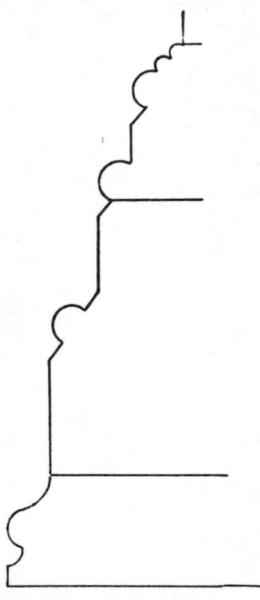

FIG. 127 — Hereford.

The choir of Exeter (circa 1270-1307) follows, with variations, the thirteenth-century English scheme as embodied in Lincoln nave and Presbytery. Its most noticeable feature is the vaulting which is on the Lincoln model with the addition of more tiercerons. In Lincoln nave, as we have seen, one tierceron was inserted in each lateral cell, in the Presbytery this was omitted, in Lichfield it reappears, and here at Exeter it occurs again with the addition of two others. These three tiercerons, together with the transverse and groin ribs, are so arranged as to give an approximately semicircular shape to the vaulting conoid, extending for a considerable distance above the springing. Thus this vaulting, more than any other that we have thus far examined, approaches the form of the subsequent so-called fan vaulting. It may be well to develop this point a little farther. As we have already seen, in part (p. 133), the shape of the vaulting conoid, in horizontal section at any given level, depends on the number and the curvatures of the ribs. By varying the numbers and

[1] Published in Longman's *Three Cathedrals of St. Paul*, London, 1873.

the curves, we may, as Willis has shown,[1] make the conoid, between the springing and the crown, assume in section any form we please. In quadripartite vaulting the conoids are necessarily rectangular on plan at the crown, and if the curves of the groin ribs are such that a horizontal rod parallel with the axis of the nave, passed up and down against the transverse rib, would touch the groin ribs also at every level, and if the longitudinal rib be so curved that a rod perpendicular to the wall would touch both it and the groin rib at every level, the conoid will, of course, be square in every horizontal section, as at A (Fig. 128). But this will rarely be the case, though English vaulting often tends to this form, as in the Presbytery of Lincoln.

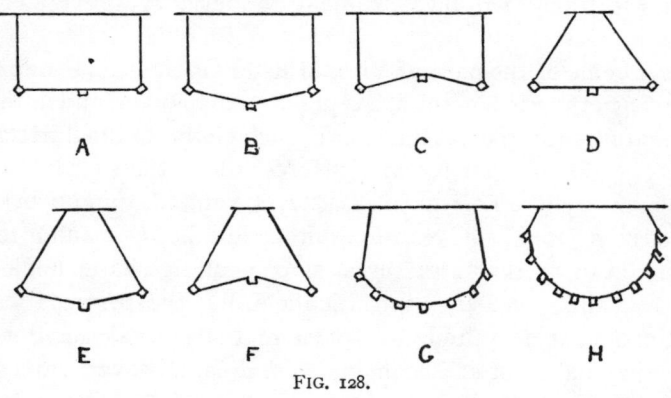

FIG. 128.

Curvature given to any of the ribs which would prevent their passing through the rod at any given level will, of course, break the square at that level. The centre, for instance, from which the curve of the transverse rib is struck may be so placed, and its radius be such, as to advance it beyond the groin ribs at the middle section, as at B, or to draw it in, as at C. If the longitudinal rib be stilted, the form will become as at D. If, at the same time, the groin ribs be so curved as to draw them in at the middle section, the form will be as at E; and if on the other hand they be advanced, the form F will result. Where there are tiercerons the form may be as at G, as in the nave of Lincoln, and where the tiercerons are multiplied, the form H will be assumed, as at Exeter.

The vaulting shafts of Exeter start from corbels, as at Lin-

[1] *Construction of the Vaults of the Middle Ages*, pp. 18 *et seq.*

coln; the group now consists, however, of five members instead of three, but, as there are eleven ribs to carry, the relation of the shafts to them is not more logical than in the Lincoln system. The orders of the great arcade are indistinctly marked — the whole archivolt becoming in effect a broad splay of mouldings in which five principal groups of members appear, while the pier, having in section the form of a square set diagonally, has five shafts on each face corresponding to the moulding groups. The capitals of these shafts are of the moulded type. The triforium arcade has four cusped arches on triple shafts, and the clerestory is heavily walled. A flat pier buttress rises through the triforium, and against it a vigorous external flying buttress is brought to bear at about the level of the crown of the vault.

The scheme of the nave of York Minster (Plate XXII) departs widely from the earlier English types of composition, and in some of its features approaches the later French Gothic of the thirteenth century, while in other features it foreshadows the so-called Perpendicular style. This nave was never vaulted, though in one respect its system provides for vaulting in a better manner than is common in English structures, since vaulting shafts not only start from the pavement as at Lichfield, but the principal ones are of sufficient magnitude to have a real structural function — which they have not at Lichfield. There is, however, only one shaft on either side of the main shaft, and this is so very small as to be ineffective both in expression and function. The wooden simulation of vaulting, with which this system was covered in the fourteenth century, need not be considered here, since it forms no part of the original scheme, and is in another style.

The most noticeable feature of this nave is the combination of the clerestory and the triforium into one composition by the carrying down of the jamb shafts and mullions of the clerestory openings to the level of the triforium string. An early instance of this occurs in the choir of St. Germain des Prés of Paris, dating from 1163, where the clerestory has a pair of shafted openings, the three shafts of which (Fig. 129) are thus brought down. This arrangement occurs also in some other early French monuments, as in St. Remi of Reims, and it is adopted in the nave of Amiens — where the jamb shafts and the central mullion of the great compound clerestory openings are brought down to the

PLATE XXII

Nave of York.

triforium string. In these examples the clerestory and triforium stages are pleasantly united while each remains well marked. But the nave of York follows a further French development (found in the nave of St. Denis, and in the choir of Troyes), where all of the clerestory mullions, as well as the jamb shafts, come down to the triforium string. In these latter French examples, the triforium is lighted, as it is not in York, but the composition is exactly the same in essential particulars. It is not, however, the same in its relation to the building — for in St. Denis and Troyes the opening occupies the whole space between the piers of a perfectly developed Gothic system of skeleton construction, whereas at York the Anglo-Norman wall construction survives.

English writers have not recognized the French origin of this form of united clerestory and triforium, a form quite different from that of Pershore already noticed (p. 147), and even Willis appears to regard it as a novelty devised by the architect of the nave of York, though he does not affirm this. He describes the scheme as follows: "The Early English transepts are divided into pier arches, triforium, and clerestory. . . . But in the nave there are but

FIG. 129. — St. Germain des Prés.

two great divisions, of which the lower one, containing the pier arches, is 51 feet high; the upper one, 43 feet high, is occupied by a large clerestory window of five lights, with geometrical tracery and a transom across the middle. The lights above the transom are glazed, and constitute the real window, but the lights below the transom (if the phrase can be applied to openings so perfectly dark) are open, and as the roof of the side aisle abuts against the transom, the space behind them, and to which they communicate, is the interval between the stone vault of the aisles and its wooden roof; they thus serve the purpose of a triforium."[1] This description is singularly incorrect for a writer so generally accurate as Willis. To say that in the nave there are but two great divisions, and to speak of the upper one of these as occupied by a large clerestory window with a transom across the middle, is to speak from what is superficial, and to ignore the real character of the building. Structurally the three divisions of ground story, triforium, and clerestory are as fully developed in the nave as in the transept. The difference is only that in the nave the upper two stages are superficially treated as one by carrying down the vertical members of the clerestory opening through the triforium, as in the French examples just cited.

An increased elaboration is noticeable in the tracery of this nave, though, except in the west front, it retains the geometrical character. The arcades of the triforium have the gable with crockets and finial over the arch that we have noticed at Lichfield, and this feature became common after the middle of the thirteenth century. This occurs first in France about 1240, I believe, as in the triforium of the choir of Amiens. Externally the aisle openings are surmounted by such gables, as in the Sainte Chapelle of Paris, and many other French monuments of the thirteenth century and later.

The west front of York is altogether French in its proportions and general disposition of parts, except for the diminutive portals, and the great pointed window, in place of a circular opening, which differentiate it from typical French models. In the lower part of this front, which followed immediately on the completion of the nave, an extended application of crocketed gables over the small arches of the ornamental arcades, both on the wall and on the buttresses, is noticeable. An ornamental change appears in the great window of this front — which was glazed in 1338[2] — and in the tower windows of the clerestory level, in the sinuous curves of the tracery. These are, I believe, among the early examples of that flowing tracery which prevailed about the middle of the fourteenth century. The top stories of the towers are in the subsequent Perpendicular style.

The nave of Worcester Cathedral, of which all but the two western bays dates from the fourteenth century, — the north side having been begun about 1317 in a very simple form of the so-

[1] *The Architectural History of York Cathedral*, p. 22.   [2] *Op. cit.*, p. 27.

called Decorated style, while the south side, including the high vaulting, was not completed till 1377, — has, like the nave of York, a system of vigorous vaulting shafts rising from the pavement. The rib system of the vaulting is more simple than that of most English vaulting of the time. It has no tiercerons between the transverse ribs and the groin ribs, and but one tierceron in each lateral cell. It has, however, transverse and longitudinal ridge ribs. Willis[1] calls attention to a feature of this vaulting which, though plainly introduced as a makeshift, appears to have given rise to a characteristic feature of the later forms of vaulting in the Perpendicular style. This occurs on the north side only, and consists of a diminutive arch for the support of the tierceron between the groin rib and the longitudinal rib, just above the springing (Fig. 130). The springing blocks, as Willis explains, belong to the earlier work of the whole north side, and appear to show that it had been the intention to cover the nave with vaulting having no tiercerons. When this point in the construction was reached, Willis supposes that the work was stopped, and that no more was done for a considerable time. On resuming, the idea of inserting tiercerons was conceived, and in order to get them in without reconstructing the springing blocks, the device of the small arch was resorted to. On the south side, where the work was all new, the tiercerons start from the main impost in the manner that had before been common. This theory seems to explain the facts, but it supposes a mode of procedure that was apparently uncommon in mediæval building. A nave appears usually to have been built bay by bay, complete on both sides from end to end — which is certainly the more natural, and the easier way. We shall see, in the next chapter, that this small arch between the ribs, introduced as a makeshift, gave rise to a new method of arranging the ribs in what is known as fan vaulting.

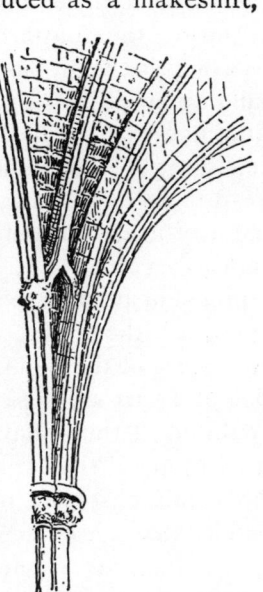

FIG. 130 — Worcester Nave.

[1] *Architectural History of Worcester Cathedral*, London, 1863, pp. 29–30.

In this nave the passageway survives in the clerestory, and the heavy wall construction of the older building prevails throughout. Of the whole monument Willis truly remarks[1] that "the general design of Early English, Decorated, and Perpendicular severies is the same, and probably derived from the Norman." This is significant, and applies to the pointed architecture of England generally, as our foregoing analyses have shown. This architecture is not only derived from the Norman, but retains to the end the Norman characteristics of construction.

During the fourteenth century, with the growth of secular interests and luxurious tastes, the finer inspiration of the earlier building epoch was gradually lost, and the architecture of England, like that of the Continent, grew more and more florid as time went on, while the quality of the ornamental elements as steadily declined, and a factitious spirit in design began also to manifest itself. A notable instance of this appears in the well-known octagon, of Ely Cathedral. In this octagon, which was begun shortly after the fall of the Norman crossing tower in the year 1322, the architect conceived a feature not in keeping with the nature of the building into which it was interpolated. The idea of a vast area opening out of the nave of such a structure, would not, I think, have found favour with the builders of northern Europe of the twelfth and thirteenth centuries. But under the conditions that now prevailed, and with the striving for novelty that marks periods of artistic decline, the impropriety of such a feature was not felt, and a scheme more conformable with Roman and Byzantine design was engrafted on the Norman and Early English work.[2] The covering of this octagon has been called a Gothic dome,[3] or cupola. But it is not a dome in the sense of a cupola, and, as I have elsewhere[4] shown, there can be no such thing as a Gothic dome. The principles of Gothic vaulting are opposed to those of any vault that can properly be called a dome. Moreover, the elaborate covering of the Ely octagon is not vaulting in a proper sense. It is made of wood,

[1] *Architectural History of Worcester Cathedral*, p. 33.

[2] More conformable, that is to say, as to the idea of a great circular, or polygonal area covered with a ceiling unsupported from the pavement, save in the periphery.

[3] Fergusson, *History of Architecture*, etc., vol. 2, p. 135.

[4] *Character of Renaissance Architecture*, New York, the Macmillan Company, 1905, pp. 56–58.

and while it imitates some features of stone vaulting, it has a form that could hardly be executed in stone — certainly not with safety. For the conoids, springing out of the angles, terminate on the straight sides of a large octagonal opening with nothing to withstand their thrusts against these sides. In the timber construction this form is, of course, perfectly safe, but to make such a vault secure in stone, the opening would have to be circular. It is true that in the dome of Florence we have a stone vault with an octagonal opening, but the opening there is relatively small, and the short and thick sides of its curb, being monolithic, are strong enough to resist the thrusts. But even so, the form is a bad one from the point of view of right principles of construction. A polygonal vault ought not to have such an opening. The dome of St. Peter's, with its circular opening, is in this respect on right principles; but, of course, the wooden covering of the octagon of Ely has nothing of the form of a dome. Nor has it the form of a Gothic vault over such an area. A Gothic vault would have eight groin ribs converging on a single point at the crown, and a stilted arch on each side of the octagon reaching to about the same level. Such a vault would require abutments against each angle, either in the form of a solid wall set edge on (which would block the aisles) or of flying buttresses carried over the aisles. But however it might be covered, this polygonal area, exceeding the width of the nave, is out of place in such a building. The lanterns and small domes that were so numerous over the crossings of mediæval churches in Italy and Gaul, where the traditions of Roman and Byzantine art prevailed, did not exceed in span the width of the nave. At Siena, however, a scheme analogous to that of the Ely octagon had been carried out. Here the space at the crossing has the form of a hexagon with a span that exceeds the width of the nave. It is not improbable that the designer of the Ely octagon got his idea from Siena, but the introduction of such a feature shows, in both cases, a misapprehension of the nature of Gothic design and construction. There is, I think, apart from its incongruity, no reason for such a feature in a building of this kind. The crossing is not the sanctuary, and there is nothing to call for special emphasis or dignity in this part of the church. I would not speak dogmatically, but this octagon appears to me an inconsistent interpolation, and a manifestation of that factitious spirit in design that came more extensively into play in the architecture of the Renaissance.

The factitious character of this composition is shown further in its ornamental details. The oblique sides are each pierced with a large opening at the clerestory level, and on the wall surface beneath the opening are three sunk panels, framing sculptures in high relief, with a pointed arch of double flexure, ornamented with cusps, crockets, and finials, over each. These so-called accolade arches, earlier instances of which appear to have been produced in the windows of the Lady Chapel of Lichfield (circa 1296–1322), became common features of English architecture during the first half of the fourteenth century, and seem to have given rise to that flowing tracery which is the distinguishing feature of what is called by Sharpe[1] the Curvilinear style, and which appears in the large openings here, as well as these panels. These clerestory openings have arches in two planes, the inner one of which is shaped like those of the arcades of the north transept of Hereford (cf. p. 168) and thus, though springing from the same level, has its crown lower than that of the outer plane. Over this is another arch (of normal shape like the one in the outer plane) forming a wall rib to the wooden vaulting, and the space between the two is filled with open tracery.

The openings into the aisles on the oblique sides are noticeable for the treatment of their archivolts and jambs. The archivolts are of three orders, of larger profiling than had been common, and the middle one is carried down into the jamb without change of profile, and without any capitals or impost mouldings — an early instance of that form of continuous impost which subsequently became a characteristic feature of the so-called Perpendicular style.[2] The two other orders are shafted, and their capitals have a low cushion shape, with round abaci and involved carved ornament.

The choir, which appears to have followed immediately after the octagon, shows further development of the florid ornamenta-

---

[1] *The Seven Periods of English Church Architecture*, p. 29.

[2] Continuous imposts are met with, of course, even in Norman works, as in the south portal of Malmesbury Abbey, the west bays of Worcester, and elsewhere, but in the Perpendicular style they become more common, and have peculiarities of profiling that are foreshadowed here.

tion that was beginning to characterize the art. The vaulting especially presents new features that are significant of the approach of the last phase of English mediæval architecture. The rib system is primarily like that of Exeter, save that there are only two tiercerons in each lateral cell instead of three, but these are supplemented by an increase in the number of liernes used in new ways. Hitherto we have found liernes only in the crowns of the lateral cells, but they are now applied to the vault surface. In addition to the longitudinal ridge rib there are in this choir vault, transverse ridge ribs, instead of short liernes,[1] and from the point of intersection (*a*, Fig. 131) of the groin ribs, four liernes branch out

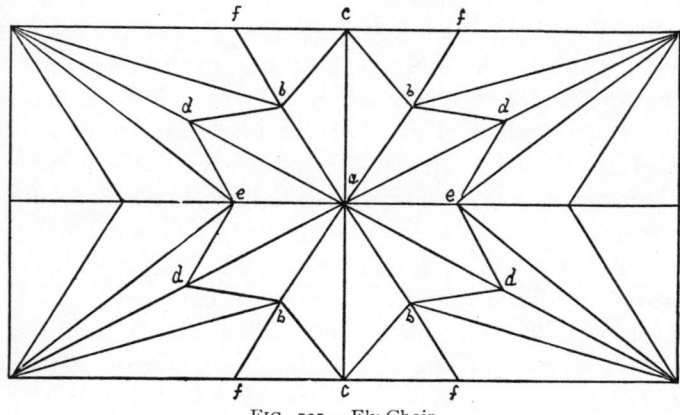

FIG. 131 — Ely Choir.

to meet the tiercerons that lie between the groin ribs and the transverse ribs in the points *b*, where these tiercerons are stopped. From the points *b* other liernes are carried back to meet the longitudinal ridge rib in the points *c*. Again, from the points *b* liernes reach to the groin ribs, meeting them in the points *d*, from the points *d* others are directed to intersect the transverse ridge rib in the points *e*, where the longer tiercerons of the lateral cell meet this rib, and again from the points *b* still others are carried to intersect the transverse ribs in the points *f*. The point of intersection of the groin ribs is marked by a large sculptured boss, and the points where the liernes meet are marked by smaller bosses.[2] The principal ribs are gathered on the capitals of three vaulting

---

[1] The transverse ridge rib occurs also in the transept of Lichfield.

[2] The wooden vaulting of the nave of York, which followed soon after the choir of Ely, is a variant of this scheme.

shafts more slender than those of the presbytery, and the abaci of these capitals, as well as the tall plinths of the bases, are now made octangular on plan.

The ground-story piers differ considerably from those of the presbytery. As in the presbytery, the arches of the great arcade are of three orders, but the middle one is treated like that of the oblique sides of the octagon already noticed, — being carried down, with continuous imposts, to the pavement, so that the jambs of this order take the place of the round shafts in the corresponding order of the presbytery. The clerestory retains the Norman passageway, but the inner plane of this passageway has but one shafted arch, embracing the whole width of the bay, with a cusped intrados in open tracery of sinuous curves; while in the outer plane there are two pointed arches springing from a large central mullion, the space beneath each arch being subdivided by a secondary mullion and sinuous cusped tracery, while similar tracery fills the space over the principal arches and under the crown of the great encompassing arch. The triforium is high over the outer wall, like that of Westminster, and is lighted by a wide-mullioned opening in each bay. This opening has a round arch, and is subdivided primarily like that of the clerestory, but the mullions are here all of the same magnitude, and the secondary ones are continued upward, through the imposts of the lesser arches, halfway to the soffit of the great arch where they branch into tracery, a step in the direction of the Perpendicular treatment. Externally, beneath each of these openings, the mullions and jamb mouldings are carried down in relief on the face of the wall, and a moulding of the same profile crowns this part of the wall — crossing the mullions like a transom, as in the triforium of York. The aisle openings are round arched, and have each three mullions, of equal magnitude, branching into cusped tracery of sinuous curvature. All of these openings have continuous imposts, and each of them fills the whole width of a bay.[1]

[1] This development of the opening so as to fill the entire width of the bay does occur occasionally in the later mediæval buildings of England. It occurs to some extent in the earlier presbytery of Ely, as well as here in the choir. But the clerestory passage of Norman art survives in both parts, and the double archivolt of the opening is distinct from the longitudinal rib of the vault. Such exceptional instances of approach in some details to French Gothic treatment do not make even such pointed art of England akin to the Gothic of France as to

It is unnecessary to pursue further the ornamental redundance, and the capricious innovations and readjustments in composition, that characterize the art of the later thirteenth century, and the early part of the fourteenth. They were tending to bring about the final phase of mediæval architecture in England known as the Perpendicular style — which will be considered in the next chapter.

<small>the total and essential structural system. Notwithstanding that both presbytery and choir of Ely are furnished with vigorous flying buttresses, the system of both is far from having French Gothic character in the fundamental feature of the vaulting, and in the absence of the pier as a continuous member logically adjusted to the vaulting.</small>

## CHAPTER IX

### THE PERPENDICULAR STYLE

THE havoc wrought in the fourteenth and fifteenth centuries on monuments of earlier times was great and deplorable. The remodelling of the choir of Gloucester and the nave of Winchester, the mutilation of Tewkesbury, Malmesbury, Norwich, and many other Norman structures, have deprived us of knowledge of much church architecture in England of great importance. That the designers of this uninspired epoch could not have found scope for the exercise of their architectural fancies in wholly new buildings, and refrained from laying violent hands on the works of their predecessors, is much to be regretted. A view, to-day, of one of the great Norman apses — as of Canterbury, Gloucester, Norwich, or Durham — would be a great privilege to the student of Anglo-Norman art; but not one of them has survived,[1] and few naves, choirs, or transepts have wholly escaped the mania for remodelling that prevailed at this time. This remodelling was, indeed, generally superficial. The elaborate Perpendicular work in the choir of Gloucester, and in the nave of Winchester, is a mere overlay in the one case, and largely a re-working in the other — the old Norman structure in both remaining more or less beneath the surface. But complete demolition would hardly have wrought more damage in either case in so far as what can be seen from the central aisle is concerned.

The peculiarities that distinguish what is known as the Perpendicular style had, as we have seen, begun to take form in some of the later buildings described in the last chapter, — the introduction and multiplication of tiercerons and liernes in vaulting, the prolongation of the clerestory mullions downward over the triforium wall, with a horizontal member, like a transom, crowning this wall, as in the nave of York; the same arrangement in the

[1] The apse of Norwich is, indeed, nearly intact up to the clerestory string.

PLATE XXIII

Choir of Gloucester.

outer triforium openings of the choir of Ely, together with the additional prolongation of two mullions upward through the imposts of the smaller tracery arches, and a tendency to prismatic profiling, as in the jambs and archivolts of the arcades of this choir. From such beginnings the progress to further complications in the ribs of vaulting, to the systematic prolongation of mullions to intersect the arch of the opening, to the introduction of transoms in the opening itself, the extensive application of panelling to wall surfaces, and the prevalence of prismatic profiling in vault ribs, jambs, and archivolts — which characterize the Perpendicular style — was rapid.

The remodelled transept and choir of Gloucester (circa 1331–1377) appears to be the earliest instance of the Perpendicular style in its distinctive form, and on a large scale. According to the natural order, we may begin our examination of it with the vaulting, though there is little structural significance in its forms and adjustments to make it of material consequence where we begin. The vaulting of the south transept follows earlier vaulting to the extent of retaining the distinctly quadripartite form, having groin ribs that intersect normally in the centre of each compartment. And it is worthy of notice that the principal ribs here — the transverse ribs, the groin ribs, and the longitudinal ribs — have each its own support in the shaft group, so that the system is in this respect more logical than English vaulting is generally. There is no stilting of the longitudinal ribs, and the shapes of the transverse ridge ribs, together with the arrangement of the liernes, which now form a network over the whole vault, are such as to give rise to some peculiarities of conformation in the surfaces which, however it is not worth while to describe, and we may pass on to the consideration of the very different vaulting of the choir.

In the rib system of this choir vaulting (Plate XXIII) the liernes are so increased in number that they form a close and complicated network over the entire surface, and the conformation of the vault is widely different from that of any true Gothic work. It may be roughly described as a pointed barrel vault with cross cells interpenetrating below the level of the crown. As far as is compatible with this, the rib system is primarily like that of Lincoln nave — having one tierceron between the transverse rib and the groin rib, and one between the groin rib and the longitudinal rib. The groin ribs, since they have to intersect below the crown of the barrel vault, are prolonged, beyond the point of intersection, to meet the longitudinal ridge rib in the points where this rib is crossed by the transverse ribs. They thus become surface ribs in the barrel vault from the point where they intersect. The primary tiercerons meet the ridge rib midway between the transverse ribs, and thus occupy the place on plan that would be taken by the groin ribs in normal quadripartite vaulting. Two other longitudinal ribs, one on either side of the ridge rib, and but a little way below it, are carried from end to end of the barrel vault, and a maze of liernes, the places and directions of which it is not worth while to follow, complete the system. All of the main ribs interpenetrate at the springing so that their total bulk is not greater than that of the transverse rib alone where it is free, and are gathered upon the capital of a single vaulting shaft which rises from the pavement. Grouped with this shaft, but separated from it by a hollowed member with a fillet, is a smaller shaft which carries a member of the moulded clerestory archivolt, the lower members of this archivolt starting from another shaft placed at a considerable distance from the vaulting shaft, and reaching to a higher level where it intersects the curve of the upper member, a strip of wall filling the space between this shaft and the vaulting shaft. In other words, the clerestory archivolt is a segmental one, like that of the north transept of Hereford, with an upper moulding sent down against the wall, without change of curvature, to the level of the vaulting impost. Close against this jamb shaft of the opening is another shaft, which carries a moulding in the form of a half-blind arch that intersects the larger arch springing from the level of the vaulting impost, and thus making a small blind arch on the strip of clerestory wall.[1]

The Norman structure had a low aisle on the ground story, a triforium gallery, and a clerestory; but the clerestory was demolished and rebuilt on this remodelling, while the aisle and gallery remain. The Norman piers of the ground story and of the triforium gallery are massive round columns, against which the exist-

---

[1] I realize that it may be found difficult, except in the building itself, to follow this description without an elaborate diagram. But such a diagram would cost more labour to prepare than I think the subject is worth.

ing shafts of the choir are set, while the bays are filled with elaborate trellis screens, the details of which are a development of the clerestory and triforium of the nave of York, the mullions being brought down in front of the triforium openings, over the wall surface beneath, and in front of the upper parts of the ground-story openings, where they terminate on a depressed skeleton arch. The semicircular curves of the Norman archivolts of the ground story and triforium are marked on this overlay by mouldings having the same profile as the mullions, and the clerestory and triforium openings have each a transom, while other horizontal members are introduced — one at the bottom of the clerestory lights, one passing through the crown of the triforium arch, one at the triforium ledge and another a short distance below it, and one through the ground-story arch a little way below its crown. The upper part of each small rectangle of this trellis-work is filled with a diminutive cusped arch, and the clerestory window head is filled with tracery composed of two pointed arches, each embracing two small depressed accolade arches, with short vertical members, as in the outer triforium openings of Ely choir above noticed, all but one of which, however, now intersect the arches in true Perpendicular fashion.

In the vast opening, which fills the entire east end the Perpendicular idea is more completely developed. The space (cf. Plate XXIII) is divided by two great mullions into three parts, of which the middle one is wider than the other two. Then this middle space is subdivided by secondary mullions into three equal parts, and all of these mullions are carried up to intersect the great archivolt. From the outer side of each great mullion, at the level of the springing of the great archivolt, a half-skeleton arch is sent off which, intersecting the great archivolt, forms a pointed arch over each lateral compartment, and beneath it are two smaller arches, the inner sides of which spring from a secondary mullion dividing the compartment into two parts. All of these lesser divisions are again subdivided by tertiary mullions into two parts each. Then the great middle compartment is crossed by eight transoms — the first at the level of the lowest transom of the choir bays, the second and third at the levels of those at the bottom of the triforium, the fourth, fifth, and sixth at equal, and greater, distances apart, and the seventh and eighth at still greater, and unequal, distances apart. All of those below the impost of the great arcade are continued across the lateral divisions, and thus the whole space is divided into a multitude of small rectangles — the upper parts of which are filled with diminutive cusped skeleton arches. The great mullions of the middle compartment send off branches at the top, forming three pointed arches, and the smaller mullions branch, beneath these arches, into small trefoil arches, from the crowns of which vertical members rise to intersect the great archivolt — skeleton cusps being set in the angles. The heads of the lateral compartments are treated in a similar manner.

A glazed framework of slender members on so vast a scale needs to be well fortified against the force of winds, and accordingly the two great mullions are made very deep. But they are shaped like buttresses with set offs, and their salience is external rather than internal. They are thus false in expression — giving the suggestion of resistance to internal pressure which does not exist. This glazed expanse is further strengthened by its shape on plan, the middle compartment being advanced outward a little, and the lateral compartments set obliquely so that salient angles are formed externally, which must considerably increase its power of resistance to wind pressure.

In the rebuilding of the choir of York (begun with the presbytery in the year 1361 [1]) the scheme of the nave of the same building already described (pp. 172-174) is continued with variations of detail in which Perpendicular characteristics are further developed. The leading structural forms, the larger divisions, and the profiling are nearly the same as in the nave, but the smaller vaulting shafts are lengthened to a height considerably above that of the principal one, thus stilting the longitudinal rib of the vault; the larger shaft is prolonged above its capital — the vault ribs interpenetrating so as to die away on its surface, and the hood mouldings of the great archivolts interpenetrate the smaller shafts in like manner. In the clerestory and aisle openings the geometrical tracery of the nave is replaced by an intermixture of sinuous members with small mullions — some of which are prolonged so as to intersect the archivolt. The capitals are low, and have octagonal abaci and bossy foliation of the crumpled kind that was now coming to prevail. Those of the great vaulting shafts are peculiarly irrational and ungraceful, having each

[1] Cf. Willis, *The Architectural History of York Cathedral*, p. 34.

an appendage with miniature corbels and arches, as in a corbel-table, surrounding it.

The east end enclosure is but a variant of that of the west end. The opening, though much larger than the western one, has the same general shape, and the same non-conformity of its acutely pointed arch to the arch of the vault — the one not being concentric with the other. In its tracery the sinuous lines of the so-called flowing style are mixed with the vertical lines of many mullions carried up to intersect the archivolt, while below the springing of the arch the mullions, which are here larger and fewer, are crossed by two transoms. At the west end the wall on either side of the opening is ornamented with several tiers of rectangular panelling framing gabled arches; but here in the presbytery these give place to two tall panels reaching from top to bottom, and subdivided by ornamented corbels, shaped beneath into canopies, so as to form four tiers of tall niches. The jamb mouldings of the opening are carried up through the impost, and, interpenetrating the mouldings of the archivolt, intersect the arch of the vault. This is an early instance of a kind of interpenetration of mouldings that became common in the French Flamboyant style.[1]

On the outside two members like mullions are set between the flat buttresses in front of each clerestory window. These mullions reach to the cornice and, together with the buttresses, form three tall rectangular openings — which are crossed by a transom, and have their heads ornamented with cusped tracery, as in the trellis screen work of Gloucester choir. The aisle windows have richly crocketed hood moulds, and are crowned by finials which rise from the archivolts in reverse curves, and give a suggestion of the accolade form. The great east window has a hood mould of pronounced accolade shape, as in the east window of Gloucester and elsewhere. In the east front the sloping lines of the roofs are not expressed. These roofs are, indeed, of very low pitch, but in the façade the compartments, answering to the divisions of the interior, terminate in horizontal lines surmounted by crocketed gables. There are no flying buttresses in any part of the building. Prominent wall buttresses, however,

---

[1] There is, I believe, good reason to suppose that the French Flamboyant style was derived largely from England. Cf. C. Enlart, *Origine Anglaise du Style Flamboyant*, Caen, 1906.

crowned with tall pinnacles, give the suggestion of a vaulted structure. The western part of the choir (circa 1380–1400) is a continuation of the scheme of the presbytery with unimportant variation of some details.

The choir of Gloucester and the presbytery of York were followed by the naves of Winchester and Canterbury, which are, for the most part, nearly contemporaneous works, though a beginning was made at Winchester by Bishop Edingdon, who died in 1366, and the nave of Canterbury was begun about 1380.[1] But Edingdon's work at Winchester was confined to the west end, and comprises the western façade with exception of the great gable, — the west window being a copy of the great east window of Gloucester, two bays of the north aisle wall, and a part of one bay of the south aisle wall. The rest of the nave, except the outer face of the south aisle wall — which is Norman with Perpendicular windows interpolated — is the work of William of Wykeham, begun in the year 1394. Of Bishop Edingdon's scheme for the remodelling of the Norman nave we have no knowledge beyond what is shown in the parts just mentioned, but the refashioned windows and buttresses of Edingdon were followed, with some variations and refinements, by William of Wykeham,[2] and it is reasonable to suppose that in the rest of the work Wykeham likewise followed the project of his predecessor. That Edingdon's work was largely inspired by the choir of Gloucester is, I think, probable. The intersection of the mullions with the archivolt, the multiplication of transoms, the filling of the heads of the rectangles with cusped skeleton arches, and the broad, hollow, and sharp-edged profiling of the jambs and archivolts — passing continuously one into the other — are features of the earlier work at Gloucester. The form of the window arch is new, though it is only a variant of that of Hereford north transept. As at Hereford, it is composed of curves struck from centres below the impost level, and thus forming angles at the springing; but these curves are struck from points still lower down, and the arch is obtusely pointed, so that it would require only to have the impost angles rounded off to give the four-centred form of the later Perpen-

---

[1] Cf. Willis, *The Architectural History of Winchester Cathedral*, p. 67.

[2] For a detailed comparison of the works of Edingdon and Wykeham see Willis's *Architectural History of Winchester Cathedral*, pp. 54 *et seq.*

dicular style. A noticeable detail of the profiling of the jambs and archivolts of Edingdon's windows is the so-called brace (AB, Fig. 132) which reappears in the work of Wykeham, in Canterbury nave, and in many other works in the Perpendicular style. In the new bases of the aisle responds the ogee moulding and the octagonal plinth of Gloucester choir are reproduced.

In Wykeham's nave the Norman structure was not merely masked, as Gloucester choir was; it was transformed in a curious manner. The Norman system was uniform, and the bay (Fig. 133, which I reproduce from Willis's admirable drawing) had the three stages — ground story, triforium, and clerestory — in the characteristic Norman form. A pilaster strip with an engaged shaft rose from the pavement in each pier, those of the easternmost three piers reaching to the top of the wall, as we have seen that they generally do in Norman buildings, but westward of these only every other one was thus carried up, the others stopping, as Willis has shown [1] and as may still be seen above the present vaulting, at the clerestory string. The pier section of the ground story (Fig. 134) was made up of round and square members answering (save in the high vaulting shafts, which had no function since there was no high vaulting) to the archivolts of the great arcade, to the upper archivolt of the triforium gallery, and to the vaulting of the aisles. These piers were now altered by William of Wykeham by chiselling away the surfaces of the round shafts, reducing their bulk, and by cutting off the edges of the square members and shaping them into hollow chamfers. The parts between the piers were subjected to more radical alteration. The ground-story archivolts with the vaulting of the aisles were demolished, the twin-arched sub-order of the triforium, with its central supporting shaft, both orders of the triforium archivolt on the nave side, together with their supports, the ashlaring of the triforium spandrels, and the inner plane of the clerestory passage, were removed. The ground-story archivolt shafts were then lengthened to the level

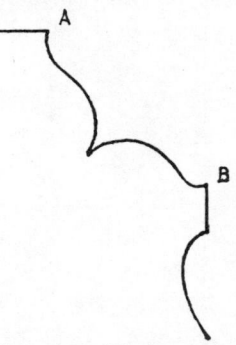

FIG. 132 — Winchester.

[1] *Ibid.*, p. 74.

of the former triforium ledge, and sharply pointed, four-centred arches were sprung from them. Directly over the crowns of

FIG. 133 — Nave of Winchester.

these arches a corbelled string-course, supporting an open parapet, was inserted, and what had been left of the Norman triforium and clerestory wall was reashlared. In other words the existing wall of the clerestory and triforium, which are treated, in the new fashion, as one stage, is the outer wall of the old Norman clerestory and the outer part of the Norman triforium wall, this last wall having been reduced in thickness so as to bring its inner face flush with that of the outer wall above. This altered wall thus stands in retreat of the ground-story spandrels (which retain the original Norman thickness) and the interval between it and the parapet forms a balcony.

The wall arch of Wykeham's vaulting is four-centred and the archivolt of the clerestory opening is concentric with it, but, since the opening does not nearly fill the width of the bay, its jambs intersect the archivolt at sharp angles, in points above the smaller curves of the wall arch, and thus the archivolt is not four-centred.

FIG. 134 — Winchester.

The opening has a skeleton pointed arch springing, with continuous imposts, from the jamb mouldings, and two mullions which are carried up to intersect the arch. From the outer sides of these mullions small half arches spring, and, intersecting the large arch, form a lesser pointed arch in each of the lateral lights. Beneath each of these is a small cusped arch, and an almond-shaped opening fills the space between it and the upper arch. In the central light a cusped arch is set a little higher than the lateral ones with a cusped almond above it. As in York nave the jambs and mullions are brought down over the triforium wall, and a transom-like member marks the window-sill, with cusped arches in the panels beneath. The wall solid on either side of the window is panelled with members like those of the lights.

The vaulting, built after Wykeham's death, is a simplified variant of that of the choir of Gloucester, and an improvement on it — for although, as at Gloucester, it is a pointed barrel vault with cross cells interpenetrating below the level of the crown, the longitudinal ribs are stilted, as they are not at

Gloucester, and there is nothing of the fan-vaulting character in the conoids. The springing level, too, is relatively lower, so that the vault has not the depressed form of the Gloucester vaulting, but rises with a soaring expression from its stately shafts. As there is but one shaft, however, in each pier, the ribs of the vault are again all gathered on a single capital. The vaulting capitals have a bulging outline with foliation and round abaci, while those of the great arcade have octagonal abaci with no foliation — as in the choir of Ely. All of these capitals are low in their proportions, the fine corinthianesque outline of the Early English capitals being now wholly lost.

Externally the flat Norman buttresses are retained in the clerestory, and the thick Norman wall gives deep splays to Wykeham's openings. These openings have hood moulds shaped to the angles at the springing of their segmental arches and carried part way down the jambs, terminating in bosses. This feature, which became common in later Perpendicular work, does not appear in Edingdon's aisle windows. Wykeham's aisle buttresses follow those of Edingdon, save that they are less salient, have fewer offsets, and are crowned with more slender pinnacles. No flying buttresses appear over the aisle roof, but under this roof such buttresses are inserted — springing curiously, from the crowns of the transverse arches of the aisle vaulting.

The Perpendicular style in its earlier form culminates in the nave of Canterbury. Willis has remarked the similarity of its composition to that of the nave of Winchester, though the construction is lighter, being wholly new work — the Norman nave of Lanfranc having been demolished in 1378 because it was thought to have become insecure. The nave of Canterbury is, in fact, the first and only great nave that was entirely built in the Perpendicular style. That the schemes of both Wykeham and Chilenden [1] were derived from Edingdon's beginning at Winchester there can, I think, be little doubt.

The proportions of the nave of Canterbury are very different from those of the earlier English churches, and are more like those of the Continent. The vaulting shafts rise majestically

---

[1] The design of the nave of Canterbury has generally been ascribed to Prior Chilenden, but it is not certain that he was the architect. Cf. Willis, *The Architectural History of Canterbury Cathedral*, pp. 119 *et seq.*

from the pavement, and the lines of the vaulting are well adjusted to them. An effect of altitude appears to have been sought by these later English builders. This effect is got in Gloucester choir by raising the clerestory far beyond the height of the original Norman one, at Winchester — where the Norman clerestory was retained — the ground-story arcade was raised, and at Canterbury the height of the ground story is increased to an exceptional extent — so that the triforium and clerestory are crowded into a comparatively narrow space.

The nave of Canterbury, being a homogeneous work in the Perpendicular style, naturally exhibits a consistency throughout its system that is wanting in Gloucester and Winchester. But the relationship of its parts is not wholly logical, and what it embodies of the Gothic idea is confused with survivals of Romanesque tradition. The vaulting is in wide oblong compartments, the longitudinal ribs are much stilted, and some of the other ribs are more or less so. There is a tierceron between the groin rib and the transverse rib, and two such ribs between the groin rib and the wall rib — the one nearest the wall rib being much stilted and the other one less so. The mutual adjustment of these ribs is such that the conoid of the vault in horizontal section is much narrowed against the pier. There are both longitudinal and transverse ridge ribs — and these ribs are straight in elevation, making the crown of the vault level lengthwise, but as the keys of the wall ribs are a little higher than the keys of the groin ribs, the crowns of the lateral cells incline downward slightly towards the centre of each compartment. The rib system is supplemented by liernes, but these are confined to the upper part of the vault and form a more simple reticulation than occurs in the vaulting of Gloucester and Winchester. The transverse ribs have the profile A, and the ridge ribs, liernes, and tiercerons, the profile B (Fig. 135). Notwithstanding that three vaulting shafts rise from the pavement, the principal ribs are all gathered by interpenetration on the capital

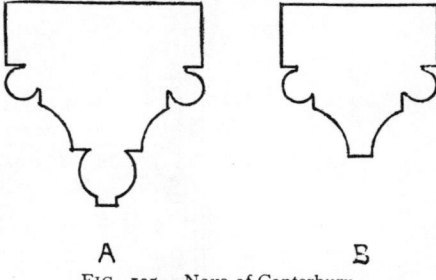

FIG. 135 — Nave of Canterbury.

o

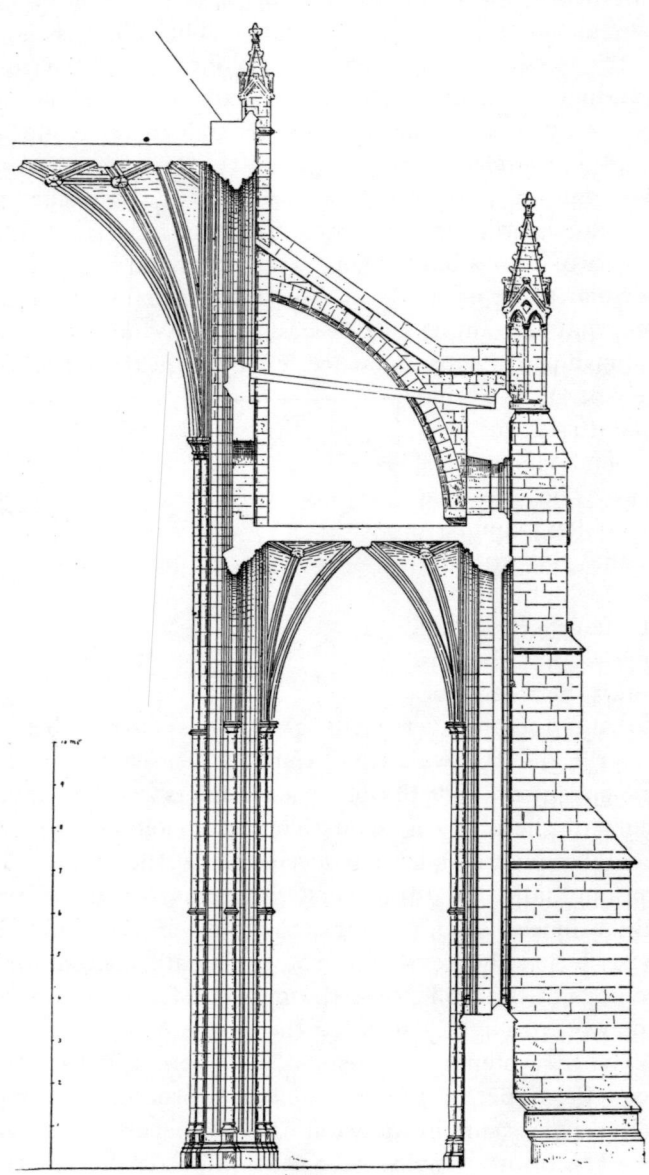

FIG. 136.—Canterbury Nave.

of the middle shaft, while each lateral shaft supports only the the wall rib and the tierceron that comes next to it — this last interpenetrating so as to die away completely far above the impost. No logical correspondence subsists, therefore, between the ribs of the vaulting and their supporting members. The vaulting of the aisle is similar in character to that of the nave, save that it is simpler, having fewer surface ribs. The cross-section (Fig. 136) will further explain the system. It will be seen that the brace-like profile at *a* (Fig. 137) is that of an arch in the clerestory, forming a sub-order to the wall rib of the vault, which is brought down continuously to the pavement. The corresponding profile, *b*, on the aisle side, is that of a sub-order to the longitudinal rib of the aisle vault brought down in like manner. It is worthy of notice that the diameter of the pier is a little greater transversely than it is lengthwise of the nave, but the difference is only eight centimetres — which is hardly enough to augment materially its power of resistance to the vault thrusts. The great buttress has deep set-offs, and a single flying buttress is brought to bear on a square pier buttress at a level above that of the haunch of the vault. Below this the pier has no reinforcement except that of the aisle vaulting — which, however, is very high, falling only a little below the springing of the great vault. The clerestory is low, and its opening is substantially like that of Winchester, with its dividing members brought down over the triforium wall. The aisle openings are large, reaching up almost to the vaulting, and they nearly fill the width of the bay. Some solid wall remains, however, on each side, and this wall is thick — giving a deep inner splay, and a deep external reveal. This wall is carried up, in full thickness, above the aisle vaulting, and is there pierced with a small square window in each bay which lights the triforium. Thus, while having, in its tall proportions, the comparative lightness of its piers, and

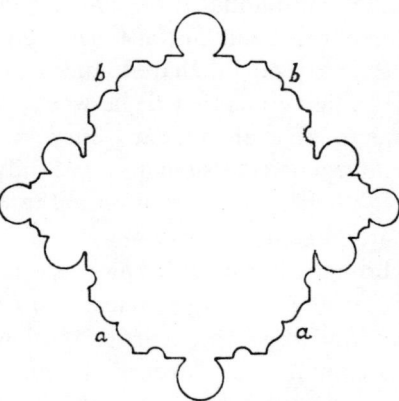

FIG. 137 — Canterbury Nave.

in its flying buttresses, some appearance of Gothic, the nave of Canterbury has little of the character of a true Gothic system; and in its enclosing walls, notwithstanding the magnitude of their openings, it manifests its Anglo-Norman character.

The nave of the large parish church of St. Mary Redcliffe at Bristol, built about the middle of the fifteenth century, embodies this phase of the Perpendicular style with marked differences of proportion and detail. The vaulting is a variant of that of York choir, differing mainly in having no longitudinal ridge rib, and the springing of the tierceron of the lateral cell from its usual place in the main impost instead of from the higher impost of the longitudinal rib. This brings it out farther in the conoid so that the vault surface between it and the longitudinal rib is strongly ploughshared, and the curves of the transverse ribs, and the tiercerons that lie between them and the groin ribs, are such as to give an outward curve to the conoid section. The ribs interpenetrate so as to leave only their soffit mouldings free at the impost, and are thus gathered upon a group of excessively attenuated supports — which are merely the same soffit mouldings brought down to the pier bases, the impost being marked by a narrow moulding in place of a capital. A larger shaft on either side of this group carries the longitudinal rib, and this shaft has a capital at the level of the main vaulting impost, although the rib it carries is stilted, and its true impost is thus at a higher level, and is continuous. It hardly needs saying that thus to give a larger shaft to one of the smaller ribs in a vault, and to place a capital where none is required, omitting this member where it properly belongs, is a freakish and irrational mode of design. Next to the larger shaft is a group of mouldings, in total bulk equal to that which stands in the place of main vaulting shafts, rising from the pavement and passing into an arch with continuous imposts, which forms a middle order between the longitudinal rib of the vault and the archivolt of the clerestory opening. The lower mouldings of the first order of the ground-story archivolts are those of the inner part of the same group, and are continuous with them; but the other mouldings of this archivolt intersect those of the pier group. The mouldings of the pier on which these archivolts intersect are in high relief against the wall spandrel, and these archivolt mouldings are thus also necessarily so, and are, in fact, hood mouldings.[1] The archivolts have two lesser orders, of which the lower one is carried by a group of three shafts, each larger than any of those which carry the high vaulting, and the middle order is supported by one shaft on each side of the group of three. All of these archivolt shafts have capitals, and each shaft and group of mouldings in the pier has a member to itself in the compound base — which has no common plinth.

The now usual scheme of combined clerestory and triforium is carried out here with an opening that fills the whole width of the bay, and the mullions in this case are brought down to intersect the extrados of the great archivolt of the ground story. It will be seen from this analysis that while the opening fills the whole bay so that practically no wall remains (a condition seldom reached in English building) yet the structure does not become a logical organic skeleton. Its parts have no proper and expressive adaptation to their functions, and the characteristic dryness of the Perpendicular style is more marked here than usual. Externally the buttresses are crowned with tall pinnacles, and a system of flying buttresses reinforces the piers. The pitch of the roof is very low (a common characteristic of Perpendicular design), so that an open parapet which surmounts the cornice is outlined against the sky.

The great Norman nave of Norwich Cathedral was vaulted (circa 1463–1472) in the Perpendicular style. This vaulting is much like that of the the nave of Exeter, with the addition of liernes at the crown, but this addition greatly changes the form of the vault. The curvatures and adjustments of the principal ribs are such as to produce in the conoid a nearly semicircular middle section, and by means of the liernes the form is made rectangular at the crown. The longitudinal ridge rib is level and only two of the principal ribs meet this rib in unbroken curves. The others cannot meet it, since they are all, except the transverse rib, of longer span, which would bring them up to higher levels, while the transverse rib, having a shorter span, would fall lower. These other ribs are, therefore, con-

---

[1] It is not easy to make such details intelligible without elaborate lettered illustrations, but the time and labour necessary to make them would be greater than the importance of such architectural composition would justify. In the building itself, or with a photograph, they may be readily followed.

nected with the ridge rib by liernes. That is to say, their continuous curves come to an end before the crown of the vault is reached, and a short piece, which, for want of a better term, I may call a lierne, meeting each of them at an angle, and reaching to the crown, is inserted. It is remarkable that the principal ribs, *i.e.* the transverse ribs and the groin ribs, should be thus broken and consequently weakened. This would endanger the stability of the vault were it not that the other ribs (which in normal vaulting would be superfluous) retain their continuous curves. The tiercerons of the lateral cells all meet the transverse ridge rib without being broken, but in order that they may do so, this ridge rib has to be arched in elevation on an inclined chord; for, since the tiercerons must be of different lengths, they reach, necessarily, different levels, falling away in height from the crown of the vault to the crown of the clerestory arch.

A very different form of Perpendicular vaulting occurs in St. George's Chapel, Windsor, dating from the close of the fifteenth century. This vaulting is on four central arches, and has square conoids abutting on a flattened barrel vault which is equal in span to about one-third the width of the nave. The ribs appear to have all nearly the same curvature, but in order to shape the conoid to the horizontal straight edge of the barrel vault, liernes have to be adjusted to most of them. The middle rib of each conoid, occupying the place of a transverse rib, reaches naturally, without liernes, to the line of junction with the barrel vault, and is continuous with the curve of this vault; but as the groin rib, having necessarily a longer span, would, if continued unbroken, reach too high, it is stopped on a boss at a short distance below the top of the conoid — a lierne being inserted to connect it with a longitudinal rib which follows the edge of the barrel vault, and receives all of the ribs and liernes of the conoid. There are two tiercerons on either side of the transverse rib, and in order to connect these with the longitudinal rib, the first is stopped on a boss, where it is met by a pair of liernes which fork to meet the longitudinal rib, just mentioned, in bosses where the transverse rib and the second tierceron meet it. The second tierceron is made to reach the required height without a lierne by having the upper part of its curve straightened to almost a right line. A lierne from the boss of the groin rib to the one on which the second tierceron meets completes one-half of that face of the conoid which is parallel with the long axis of the vault. In the lateral cells no liernes are used to lengthen the ribs, and thus, as they have the same curvature while differing in span, they reach different levels — falling away in height from the intersection of the groins to the crown of the longitudinal arch. The crown of each cell is thus in elevation a curve on an inclined chord, as at Norwich. The middle part of the vault, which has the shallow cylindrical form, is decorated with a maze of liernes, and with pendants suspended from its crown. The great eastern opening fills the whole width of the nave, and its four-centred archivolt is concentric with the vaulting. St. George's has aisles, and the architectural treatment of the bay system is a variant of that of St. Mary Redcliffe, reinforced by a system of flying buttresses.

It is not worth while to consider further this phase of Perpendicular design — which is embodied in few other entire vaulted buildings. We may therefore now turn to the later developments in which what is known as fan vaulting occurs. This form of vaulting appears first, I believe, in the cloister of Gloucester Cathedral, and dates from about 1381 to 1412.[1] Willis defines fan vaulting as that in which the radiating ribs are all of the same curvature and elevation, so that the conoid (which he calls the spandrel solid) becomes a solid of revolution — the ribs being bounded at the crown of the vault by a horizontal semicircular rib, and every horizontal section being semicircular. The spaces between the semicircles are flat, or nearly

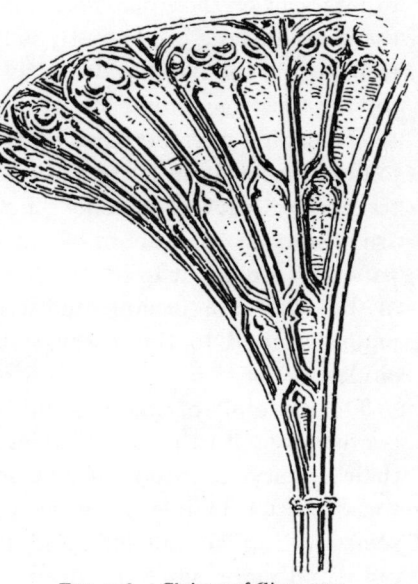

FIG. 138 — Cloister of Gloucester

---

[1] Cf. Willis, "On the Construction of the Vaults of the Middle Ages," p. 55, published in the *Transactions of the Royal Institute of British Architects*, London, 1842.

flat, panels of large stone slabs. In the conoids of Gloucester (Fig. 138) only three of the radiating ribs, namely, those which correspond to the longitudinal and transverse ribs in normal ribbed vaulting, start from the impost of the vault. Another rib, midway between these, starts from a diminutive arch of double flexure which spans the interval at a short distance above the impost, as in the north side of the vaulting of the nave of Worcester (cf. p. 175), two more ribs start from similar arches a little higher up, and four smaller ones spring from as many more arches at a still higher level. The head of each interval between the primary and secondary ribs is filled with an arch embracing a trefoiled panel, and a pair of smaller arches is formed between the secondary and tertiary ribs. In other words, the ornamental skeleton of the upper part of each conoid is composed like the mullions and tracery of the window openings in the so-called Decorated style, save that the secondary ribs are carried through the imposts (as the mullions in Decorated tracery would not be) to intersect on the great horizontal semicircular rib that bounds the conoid at the crown. In such vaulting the rib system ceases to be an independent skeleton sustaining the vault, and becomes, for the most part, mere surface ornament. Here the lower part of the conoid and the parts near the crown are constructed of jointed masonry, in large stones on which the simulated ribs and tracery are carved in relief; but between these parts the ribs are still made in skeleton — the intervals being filled with large panels of stone cut to fit them. The flat surfaces at the crown of the vault are ornamented with cusped circular panels, and panels shaped to the intervals between these and the conoid circles.

The principle of shaping and adjusting the parts of a vault in conformity with the simple demands of construction — making their beauty to reside primarily in the artistic expression of function (a principle never very strictly observed, as we have seen, by English builders, and from which they had departed more and more, since the twelfth century) finds here no embodiment. The designer now works with an artificially ornamental purpose, and his methods, having no foundation in straightforward principles of construction, are fanciful and capricious. But while his methods are not based on natural modes of construction, they are governed, as the methods of the older builders were not, by a conscious science. The vault builders of the fifteenth and sixteenth centuries were mathematicians, and their mathematical science led them into pedantry, which often finds expression in what may be called architectural jugglery — as in the pendants of Henry VII's Chapel at Westminster. The great art of the Middle Ages was wrought largely by what modern architects would call rule of thumb. Very little science of geometry or of statics were needed by the mediæval craftsman. His processes were based mainly on a quick instinct of construction, guided by experience, and by artistic judgment and imagination; and with the works that he thus achieved science and mechanical methods have produced nothing to compare.

A variant of the vaulting of the cloister of Gloucester occurs in the east end of Peterborough, dating from about 1440. But the conoids of this vaulting do not remain complete all the way up, as they do at Gloucester, and they do not, therefore, trace full half circles on plan. They interpenetrate toward the crown, and each having three horizontal circular ribs, instead of only one, the interpenetration begins at the level of the lowest of these ribs — which accordingly is the only one that traces a complete half circle on the plan. Where the conoids intersect a reëntrant groin is formed, which in elevation is necessarily curved and inclined upward from the wall toward the centre of the vault. The main ribs here all spring from the vault impost, and, interpenetrating, are gathered on the capital of a single vaulting shaft. The tracery between the ribs has more cusps than at Gloucester, and a series of crocket-like ornaments is ranged on the outer circumference of each circular rib. The total effect is thus more florid than that of the Gloucester vaulting.

A notable instance of fan vaulting, and on a larger scale, is that of King's College Chapel at Cambridge, dating from 1513. Here pronounced transverse ribs, in the form of depressed four-centred arches, divide the vaulting into rectangular compartments, and the number of horizontal semicircular ribs is increased to four. To form supports the transverse ribs are carried down the wall, without change of profile, to corbels placed at about mid-height of the jambs — the impost being marked by very small mouldings instead of capitals. The wall spaces between the windows are of considerable width, and are panelled beneath the corbels. The windows have continuous imposts, and reach only a little way above the vaulting impost. A horizontal moulding passes through the crowns of their arches, the lunettes above are ornamented with blind arcading, the spandrels with blind tracery, and the splayed jambs and arch soffit are panelled. In this single-aisled building, wholly constructed in the advanced Perpendicular style, the great eastern window has its archivolt concentric with the arch of the vault, and the mullions all intersect the arch. Externally a series of

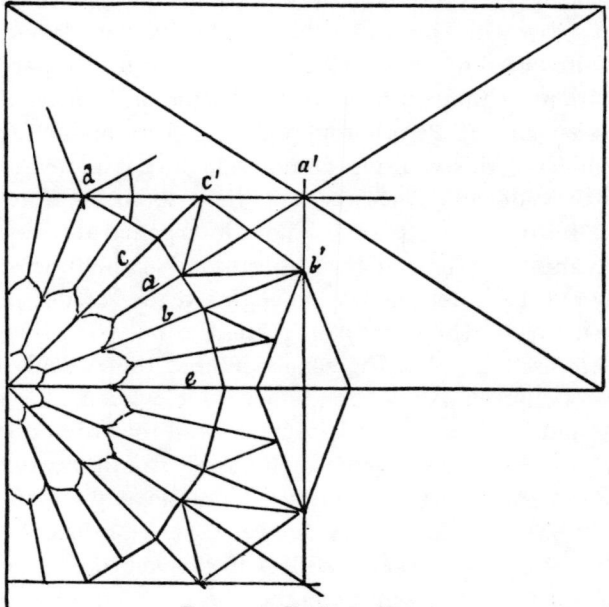

FIG. 139—Sherborne Nave.

vigorous buttresses, with pronounced set-offs, and capped with tall pinnacles, stands against the walls.

In the nave of Sherborne we have (Fig. 139) a combination of fan vaulting and lierne vaulting, dating from the close of the fifteenth century. Sherborne was a Norman structure, but was almost entirely rebuilt in the later Perpendicular style. The fans in this case are polygonal on plan, the panels being straight sided at the crown, since the semicircular horizontal rib is replaced by a series of short straight ones set on the curve. In the radiating ribs the scheme of the Gloucester cloister recurs in the lesser members starting from diminutive arches between the greater ones. The lierne part may be described as a very shallow barrel vault with cross cells, but with irregular surfaces, since its conformation is given by the network of ribs, of varying inclination and curvature, on which it rests. There are a level longitudinal ridge rib and transverse ridge ribs; the latter, since they must start from the lower level of the fans and pass through the longitudinal ridge rib, are slightly arched. The small rib, $a$, of the fan falls where a groin rib, in normal vaulting, would come, and this, and the corresponding ribs of the other fans, are produced so as to form segmental diagonal arches intersecting in the longitudinal ridge rib. The larger rib, $b$, is prolonged to meet the longitudinal ridge rib in $b'$, and the rib $c$ is carried on to meet the transverse ridge rib in $c'$. These ribs being all of the same curvature but of different lengths, reach to different levels, and the point $c'$ is thus lower than the point $a'$ and higher than the point $d$, where the transverse ridge rib starts from between the fans, and since this last rib must pass through these points, it assumes necessarily the rampant arch form. The rib $e$ occupies on plan the place of a transverse rib, but it cannot be produced, without change of curvature, to meet the longitudinal ridge rib because, the span being shorter, it would not reach high enough. A lierne of steeper inclination, forming an angle with it, is therefore joined on to it. The numerous other liernes, of varying lengths and inclinations, divide the vault into very small panels which, together with the panels of the fan conoids, are filled with small stones, each reaching from rib to rib, instead of the large stones, each filling a whole panel, as in most other fan vaulting.

There is no developed pier in Sherborne, but a considerable strip of thick wall with a member of prismatic section on its face, having three round mouldings and a compound capital for the vault support, rises from the pavement, and the clerestory archivolt mouldings are brought down continuously to the triforium ledge. The mullions of the clerestory are brought down over the triforium wall, as at York and elsewhere, and a deep-splayed and panelled reveal takes the place of a passageway. The ground-story piers and archivolts are heavy and continuous, with two splayed orders, the jambs and soffits, as well as the splays, being panelled. The walls of the clerestory give a considerable external reveal, and a simple buttress reinforces the wall.

In the choir of Bath Abbey (circa 1500–1539) the fans are semicircular on plan, and meet on the long axis of the vault, but intersect transversely, as in King's College Chapel. Here again a wall with a deep splay takes the place, above the ground story, of a proper pier, but a vaulting shaft is set against it rising from the pavement. The scheme of the combined clerestory and triforium, which had become so common in the Perpendicular style, is here replaced by one great opening reaching from the ground story to the crown of the vault — the roof of the aisle being now of such low pitch as to eliminate the triforium as a stage in the composition. The ground-story pier has a member with the brace profile (cf. Fig. 132, p. 189) on either side which passes continuously into the archivolt. At the impost of the great arcade the vaulting shafts are banded with a ring of mouldings, and similar mouldings mark the impost of a member with hollowed bevels on the soffit of the archivolt. The great archivolts are four-centred, and have ogee hood moulds, which intersect the vaulting shafts, dying away on their surfaces just above the impost.

Very steep flying buttresses with pierced spandrels rise over the aisles, and the great development of the clerestory, suppressing the triforium, as we have just seen, gives an unusual proportionate height to the building above the aisle roof. Bath Abbey Church is, I think, in external aspect, one of the happiest compositions in the Perpendicular style. The parts are finely proportioned, and in the general view from the northeast it has great dignity of aspect. The angle buttresses of the transept rise grandly from the ground, and the upright lines of the crossing tower carry out the aspiring expression. Few other monuments of this epoch seem to me so fine in total external effect.

Another phase of the Perpendicular style is embodied in Henry VII's Chapel of Westminster, begun in 1502. It is hard to speak in measured terms of such a composition. It appears to me an instance of mechanical jugglery in which every noble quality of architecture is sacrificed to constructive pedantry and ornamental excess without any fine quality of ornament. Its fan vaulting manifests great science in far-fetched construction designed to trick the eye, and great skill in the mechanical art of stone cutting; but of rational composition it

## THE PERPENDICULAR STYLE

has none. An earlier instance of a similar scheme is found in the Oxford Divinity School (1445–1480), where heavy transverse ribs, in the form of depressed four-centred arches, are visible, as in normal vaulting, throughout their entire span, and give some sense of security, notwithstanding the conoid pendants which puzzle and disquiet the beholder who does not readily perceive the principle on which they are made secure. Here at Westminster the transverse ribs (which are pointed arches) pierce the vault where they meet the pendants and disap-

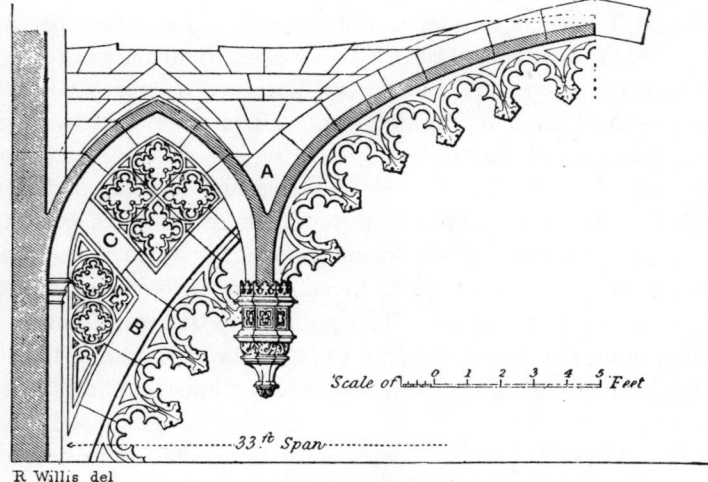

FIG. 140 — Henry VII's Chapel.

pear from view. The wall conoids are of the same magnitude as the pendants, and both have the springing level high above that of the transverse ribs (each of which would be one of the ribs of a larger conoid in ordinary fan vaulting), and thus these ribs become free skeleton arches between the pendants and the walls. The section (Fig. 140) shows the principle of construction.[1] The lower part of the pendant A is a voussoir of the transverse rib B, which, beyond the pendant, does not appear on the under side of the vault. This pendant, the security of which so puzzles the general beholder, really strengthens the vault by weighting its haunch in much the same way that filling the pockets does in normal vaulting, and between the pendant and the springing the transverse rib, being free of the vault, is

[1] Figure 140 is reproduced from Willis.

stiffened by the branch C, which rises to meet the wall conoid, and by the tracery with which the intervals are filled. The masonry of the upper part of the pendant is, of course, built up from the part which is keyed into the transverse rib, and is thus suspended only in appearance. In principle of construction the scheme is sound, though involved; but as architectural composition it is indefensible. For it may, I think, be affirmed as a principle that in architecture stability must be apparent, as well as real. These hanging masses of masonry, if not actually disturbing to the beholder, only excite wonder as to how they are held up, but such wonder is not a feeling that noble architecture tends to awaken. In good architecture structural forms and adjustments are not unnecessarily elaborate, nor are they needlessly concealed or falsified in appearance. They are straightforward and intelligible.

The longitudinal ribs of this vaulting are depressed, four-centred arches with continuous imposts, their supports having the same profile carried down to the pavement. The archivolts of the openings are sub-orders to these ribs with their mouldings also carried down the jambs. The main supports are, as in the preceding monuments of the Perpendicular style, narrow strips of wall on which these members are worked, rather than well-composed piers.

Henry VII's Chapel has aisles with flying buttresses over them. The great outer buttresses are octagonal on plan — an unsuitable form, since it does not offer resistance in the direction of the vault thrusts, with economy as to bulk; and does not express the direction of the thrust to which it is opposed as the narrow rectangular Gothic buttress does. The flying buttress has two arches with pierced spandrels, and with tracery in the interval between them. The back of the upper one is shaped to an upward curve where it meets the slender clerestory wall buttress, with which it thus becomes tangent. This abutment reaches only to about the level of the springing of the conoids, but the system is weighted with a heavy attic wall.

In the general outside view an instructive comparison is afforded with the nobler early work. Viewed from the southeast the simple and expressive forms of the great choir and transept may be seen in contrast with this overwrought and shapeless work of an architecturally uninspired age.[1]

The choir vault of Oxford Cathedral is a curious variant of both the Divinity School and Henry VII's Chapel. The transverse ribs, which appear to be semicircular, pierce the vault at the pendants, as at Westminster. These ribs, below the pendants, have solid spandrels, and from these a very short segmental section of barrel vaulting on ribs is sprung against the wall in each bay. There are thus no wall conoids. The fan pendants, which are, of course, keyed into the great transverse ribs, as in the Divinity School and Henry VII's Chapel, are not bounded at the top by a horizontal semicircular rib. They are, however, in other respects, true fans, having their ribs all of the same curvature (two-centred curves) up to the level, where they would usually meet a circular horizontal rib. At this level they are connected with liernes which follow the same direction on plan and intersect a longitudinal ridge rib and transverse ridge ribs. These liernes, being of different lengths, are inclined at slightly different angles with the respective fan ribs, and shorter liernes, set obliquely between them, form a network pattern at the crown of the vault.

It is not worth while to follow the capricious variations of such vaulting any farther, but we may in the next chapter give some attention to the timber roofing that so often took the place of vaulting in the English Perpendicular style.

[1] The entire exterior of Henry VII's Chapel is now the work of the modern restorer, but it reproduces, I believe quite faithfully, the original work of the early sixteenth century.

# CHAPTER X

### TIMBER ROOFS

In England during the Middle Ages extensive use was made of timber roofs without vaulting. Such roofs are of three kinds : (1) those having a form that simulates stone vaulting, (2) trussed roofs with tie beams, and (3) imperfectly trussed roofs without tie beams. The first class need not detain us, since roofs of this kind are both exceptional and abnormal. To fashion a wooden roof in a form proper to stone vaulting, as at York and St. Albans, is to violate every principle of timber construction, and of reasonable design. The only right manner of building a timber roof is that of straightforward trussing which meets every tendency to deformation, and subjects the supporting walls to crushing weight only. This requires the use of a tie beam.

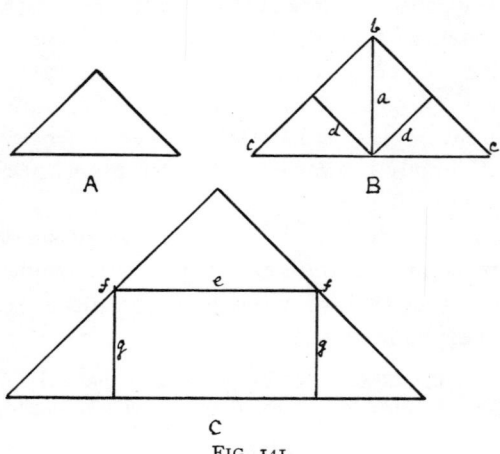

FIG. 141.

In examining the timber roofs of the Middle Ages the following elementary considerations should be kept in mind : the simplest form of truss is composed of three members put together in the form of a triangle (A, Fig. 141), the horizontal member forming a tie, and having no other function. But a truss of this simple form may, in a roof of any considerable span, be deformed by flexion. The tie beam may sag. To prevent this (B, Fig. 141) a king post $a$ is suspended from the point $b$ and pinned, or strapped, to the tie beam, which is thus held up. The rafters $bc$ may also be long enough to sag, in which case struts $d$ will be required to brace them. These struts are firmly supported at the base of the king post, since the point $b$, from which the king post is suspended, is immovable so long as the feet of the rafters remain secured to the tie beam. Over wider spans more members may be required, and a collar beam $e$ (C, Fig. 141) may be inserted, which acts both as a tie and as a brace. Then from the points $f$, which are immovable so long as the great triangle is securely pinned together, queen posts $g$ may be suspended to hold up the tie beam in two points. Many other parts may be required according to circumstances, but in sound roof construction trusses are always composed on this principle.

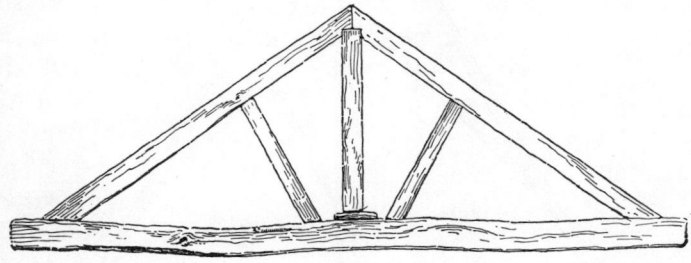

FIG. 142 — Grasmere.

In England during the Middle Ages the function of the tie beam appears not to have been well understood. A marked illustration of this is found in the rude trussing of the small parish church of Grasmere [1] (Fig. 142), where it will be seen that the king post instead of being suspended, so as to hold up the tie beam, is made to rest upon it — a block being interposed like a rude base of a column. In place of struts, set in the angles formed by the king post, where, if the beam were properly held up, they would find unyielding points of support, they are, like the king post, made to rest on the beam, and at some distance from the king post.

The English carpenters of the Middle Ages appear thus to have regarded the tie beam as a support for the king post, and also for other members of the framework, as at Charney, Berk-

[1] I do not know the date of this truss. It may well be modern, but it illustrates the kind of misunderstanding of the function of the tie beam that is found, in one form or another, in many mediæval English churches.

P

shire (Fig. 143), where the king post reaches only to a collar beam and carries a longitudinal beam and four struts — two of them in the plane of the truss, and the other two perpendicular to it, so as to brace the roof in the longitudinal direction. Used in this way the tie beam requires to be enormously heavy, and it is often, as in this case, slightly arched in order to increase its rigidity. But properly, being subject to tension only, it need not be heavy, and may be very light. On

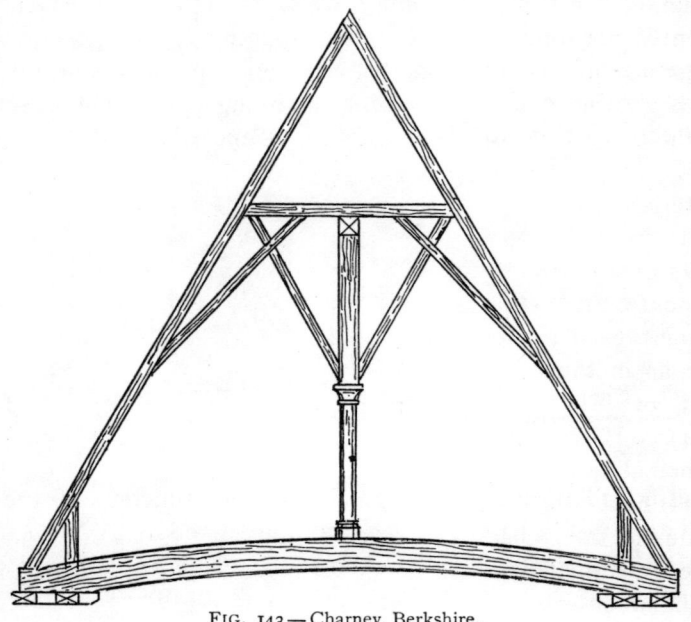

FIG. 143 — Charney, Berkshire.

such misuse of the tie beam Viollet le Duc remarks: "On concevra que des constructeurs qui comprenaient si mal la fonction de l'entrait aient cherché à se priver de ce membre."[1] And accordingly we find that from the fourteenth century, when the construction of ornamental timber roofs became a great preoccupation of the English builders, the tie beam rarely appears. Moreover, it is evident, from the numerous roofs remaining, that a gabled, or an arched, form was preferred for the general outline of the under side of the roof, and on this account also they sought combinations which would enable them to dispense with the tie beam, at first by reliance on collar beams and inclined

[1] *Dictionnaire Raisonné de l'Architecture Française*, s.v. Charpente, p. 36.

ties, and later by an elaborate system of triangulation which overcame thrust, though at an enormous cost of labour and material. Thus a great variety of ornamental timber roofs were produced in England, many of which are admirable specimens of ingenious carpentry, though not of straightforward and economical construction and consequently not of the finest art. The finest art is not tortuous in method, or needlessly prodigal of material.

In many cases roofs were framed without either collar beams or diagonal ties, as in the transept of Ely (Fig. 144). Here the principal rafters are stiffened against flexure by the arched piece *a* framed into a hammer-beam *b* and a short king post *c*. There is a ridge beam *d*, two purlins *e*, and two wall plates *f*. The spandrels are filled with upright planks, which contribute to the rigidity of the rafters.

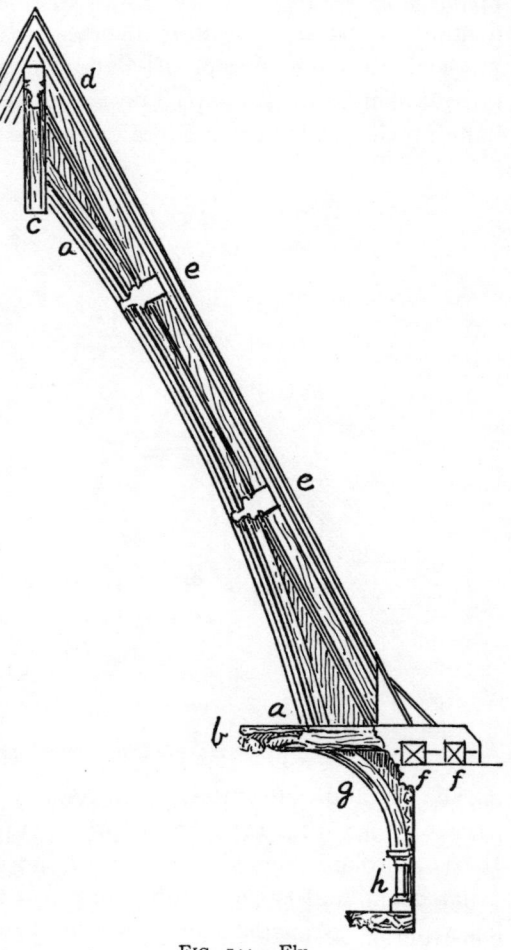

FIG. 144—Ely.

Such trussing has no effect against thrust, the two sides acting against each other just as two plain rafters would act, and they depend for stability on the strength of the heavy Norman walls, against which their thrusts must be powerful, notwithstanding the high pitch given them. To prevent pushing off the wall the brace *g* (which also supports the hammer-beam) and the wall post *h* serve. At Brinton, Norfolk, a simplified variant of the roof scheme of Ely transept occurs. Here the curved members are each of one solid piece of timber shaped so as to fit against the rafter, and against the wall, like a knee of a ship. In this manner the hammer-beam is dispensed with. At St. Stephen's, Norwich, the schemes of Ely and Brinton are combined, the knee timber being supported on a hammer-beam, and, far overhanging the wall, stopping against a post framed into the ham-

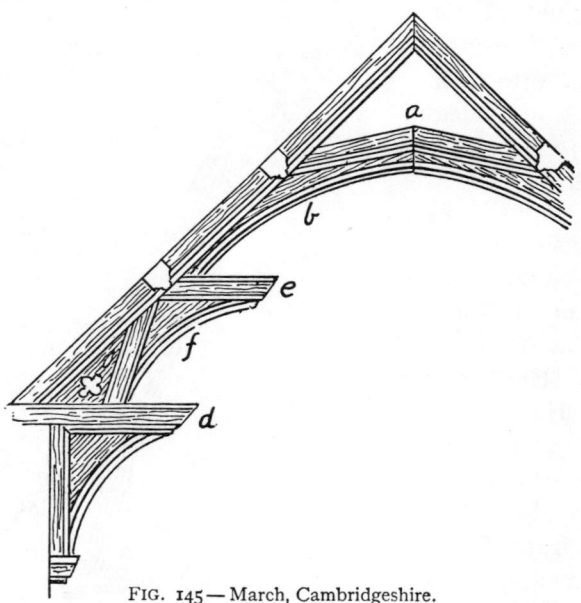

FIG. 145 — March, Cambridgeshire.

mer-beam and the rafter. At March, Cambridgeshire, we have a truss (Fig. 145) of singularly unreasoned composition. It has a broken member *a*, shaped to an angle, in the place of a collar beam, and is thus ineffectual as a tie. Beneath this is a knee piece *b*, reaching only to the lower purlin *c*, where it stops against the principal rafter. The hammer-beam *d* supports an inclined brace reaching to the lower purlin, and a second hammer-beam *e*, which has no function, is supported by a knee piece *f*. There can be no wonder that such a combination has had to be secured by strong iron ties. An arrangement (Fig. 146) illustrated by Viollet le Duc[1] is hardly more

[1] S.v. *Charpente*, Fig. 29.

rational. The member *a*, pinned into the rafter, receives the abutting ends of the arched pieces, but little strength is given to the rafter by such a combination, and there is again no tie whatever. The arrangement would be effective against upward pressure on the rafter, but is ineffective in the direction in which rigidity is required; and there is no effective security against thrust in the truss as a whole. Wandswell Court, Gloucester, has a roof that is trussed in a better manner. The collar beam here (Fig. 147) is straight, and is placed low enough to act somewhat effectively as a tie ; and this, together with the heavy-arched knee timber secured to its under side, and reaching

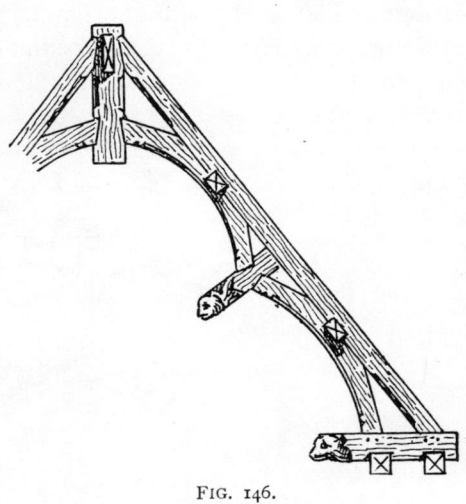

FIG. 146.

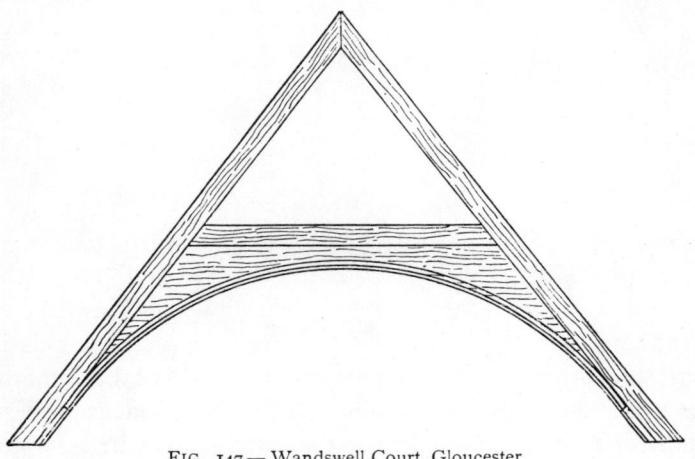

FIG. 147 — Wandswell Court, Gloucester.

down almost to the feet of the rafters, to which it is securely fixed, makes a combination that is practically unyielding. But such a truss is practicable on a small scale only, since each member must be of a single piece of very heavy timber. The

Hall of Sutton Courtenay, Berkshire (Fig. 148), has a broken member shaped to an angle, as at March, with heavy curved timbers beneath, forming a pointed arch. Higher up is a straight collar beam with short braces reaching to the rafters. A king post supports a longitudinal beam just beneath the

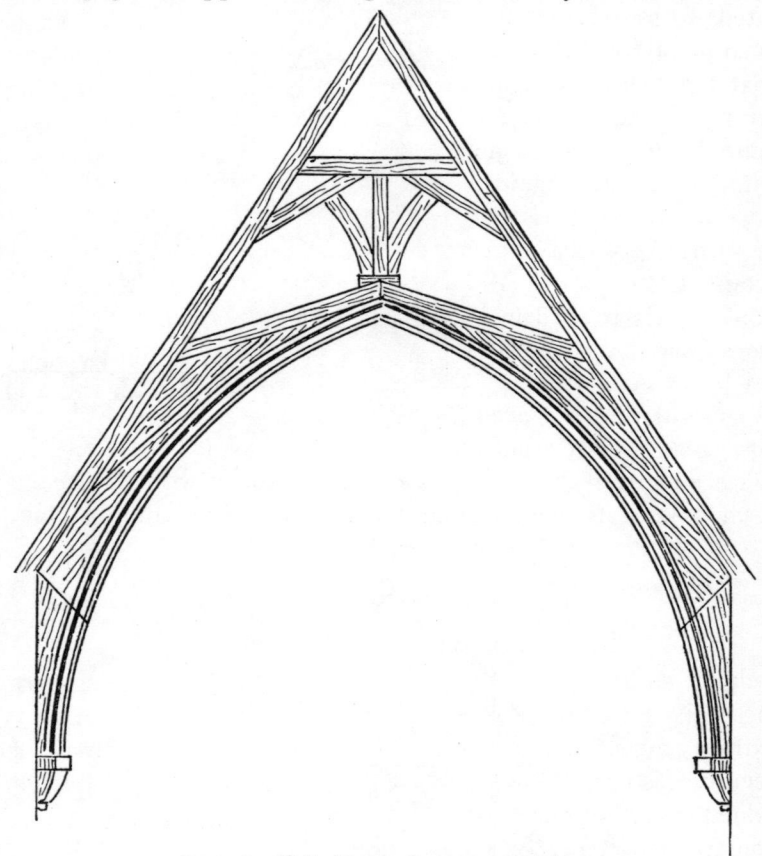

FIG. 148 — Hall of Sutton Courtenay, Berkshire.

collar, and struts from this post meet the collar braces. The true principle of the truss finds little embodiment here. A variant of this occurs in Nursted Court, Kent, where supports from the floor rise to the purlins, and the arched timbers spring from these supports.[1] Figure 149, from Malvern Priory, is an ornamental example on the principle of a collar tie which, on a small scale, with heavy timbers and strong tenons, may be secure

[1] Figured in Parker's *Domestic Architecture of England*, Oxford, 1859.

enough; but all contrivances for doing away with the tie beam are either vicious in principle, or wasteful of labour and material.

The great roof of Westminster Hall [1] is securely trussed without a tie beam. A collar beam firmly ties the upper part of this elaborate truss, and the parts below are so effectively triangulated, so strongly framed into the upper part, and the whole is so powerfully stiffened by filling with small upright members, that the roof acts on the walls with little more than crushing

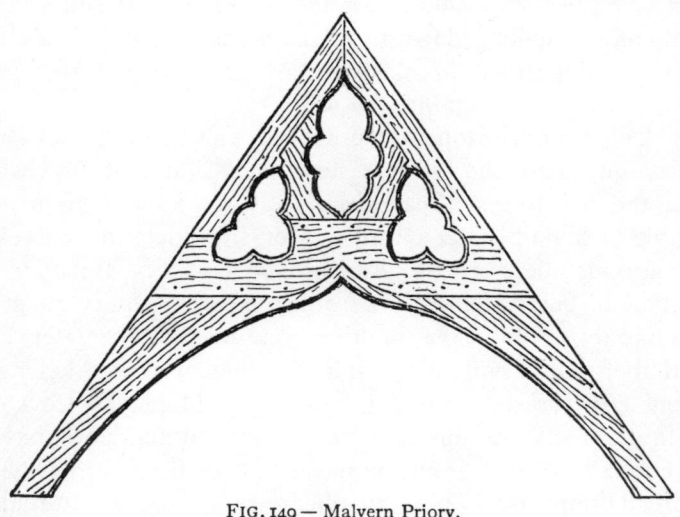

FIG. 149 — Malvern Priory.

weight; so enormous is this weight, however, that the supporting walls have to be of great thickness. But while on this extravagant principle the roof of Westminster Hall may be secure, it is not, I think, good design, because its strength is obtained in an indirect way. The true principles of timber roof construction are embodied in the basilican churches of Rome, and in the numerous derivatives of these churches in Western Europe. The roofs of these churches are light, and have no thrust, so that the thin, unbuttressed walls support them perfectly. The pitch of such a roof may be high or low, as conditions may require, and the use and combination of posts, struts, and collar beams may vary considerably according to span and pitch, but no departure from the principle on which they are framed is compatible with sound construction or good art.

[1] Analyzed and illustrated by Viollet le Duc, s.v. *Charpente*, pp. 41 *et seq.*

Timber roofs of better form are sometimes met with in England, as at St. Michael's, Coventry, where, although the pitch is low for a northern climate, the truss is properly constructed with a tie beam, which appears to be held up by a suspended king post. A ridge beam with two purlins on either side form, together with the rafters and the external covering, an agreeable panelled ceiling. In St. Margaret's, Westminster, a wooden roof of still lower pitch has transverse beams shaped to the double incline, and beneath them are solid knee timbers meeting in the middle and extending down the walls on either side. They thus form very depressed four-centred arches. Such a roof must exert strong thrusts against the walls.

At Chipping Norton, Oxfordshire, a true form of truss occurs, but with the useless addition of arched braces beneath the tie beam. Apart from this we have here a good example of a simple open timber roof, in which the necessary structural members alone give an agreeable effect. But churches designed to carry timber roofs alone do not require substructures like those that have vaulting, yet most of the later English timber-roofed buildings retain the members that belong to vaulted structures. Chipping Norton, St. Michael's, Coventry, St. Margaret's, Westminster, Cirencester, and many others have vaulting shafts rising from the pavement, or from corbels above the arcade imposts. These members are, indeed, so attenuated as to suggest an ornamental, rather than a structural purpose — which, as we have seen, is the case also in most English vaulted churches. But for timber roofs no such supports are wanted; such roofs are securely carried by the walls. It is true, as we have seen, that they are frequently found in unvaulted Norman structures, but this, as we have also seen, is apparently due to misunderstanding of the use of such members. The trusses do, indeed, bear more heavily on the walls than the intervening parts of the roof, and in good construction the places where they fall are, therefore, fortified by larger blocks, or templates, of hard stone, which distribute the weight enough to prevent disintegration that might result from too much pressure on single points, especially when the walls are built of brick or small stones. And it may be well to mark these reinforcements by shaping them into corbels, but there is no propriety in groups of shafts like those which the ribs of stone vaulting call for.

A model of excellence in the design and construction of a great timber-roofed church of the Middle Ages is that of San Francesco of Siena. A grandly proportioned nave without aisles and a transept at the extreme east end are there covered with a timber roof of admirable character. The tie beams of the trusses rest on short wooden corbel blocks, but the walls beneath are unbroken save by narrow pointed windows high above the pavement. The architectural character of the building depends entirely on its noble proportions, and on the simple structural framing of its open roof. Notwithstanding that it is now despoiled of the fresco painting with which its walls were formerly illuminated, it is still a grand and impressive interior.

I do not know of any timber roofs in England formed on so excellent a model.

# CHAPTER XI

### CONCLUDING SUMMARY

I THINK it will be seen from the foregoing analyses that in the mediæval church architecture of England the principles of Norman art, introduced by the conquerors, formed the local building habits so completely that all later influences from other sources were powerless to modify them essentially. Even the great importation of Canterbury failed to produce, in the works which followed it, any material change in the established modes of building. In our examination of the round arched Norman art we found a lack of structural logic so constant as to become a characteristic of the style, and the inconsistencies of this earlier art were, as we saw, carried over into the Early English, which, therefore, never became a logical style. No appreciation which ignored these facts can present the mediæval architecture of England in a true light.

Yet the so-called Early English style, like the older Norman style has, I think, qualities that are worthy of great admiration, which I would fain set forth, if I could, in a way that would help to make them justly felt. This style is not, in any sense, either a copy of French Gothic, or a result of merely engrafting French details on Anglo-Norman structure. Its characteristic details, as well as its structural system, are, as we have seen, entirely unlike those of the French Gothic. Whatever the Anglo-Normans derived from the French source was, in Early English, recast according to their own genius, and so completely transformed as to lose its French character. But nevertheless the changes which made the Early English style out of the Norman were largely determined by the French influence, mainly through Canterbury. It may be well here to recapitulate the main points of likeness between Lincoln (in which the first strong manifestation of the changes appear) and Canterbury, to summarize the distinctive features of Early English, and briefly to consider what may be called the Early English ideal.

## CONCLUDING SUMMARY

The plan of Lincoln follows that of Canterbury in having two transepts and two small apses on the east side of each arm of the eastern transept, while the oblique sides of St. Hugh's apse recall the narrowing part of Canterbury choir. The sexpartite vaulting of Canterbury is followed in both transepts of Lincoln, though without the Canterbury logic in their relation to the piers — which are those of a uniform system, and thus unsuited to such vaulting. The vaulting shafts of the choir of Lincoln are single, as in the intermediate piers of Canterbury, but here also the logic of Canterbury is wanting, since each of these shafts is charged with a group of vault ribs, whereas in Canterbury there is only one. The ground-story piers of Lincoln choir were, before alteration, composed on the model of those piers of the oblique part of Canterbury in which four auxiliary shafts occur. The cross-section of this choir conforms to that of Canterbury choir almost exactly in essential particulars. The peculiar five-celled vaulting of the aisles of Canterbury is reproduced in the Lincoln aisles. The responds and the passageway of the Lincoln choir aisle follow substantially those of Trinity Chapel. Lincoln choir follows Canterbury, also, in the use of Purbeck shafting, in the banding [1] of the shafts, in the composition of the crossing piers of the eastern transept, in the obtuse pointing of the great archivolts, in having two orders in these archivolts, and in the absence of hood moulds over them. The triforium scheme, too, follows that of Canterbury, and the clerestory is a variant of that of William of Sens; this last, however, is, as we have seen, derived from the Norman Romanesque, and is quite unlike that of the French Gothic.[2] In nearly all of these points the architecture of Canterbury choir is unlike any preceding architecture of England, and that the occurrence of the same features in Lincoln is due to direct imitation, there can, I think, be no question;

---

[1] This banding of the shafts at Canterbury appears (by the profiling, and other points) to derive from Sens (cf. p. 104). I do not know when the banding of shafts first appeared in England, but there is a rude instance of it in the responds of the aisle of the Norman transept of Winchester, and there are, I believe, some other Norman instances.

[2] There are, in French Gothic, some exceptional instances of a clerestory ledge, with openings through the piers, for circulation, as in the early church of St. Germer de Fly, near Beauvais, and in Notre Dame of Dijon. But even these are very different from the Anglo-Norman clerestory passage between two walls.

and from Lincoln we have traced them, with minor variations, through the most characteristic Early English monuments.

The distinctive features of the Early English style have not, hitherto, been clearly and correctly set forth, largely because the essential structural forms, in their mutual relations throughout the whole system, have not been taken as the basis of analysis and description. Rickman, for instance, the first English writer of importance, tells us that this style is "distinguished by pointed arches, and long narrow windows, without mullions; and a peculiar ornament, which, from its resemblance to the teeth of a shark, we shall hereafter call the toothed ornament."[1] His fuller description which follows is given under the headings: Doors, Windows, Arches, Piers, Buttresses, Tablets, Niches, Ornaments, Steeples, Battlements (sic), Roofs, Fronts, and Porches. Such structural members as are included in this list are not considered as to their functional forms and relationships, but only in their ornamental character. Thus under Arches he tells us that the arch generally has the lancet form, and the great archivolts are deeply moulded, and often have the toothed ornament. Under Piers he explains that they have two distinguishing marks: division by bands, and an arrangement of the shafts for the most part in a circle. Among uncommon forms, he adds, are those which consist of shafts, some of which are plain rounds, others filleted rounds, and some "whose plan is a spherical triangle (sic) with the edge outwards." He then remarks that the capitals of these shafts are various, and describes their leading forms, and those of the bases also. Under buttresses he says that there are four kinds, the flat buttress, not so broad as the Norman, often with small shafts on the angles; a narrower buttress, sometimes with one set-off, and sometimes without any, often with chamfered edges, and sometimes with angle shafts between the tablets; a long slender buttress, of narrow face and great projection in a few stages; and toward the latter part of the style a buttress was used which is distinguished by its triangular head, and he adds, " Now began to be used the flying buttress, of which Salisbury (sic) and Chichester cathedrals present various fine examples." All that he has to say about vaulting is under the heading Roofs, and the

[1] Thomas Rickman, F.S.A., *An Attempt to Discriminate the Styles of Architecture in England*, fourth edition, London, 1838.

vaulting of Salisbury is said to be the best specimen. It is described as having "cross springers, and the rib from pier to pier, but it has no rib running longitudinally or across at the point of the arches." He then describes very briefly, and not more clearly, a few other kinds of vaulting in which additional ribs occur, and merely remarks on them that the "rib mouldings of these groins are not very large, and consist of rounds and hollows, and often have the toothed ornament." In the whole description there is no word about the structural use of the pointed arch, no suggestion of any functional motive for the composition of the pier, no hint of the relation of the buttress to the vaulting, no remark on the purpose of the rib system in a vault, or on the significance of the various adjustments of the ribs, or the conformation of the vault surface.[1] Parker,[2] and most other English writers of the nineteenth century, follow Rickman's method. Sharpe[3] amplified Rickman's system, indeed, but did not depart from his method; and in his description of what he calls the Lancet style, *i.e.* the earlier phase of Rickman's Early English, he confines himself almost equally to the unessential. Sharpe's headings are: The Buttress, The Base-Course, The Windows, The Parapet, The Piers, The Capitals, The Bases, The Pier Arches, The Hood Mouldings, The Vaulting Shafts, The Triforium Arch, Triforium Piers, The Vaulting, The Aisle Arcade. In describing these features no account is taken of structural functions and relations, and it is significant that while giving elaborate and finely engraved elevations of exterior and interior bays, the author includes no cross-sections to show the relation of the one to the other. Like most other writers hitherto, Continental as well as English, he describes the exterior parts of a building first; but since the interior of an organic vaulted structure determines the character

---

[1] I would not undervalue the work of Rickman. Though not a strong writer on architecture, he has the honour of being the first to recognize the importance of the study of the mediæval monuments of England, and of breaking ground in that field of study. His failure to grasp the essential principles of the buildings he described was natural under the conditions of taste and knowledge that prevailed in his time.

[2] John Henry Parker, C.B., *An Introduction to the Study of Gothic Architecture*, fourth edition, Oxford and London, 1874.

[3] Edmund Sharpe, M.A., *The Seven Periods of English Church Architecture Defined and Illustrated*, London, 1871.

of the outside, the proper order is to take the internal composition first.

The distinctive features of the Early English style may be shortly summarized as follows: —

1. On plan the east end is square, and the transept is considerably developed north and south.

2. The building is enclosed with walls in which the solids exceed the voids in area.

3. The vaulting is quadripartite in oblong compartments, and is furnished with a complete rib system, with the addition, in some cases, of a transverse, and a longitudinal, ridge rib. One or more tiercerons may also be included in each compartment. The principal ribs interpenetrate at the springing, and are thus gathered on a single capital, or a group of three capitals. The masonry of the vault is laid in nearly flat courses from rib to rib — the courses often tending in an oblique direction, so that they are not parallel at the crown. The longitudinal rib is not stilted, and the conoid thus widens as it rises against the clerestory wall — diffusing, instead of concentrating, the thrusts.

4. The high vaulting shafts, either single or in groups of three, are excessively slender, and each shaft, or group of shafts, rests on a corbel at a greater or less distance above the head of the ground-story pier.

5. The pier is not developed as a continuous member above the ground story. It consists of a column of coursed masonry, having a general outline, in horizontal section, either circular, or in the form of a square set diagonally, surrounded by freestanding shafts, banded in the middle, and answering to the orders of the great archivolts, and to the aisle vaulting.

6. The great archivolts are of three orders of rounded section, and are subdivided into small mouldings consisting of rounds, hollows, and fillets, and are embraced by a hood mould.

7. The triforium is open, exposing to view the timber roof over the aisle vaulting; and its arcade consists of a pair of arches of several orders in each bay, with a sub-order of two arches under each of the principal ones. This arcade is richly shafted, and its archivolts, like those of the ground story, have rounded sections and small mouldings.

8. The clerestory has a passageway in the thickness of the

wall, and the arcade of its inner plane has a tall arch in the middle, and one or two subordinate arches on either side, forming a group that conforms in outline with the longitudinal rib of the vault by which it is embraced. The archivolts here are moulded and shafted, as in the arcades below.

9. Externally a rectangular buttress is set against the aisle wall opposite each respond of the interior. This sometimes has angle shafts, and sometimes it is bevelled; it may be capped with a plain set-off just under the wall cornice, or it may have a gablet rising above the cornice. The base-courses and string-courses are returned around it, and on the angles of east ends and transepts such buttresses are set, one on each face, always perpendicular to the wall, so that on plan they meet at right angles and from between them, on the wall angle, a simple pinnacle rises.

10. On the clerestory wall plain flat pilaster buttresses, with angle rounds, mark the bays of the interior, and a plain cornice on a corbel-table crowns the wall. The external flying buttress is not a feature of the Early English style.

11. The clerestory and aisle openings are of two orders, of which the first is shafted and the second is plain, with a shallow reveal and a narrow splay. Where there are three openings in a bay, they are of two magnitudes, the middle one large and the others small, as in the inner plane of the clerestory. If the opening be single, it may be flanked by two blind arches. Aisle openings are sometimes in pairs, and all window openings are tall and narrow, and without mullions.

12. Eastern façades and transept ends conform in outline with the cross-sections of the parts they enclose. The wall between the angle buttresses is plain, and is pierced with openings like those of aisles and clerestories. These openings are usually in a group of three with the middle one the taller.

13. Capitals have round abaci with rounded mouldings, of which the top member is deeply undercut. The bell is of concave outline, and of two general types, with many variations of each. The first of these is foliated with trefoil leafage — the leaf ribs having a rectangular section. There are two principal forms of such capitals, one (the most distinctively Early English) without crockets, and the other with them. In the second type there is no foliation, the bell being simply moulded.

14. Bases are profiled with rounds and deep hollows, or a succession of rounds without hollows, and have round plinths.

15. Vault ribs tend to a rounded section, with mouldings of rounds and hollows, contrasted by fillets.

16. Wall surfaces, both internal and external, may be ornamented with sunk trefoils, or quatrefoils, and with shafted arcading.

17. The spirelets of pinnacles are plain, save for a crowning finial, and angle rounds.

These, I believe, are the main features that distinguish the Early English style. Of west fronts, and of towers and spires, examples in the pure style are too few to admit of any general characterization. Such west fronts as exist on a monumental scale are either posterior to the best period, as that of Salisbury, are incomplete, as that of Lincoln, or they differ so much one from another, as the fronts of Wells and Peterborough, that no typical composition can be gathered from them. Of pure Early English towers few, if any, are complete, and of spires there are none.

The characteristics here enumerated distinguish what may be called the ideal of the Early English style. But this ideal appears never to have been completely embodied in any single monument. Like that of the pure French Gothic, it must be gathered out of different buildings where its distinctive features are associated with more or less that is foreign to its nature. It is remarkable that the Middle Ages, notwithstanding their supremely noble achievements in architecture, never produced a monument which, like the Parthenon, embodied all the qualities of its style in harmonious perfection. Thus, in order to realize the Early English ideal, we must discriminate carefully, and supply from other sources what we find imperfectly characteristic in any given work. Influences were mixed, new ideas were circulating, and the art was constantly shaping into new forms. But the Early English style had, as M. Renan has said of the French Gothic, a classic moment, and it is this that we should endeavour to lay hold of. The pure style endured for a very limited period of time. It is, of course, impossible to fix with precision the duration of any phase of artistic production, but it may be said roughly that the style we are considering did not attain its full development before about 1220, when Salisbury and Worcester were begun, and did not endure after 1245, the time of the beginning of Westminster Abbey.

This Early English style in its integrity is, as I have said, a style of much beauty, notwithstanding the manifold structural inconsistencies which to a critical eye are manifest at a glance. But apart from what we may consider its artistic merits or defects, it is important that we should realize its essential difference from the Gothic of the Ile de France. Of this difference we have had, indeed, abundant illustration in the course of this work, but a direct comparison of two contemporaneous monuments may help to make it more clearly apparent. The cathedrals of Amiens and Salisbury, both begun in the year 1220, have often been cited as typical of their respective styles; but no such comparison of them as should demonstrate their radically different nature, has, so far as I know, been made. In Amiens the Gothic idea of an organic skeleton without walls, supporting stone vaulting, is embodied on a vast scale, in utmost perfection, both structural and artistic. The vaulting is entirely straightforward and simple, and has transverse ribs, groin ribs, and longitudinal ribs — the only ribs in such vaulting that have any necessary structural function, and the only ones that are found in pure French Gothic art in its integrity.[1] The longitudinal rib is stilted, bringing the vaulting conoid into the form that gives the most effective concentration of thrusts. The pier is a compound member rising through the three stories of the building to the external cornice, and is well developed in every part. On the ground story it has the form of a cylindrical column with four engaged shafts, one on the nave side, carried up continuously to the vaulting impost, where it supports the

[1] The vault with ridge ribs and tiercerons over the crossing of Amiens has been cited by some recent writers, both French and English, as showing that such supplementary ribs were used in the best period of French Gothic. But there is nothing to justify such a conclusion. The date of this vault is unknown, but it is certainly not earlier than the transept and choir — which are subsequent to the purer work of the nave in which the true French Gothic art culminates. Viollet le Duc (*Dictionnaire Raisonné*, IX, etc., p. 18, note) says it appears to date from the close of the thirteenth century, or possibly about 1270. This may well be; but, as I have elsewhere (*Development and Character of Gothic Architecture*) tried to show, the finer Gothic impulse was spent before that time, and all except the nave of Amiens, though for the most part still on the main lines of the earlier work, belongs to the period when the French Gothic was beginning to decline. The vault of the crossing in question is one of the features which mark this decline.

great transverse rib, one on the aisle side for the support of the aisle vaulting, and two others from which spring the suborders of the great archivolts. From the ground-story capital, on the nave side, two smaller shafts rise, one on each side of the great vaulting shaft to carry the groin ribs, and from the triforium string two still smaller ones are carried up, above the main vaulting impost so as to stilt the longitudinal ribs which they support. Within the triforium, supported on the transverse rib of the aisle vault, starts a rectangular pier buttress pierced by the passageway. This buttress, above the aisle roof, takes the form of an engaged shaft and a free-standing shaft, separated by an interval for circulation corresponding to the triforium passage below. These shafts rise to the intrados of the lower arch of the flying buttress (which has two superimposed arches), while over this two shorter shafts rise to the arch above, and above this upper arch the inner member only (which now again becomes rectangular) is carried up to the main cornice. Finally, against the aisle respond, and rising far above the springing of the high vaulting, stands the great buttress, the one rigid member of the system, consolidating the whole. Between the piers nothing equal in thickness to the archivolts of the ground-story arcade is carried above the triforium ledge. The vast clerestory is in one plane of mullions and tracery, with no wall whatever, and the great aisle openings are the same. Thus no wall solids, save the insignificant ones of the arch spandrels, and the aisle enclosure, survive — the structure having become a vast open framework of piers, arches, and buttresses supporting the vaults.

Turning now to Salisbury, we find a radically different scheme, save in the vaulting, which, as we have seen, is largely of French Gothic character, and therefore not in keeping with the rest of the system. There is no pier rising through the several stories of the building, with parts functionally related to the vaulting. The pier comes to an end at the springing of the ground-story arcade. Externally the outer buttresses terminate at the level of the aisle cornice, and there is no visible buttress system above this, for the shallow pilaster strips of the clerestory wall cannot, in any proper sense, be called buttresses. Above the aisle roof the clerestory walls take the whole vault thrust, but under this roof, within the triforium, flying buttresses are turned, as in the nave of Durham.  The archivolts and spandrels of the triforium are as thick as those of the ground story, and the walls of the aisles and of the clerestory are of Norman thickness, with more solids than voids in each bay.  In short, the structural system of Salisbury is precisely like that of the nave of Durham, save that it has less of an organic skeleton within the massive wall construction.  That the systems of Amiens and Salisbury are fundamentally different one from the other must, I think, now be seen.  In the one we have a radically new art evolved, indeed, out of older systems, but become, in the whole and in every part, essentially different from anything that had before existed.  In the other we have a survival of the ancient mode of building, though adorned in a new fashion.  It is true, indeed, that in early French Gothic buildings, more or less massive wall construction survives.  The churches of St. Germer, of Sens, and of Senlis are hardly less ponderous, and have little less wall solid, than those of Ely and Peterborough.  But this massiveness was soon thrown off as the organic skeleton was perfected, and the building was freed from wall solids, until the elastic framework stood forth securely in its unencumbered strength and beauty in the nave of Amiens.[1]  Such an architectural evolution never had place in England, nor anywhere else outside of the Ile de France and a few neighbouring localities to which the spirit of this remarkable artistic centre of the Middle Ages extended.

But while radically different from French Gothic, and abounding in structural inconsistencies, the Early English is, I repeat, a style of much beauty, and nothing comparable to it in merit was, in my opinion, afterwards produced in England.  The Norman Romanesque, we should hardly call beautiful.  It appeals by its grandeur.  But the Early English, in what I consider its normal and ideal character, has, I think, the quality of beauty to a degree found in few other styles.  It is not the beauty of French Gothic, — that stands supreme, — but a beauty of its own which may even be thought to suffer little in comparison, though things so different can hardly be compared.

[1] In developing the system mere lightness was not sought by the Gothic builders.  There is no excessive attenuation in Gothic art in its integrity.  It is robust enough, in appearance as well as in reality, to be perfectly stable and monumental in effect.  Exaggerated lightness of construction belongs to the period of decline.

This Early English style had possibilities that were never fully worked out, and that might have freed it from its structural inconsistencies. But after the middle of the thirteenth century conditions in England, as on the Continent, had changed, the finer inspiration declined, and architecture became, as we have seen, increasingly florid and ostentatious — a condition that has always marked declining art — until it sank into the dry and mechanical formalities of the Perpendicular style.

# INDEX

ABACUS, French form of, 84; rudimentary Early English form of, 84, 111, 261; typical Early English form of, 223; octagonal form of, 180.
Abbaye aux Hommes, capitals of, 39; bases of, 41; clerestory of, 37.
Aisles, usually vaulted in Norman churches, 4; vaulting of, in St. Albans, 5; in Peterborough, 11, 24; in St. Etienne of Beauvais, 23, 24; in Winchester, 24; in Canterbury, 77, 101, 103; in Worcester West bays, 55, 56, 57; in New Shoreham, 62; in The Temple Church, 68; in Lincoln choir, 122; in Lincoln nave, 135.
Alternate system, reason for, 3; of Ely, 2, 3, 32; of Norwich, 2, 3, 32; of Waltham Abbey, 2, 3; of Durham, 3, 27, 28; of St. Ambrogio of Milan, 27; of Le Mans, 30.
Amiens, cathedral of, its influence on Westminster Abbey, 151; apsidal chapels of, 151; free-standing shaft in buttress of, 156; combination of triforium and clerestory in, 172; ornamental gables in, 174; described and compared with Salisbury, 225, 226; vault over crossing, 225 (footnote).
Angle spur, or *griffe*, of Canterbury choir, 87; disappears with the introduction of the round plinth, 87; of Trinity Chapel, 106; of the Ccorona, 106.
Anglo-Norman builders, principles of organic construction not grasped by, 45; their tendency to break the continuity of supports, 52; their genius not of a kind to assimilate the principles of French Gothic art, 89.
Apses, of Canterbury, 15, 97; evolution of, in French Gothic, 15; of Romsey, 15, 16; of Tewkesbury, 16; of Christchurch, 16–19; of Lincoln, 113; of Westminster, 151; of Reims, 151; of Amiens, 151.
Apsidal chapels, of Reims, 151; of Amiens, 151; of Westminster, 151.
Arcades, of Castle Acre west fronts foreshadow those of the Early English style, 38; of Lincoln choir, 124.
Archivolts, Anglo-Norman, usually of several orders, 42; Norman profilings of

42; of Canterbury choir, 83, 84, 86; of Lincoln choir, 125, 126.

BASES, of Worcester, 7, 54; of Durham, 41; of Tewkesbury, 41; of the Abbaye aux Hommes, 41; of Canterbury, 41, 87, 107; of Sens, 87; of Chichester, 112; of Lincoln, 116; of Salisbury, 138; of Wells, 65; octagonal form of, 180.
Bath Abbey, vaulting of, 204; openings of, 204; ground story pier of, 204; archivolts of, 204; buttressing of, 204; external aspect of, 204.
Beverley Minster, vaulting of, 141; supports of, 141, 142; proportions of, 142; ground story piers of, 143.
Bilson, John, *The Beginnings of Gothic Architecture*, 25 (footnote); *The Architecture of the Church of Kirkstall Abbey*, 47 (footnote); on the vaulting of Durham, 25.
Brinton, Norfolk, timber roof of, 212.
Bristol, St. Mary Redcliffe, church of. See St. Mary Redcliffe.
Burgundy, the pointed arch of Fountains Abbey an importation from, 46.
Buttress, of Durham, 35; of Canterbury, 81, 101; of Worcester, 146; of Wells, 64; of Lincoln, 117, 136, 164; of Salisbury, 141; of Westminster, 145, 146; Norman forms of, 35, 36.

CAMBRIDGE, church of St. Sepulchre. See St. Sepulchre.
King's College Chapel, vaulting of, 201; wall spaces of, 201; Perpendicular style of, 202.
Canterbury, cathedral of, vaults of the Norman crypt, 9, 10, 11; apsidal aisle vaulting of the same, 11; irregularities of, 11; its system in part illogical, 13; St. Andrew's Chapel of, 11; its vault a spherical surface with cells, 15; how it differs from French Gothic apse vaulting, 15; date of, 16; vault under the Treasury of, 21; its irregularity of plan, 21; its rib system, 21; its domical form, 21; compound supports of, 22; piers of the Infirmary, 34; piers on the same

229

principle survive in the Early English style, 34; capitals of the Norman crypt, 38; later capitals of the same, 39; choir of, exhibits the first introduction of early French Gothic art, 70; derivation from Sens, 71; plan of, largely determined by the Norman remains, 71; sexpartite vaulting of, 71, 73, 74; its departures from the system of Sens, 71; piers of, 71, 73; the longitudinal rib wanting in, 74; stilted vault surfaces of, 74; its longitudinal arch like that of Durham, 74; shafting of, 74; piers eastward of the crossing, 75; logical sexpartite system eastward of the crossing, 76; the narrowing part a consequence of the oblique positions of the chapels of St. Andrew and St. Anselm, 77; awkwardnesses in the aisle vaulting, 77; quadripartite vaulting of, 122, 123; triforium level determined by that of the old Norman clerestory, 78; evidence that William of Sens intended the eastern extension, 78; round arches in the transept archivolts, and in the transverse ribs of the aisle vaulting, 78; relation of the new piers to the old responds, 78; resulting awkwardnesses, 78; quinquepartite vaults in aisles east of the transept, 79; the triforium arcade, 79; comparison with the triforium of Sens, 79, 80; clerestory not like that of Sens, 80; buttress system compared with that of Sens, 81; triforium gallery on the south side of, 81; profiling of vault ribs and archivolts of, 81–83; capitals and bases of, 84; beginnings of Early English forms in, 84, 85, 86, 87; authorship of these forms discussed, 85; bases compared with those of Sens, 87; the dominating principle that of early French Gothic, 88; single pier shafts of, 115; eastern crypt of, has little resemblance in details to the work of William of Sens, 92; Norman features of, 92; plan of, 92; evidence of a beginning by William of Sens, 92, 93; beginnings Early English capitals and bases, 93; vaulting of, 93, 94; apsidal aisle of, 94–97; likeness to Sens in rib system of, 95; piers of, 95; archivolts of, 95; influence of, on the Early English style, 136; Trinity Chapel, remarks of Willis on, 90, 91; Gervase on, 90; intended by William of Sens, 90; similarity of its style to that of the choir, 90; level of its pavement determined by the French architect, 91; likeness to Sens of the new features of the aisles, 91; relation of its plan to that of Sens, 91; plan of the apse, 97; arrangement of ribs in the apse vault, 97; horseshoe arches in the vaulting of, 98, 99; vault supports of, 99; ground story piers of, 100; great archivolts of, not pointed, 100; peculiar forms of the archivolts of, 100; triforium of, 100; system of, derived from that of the choir, 101; buttresses of, 101; clerestory of, 101; aisle vaulting of, 101–103; points of likeness to Sens in the aisles of, 104; round plinths of, 106, 107; French bases of, 107; profiling of, 107; uniformity of its style with that of the choir, 108; corona of, intended by the French architect, 91; French style of, 91; remarks of Gervase on, 91, 92; nave of, the first complete work in the Perpendicular style, 192; its derivation from Winchester, 192; proportions of, 192, 193; exceptional consistency of, 193; vaulting of, 193; profiling of, 193; lack of correspondence of the vault ribs with the supporting shafts of, 195; aisle vaulting of, 195; buttress system of, 195; clerestory and triforium of, 195; manifest Anglo-Norman character of, 106; Canterbury compared with Lincoln, 218, 219.

Capital, Norman forms of, 6, 7, 38; of Canterbury, 38, 84; of Christchurch, 39, 40; of Chichester, 112, 113; of Worcester, 6, 7, 54, 144; of Lincoln, 116, 117, 118, 124, 125, 136, 165; of Salisbury, 138; of Lichfield, 167.

Chichester, cathedral of, the Norman system, 109; repairs of, after damage by fire, 109; shafts of, 109, 110; influence of Canterbury on, 110; Anglo-Norman impress on, 110; profiling of, 111; eastern piers of, 110; capitals of, 110; foliation of, 110; corbelling of vaulting shafts of, 112; mixture of French and Anglo-Norman features in, 112; bases of, 112; crocketed capitals of, 112, 113; rudimentary Early English capitals of, 113.

Chipping Norton, truss of, 216.

Choir, defined, 152 (footnote).

Christchurch, apse vault of, 16; alterations in this vault, 16; its unique character in Anglo-Norman architecture, 18; compared with the apse vault of St. Germer de Fly, 18; French influence on, 19; possible date of, 16; capitals of nave of, 39, 40; archivolts of, 42; buttress of, 35; vaulting of the crypt of, 20; irregularities of, 20; likeness to the vaulted structures of Southern France, 20; Cattaneo, Sig., *L' Architettura in Italia dal Secolo VI al Mille Circa*, 26 (footnote); on the date of St. Ambrogio of Milan, 26 (footnote).

Cirencester, vaulting shafts adjusted to timber roof in, 216.

Cistercian architecture, that of England essentially Norman, 46.
Clerestory, Norman form of, 37; took form in the two great churches of Caen, 37; practically constant in the Norman monuments of England, 37.
Cluny, Abbey church of, double transepts, 113 (footnote).
Corbel-table, Norman forms of, 35.
Crypts, of Worcester, 5, 7; of Christchurch, 20; of Canterbury, 9, 10, 11.

DEMAISON, M., *Les Architects de la cathedrale de Reims*, in the *Bulletin Archéologique* for the year 1894, 159 (footnote); on the mullioned openings of Reims, 159 (footnote).
Domical vaulting, Byzantine origin of, 11; not common in Norman architecture, 11; advantages of, 22; a natural result of the use of the most efficacious form of groin arch, 23; the domical form reduced to a minimum in the Romanesque architecture of the Ile de France, 23; of St. Etienne of Beauvais, 23, 24; of St. Ambrogio of Milan, 26; of Morienval, 11; of Vezelay, 11.
Durham, cathedral of, nave vaulting of, 25; its date, 25; pointed of, not used in a Gothic way, 25; lack of conformity of the vaulting with the alternate system of the substructure, 27; this vaulting backward in idea, 28; its general conformation 28, 29; its omission of the transverse rib, 30; archivolts of, 42; buttress system of, 35; clerestory of, 37; triforium of, 37.

EARLY ENGLISH style, the Norman open triforium carried over into, 38; wall arcades of Norman art foreshadow those of the, 38; beginnings of, 132; attenuation of supports in, 134; lack of organic character in, 134; increase of ornament in, 135; level of vault springing in, 142; external features of, 147; admirable characteristics of, 147, 218, 227; survival of Norman construction in, 148, 218; decline of, after the early 13th century, 162; unlikeness to French Gothic, 218; characteristics of summarized, 222, 223, 224; the ideal of, 224; duration of, 224; its possibilities not fully worked out, 228.
Edington, Bishop, his work at Winchester, 188, 189.
Ely, cathedral of, alternate system of, 2; piers of, illogical in composition, 3, 32; buttresses of, 35; clerestory of, 37; triforium of, 37; octagon of, 176; florid character of, 176; not in keeping with the building, 176; wooden ceiling of, 176, 177; not in the form of a Gothic vault, 177; ornamental details of, 178; possible derivation from Siena, 177; choir of, 178; florid ornamentation of, 178; vaulting of, 179; use of liernes in, 179; vaulting shafts of, 180; octagonal abaci and bases of, 180; ground story piers of, 180; continuous imposts of, 180; clerestory of, 180; triforium of, 180; openings of, 180; Perpendicular style foreshadowed in, 180; aisle openings of, 180; timber roof in transept of, 211.
English Gothic (so called), essentially different from true Gothic, 1, 225, 227.
Enlart, C., *Arizine Anglaise du Style Flamboyant*, 187 (footnote).
Exeter, cathedral of, vaulting of, 170; approach to fan vaulting in, 170; vaulting shafts of, 171; archivolts of, 172; moulded capitals of, 172; buttressing of, 172.

FAN VAULTING, beginnings of, 199; Willis's definition of, 199; the rib ceases largely to be functional in, 200; not straightforward in principle, 200; constructive methods of, governed by conscious science, 201.
Flying buttress, rudimentary form of, in Gloucester and Durham, 35; earlier instances of, 36; not consistent with Norman art, 36; never became a characteristic feature of English architecture, 36.
Foliation, of St. Cross, 60; of St. Mary's, New Shoreham, 62; of Canterbury, 84, 85; of Chichester, 112; of Lincoln, 116, 165; of Worcester, 144; of Lichfield, 167.
Fountains Abbey, its structural forms, 46; its inorganic Norman Romanesque character, 47.
Freeman, E. A., on Lincoln choir, 127, 128.
French Gothic architecture, characteristic triforium of, 153, 155; timber roof of triforium not exposed to view internally in, 155; double triforium arcade not found in, 156; triforium wall of, carries no superstructure, 156; clerestory of, has no passageway, 157; apsidal archivolts stilted in, 158; mere lightness of construction not sought by the Gothic builders, 227 (footnote); essentially different from so-called English Gothic, 1, 225, 227.

GERVASE, on the burning and rebuilding of Canterbury, 90.
Glastonbury Abbey, advanced phase of pointed Norman design, 63; system of,

63; French Gothic character in vaulting of, 63; French Gothic profilings of, 63; peculiarity of its bay scheme, 63; continuous imposts of, 63.
Gloucester, cathedral of, no vaulting members included in its Norman system, 2; nave piers of, 34; flying buttresses of, 35; Perpendicular vaulting in south transept of, 183; supports of, 183; Perpendicular vaulting in choir of, 183, 184; vaulting shafts of, 184; clerestory archivolts of, 184; wall surfaces of, 184; Norman piers of, 184; Perpendicular details of, 185; great eastern opening of, 185, 186; fan vaulting in cloister of, 199, 200.
Gothic architecture. *See* French Gothic architecture.
Grasmere, truss of, 209.
*Griffe*, or angle spur. *See* Angle spur.
Groin arch, of Worcester crypt, 8; of the Norman crypt of Canterbury, 9, 10; of segmental in Peterborough, 24; in Worcester, 55; in Canterbury, 77; in Lincoln, 123; parts raised by ragstone addition, 21, 55; advantage of the semicircular form, 23; semicircular in St. Etienne of Beauvais, 23; in Winchester, 24; in Durham, 25; in St. Ambrogio of Milan, 26; pointed in Le Mans nave, 31.

HAMMER-BEAM, use of, 212.
Hereford, cathedral of, influence of Westminster Abbey on transept of, 167; transept vaulting of, 167, 168; vaulting shafts of, 168; segmental ribs in aisle vaulting of, 168; segmental pointed archivolts of, 168; influence of Westminster on triforium of, 168; clerestory of, 169; west side of, 169; influence of French models on, 169; piers of, 169; capitals of, 169; influence of, on Winchester nave, 188.
Hood moulds, superfluous members when used internally, 125.

JUMIÈGES, Abbey church of, clerestory of, 37.

KIRKSTALL Abbey, structural character of, 47; aisle vaulting of, 47; no complete organic system in, 47; east end of, 48.

LAON, cathedral of, compound piers of, 76.
Lasteyrie, M. le Comte de, *Discours sur les Origines de l'Architecture Gothique*, 25 (footnote); questions Bilson's dates for the vaulting of Durham, 25.
Leafage. *See* Foliation.

Le Mans, cathedral of, its nave vaulting derived from Angers, 30; logic of its alternate system, 30; derivation of the system from the Ile de France, 30; its mixed character, 30.
Lewis, Abbey church of, capitals of, 39.
Lichfield, cathedral of, modification of Lincoln scheme in nave of, 165; proportions of the triforium and clerestory of, 166; omission of the transverse rib in the vaulting of, 166; approximation to fan vaulting in, 166; vaulting shafts of, 166; no complete organic skeleton in, 166; buttresses of, 166; openings of, 166; no passageway in clerestory of, 166; aisle arcades of, 167; degradation of foliation in, 167.
Liernes, of Lincoln nave, 132; of Ely choir, 179; of Gloucester choir, 183; of Canterbury nave, 193; of Sherborne nave, 202, 203; of Norwich nave, 198.
Lincoln, cathedral of, Norman capitals in west front of, 39; later Norman capitals in western portals of, 39; St. Hugh's work in, 113; plan of, 113; resemblance to Canterbury, 113; origin of the double transept, 113; St. Hugh's apse of, 113, 114; vaulting of the transept — its points of likeness to the vaulting of Canterbury, 114; vaulting shafts of this transept, 114, 115; illogical use of the single shaft in this system, 115; its logical use in Canterbury, 115; ground story piers of the transept, 115; compound pier of Chichester compared, 115; use of crockets in, 115; cusped longitudinal arches in the transept clerestory, 115, 116; Anglo-Norman characteristics in the transept vaulting, 116; the rib profiling here follows that of Canterbury, 116; round abaci and round plinths of, 116; Early English forms developed in, beauty of Early English capitals of, 116; new scheme of leafage in capitals of, 117, 118, 124, 125; general internal aspect of, 117; pure style of the exterior of, 117; inspiration of Canterbury manifest in, 117; St. Hugh's choir, 118–129; vaulting of, 119, 120; remarks of Prior on, 120; analysis of the system of, 120–122; ground story pier of, 122; aisle vaulting of, 122, 123; its quinquepartite form derived from Canterbury, 123; segmental groin rib of, 123; aisle responds of, derived from Canterbury, 123; corbelled shaft of, 123; twin openings of, derived from Canterbury, 124; triforium scheme of, 125; superfluous members in, 125; increased redundance in, 125; archivolt profiling of, 125, 126; survival of the Norman passageway in the clerestory of, 125; acutely pointed aisle

openings of, 125; the flying buttresses of, compared with Canterbury, 127; the exterior of, largely hidden by the later works east and west, 127; characteristics of the Early English style for, advanced in, 127; mistaken idea that this choir was a new departure in architectural design, 127; Freeman's remarks on, 127, 128; Viollet le Duc's remarks on the same, 128; vaulting of the nave, 132; Anglo-Norman characteristics of, 132; longitudinal arch of, 133; continuity of supports broken in, 134; cross-section of, 135; pier buttress of, 136; profiling of, 136; ornamental leafage of, 136; influence of on later buildings, 146; presbytery of, 161; lack of the Early fineness in, 161; scheme of, a reproduction of that of the nave, 162; vaulting of, 162; lack of correspondence of the vault ribs with their supports in, 162, 163; buttress of system of, 163; absence of the pier buttress in, 164; enlarged openings of, 164; mullions and tracery of, 164; ornamental redundance of, 164; leafage of, 165; profiling of, 165; exterior of, 165; south portal of, 165; sculpture of, 165; restoration of, 165 (footnote); Lincoln compared with Canterbury, 219.

Lombard Romanesque, the first architecture of the Middle Ages to have a consistent organic character, 26; no other, save that of the Ile de France, has the same logical composition, 26 (footnote); its system of vault ribs and supports a far-reaching contribution to the subsequent architecture of the Middle Ages, 27.

London, St. Bartholomew's church of, capitals of, 39.

St. John's Chapel in the Tower, apsidal aisle vaulting of, 13; transverse ribs of, not independent arches, 13; widening of these ribs, 13.

St. Margaret's church of, its timber roof, 216.

St. Paul's, cathedral of. See St. Paul's.

Temple Church, system of, 67; aisle vaulting of, 68.

Westminster Abbey. See Westminster Abbey.

MALMESBURY Abbey, aisle vaulting of, 49; compared with St. Denis, 50.

Malvern, Priory Church, cylindrical piers of, 34; archivolts of, 42; truss of, 214.

March, Cambridgeshire, truss of, 212.

Milan, church of St. Ambrogio. See St. Ambrogio.

Morienval, Abbey church of, aisle vaulting of, 11.

Mullions, of Westminster Abbey, 159; of the presbytery of Lincoln, 164; of Reims, 159; of Ely, 180; of York, 172, 187; of Gloucester, 185; of Winchester, 191.

NEW SHOREHAM, St. Mary's church of, combination of pointed Norman and Early English in, 61; unlikeness of its north and south sides, 61; English profilings and foliation in, 62; French profilings, abaci, and foliation in, 62; aisle vaulting of, 62.

Normans, not inventive builders, 4; did not perceive the advantages of the domical groined vault, 22.

Norman Romanesque architecture, its lasting influence in England, 1; changes in, began about the middle of the twelfth century, 1; its transformation into the Early English style, 1; its grandeur, 2; variety of systems in, 2 (footnote); admirable qualities of, 4 derivation from the Lombard source, 4 (footnote); its vaults built of ragstone, 4; little precision in execution of, 4; great irregularities of plan and elevation of, 5; domical vaulting not common in, 11; the barrel vault not common in, 20; passageway in clerestory a characteristic of, 37; triforium of not walled in, 38; first changes in, 45; no essential structural transition wrought in, 45; ribbed vaulting of essentially different from that of the Ile de France, 23; its pier not so composed as to indicate an intention of vaulting in a logical manner, 31; shafts for groin ribs in high vaulting rarely occur, 31; wall arcades common in, 38; monumental qualities of, 38; string-courses of, 42; cornices of, 42; rarely found in completeness, 43; its transepts and east ends gave the model for those of the Early English style, 43; circular forms of, 43; segmental groin ribs frequent in, 123; havoc wrought in during the fourteenth century, 182.

Norwich, cathedral of, has an alternate system, 2; M. Ruprich-Robert's theory of, 3 (footnote); composition of the piers of, 32; Perpendicular vaulting of, 197; St. Stephen's Church, timber roof of, 212.

OPENINGS, double in the apsidal aisles of Sens and Trinity Chapel, 104, 123; in the aisles of Lincoln choir, 123; with mullions and tracery in Westminster, 159; enlarged with multiplied mullions and tracery bars in Lincoln presbytery, 164; Perpendicular form of beginning in the triforium of Ely choir, 180; the same developed in Gloucester choir, 185, 186.

Organic Romanesque, the Lombard and that of the Ile de France the only perfect types of, 2 (footnote); vault compartments completely enclosed in, 30.
Oxford, cathedral of, its Perpendicular vaulting, 207.
Divinity School, vaulting of, 205; St. Peter's in the east, vaulting of, 50.

PARIS, cathedral of, compound piers in, 75; apsidal aisle vaulting of, 68.
St. Chapelle, ornamental gables of, 174.
St. Denis church of, advanced character of, 50; triforium of, 137; St. Germain des Prés, combination of triforium and clerestory in, 172.
Parker, John Henry, *An Introduction to the Study of Gothic Architecture*, 1, 107; on the French work at Canterbury, 107; on the Early English style, 221.
Perpendicular style, the beginnings of in the later pointed art, 182, 183; in York choir, 186, 187; in Gloucester transept, 183; in Gloucester choir, 183, 186; in Gloucester cloister, 199, 200; in Winchester nave, 188-192; in Canterbury nave, 192; in Norwich nave, 197; in King's College Chapel, Cambridge, 201; in St. George's Chapel, Windsor, 198, 199; in Sherborne, 202, 203; in Oxford Cathedral, 207; in Oxford Divinity School, 205; in Henry VII's Chapel, Westminster, 204-206.
Pershore Abbey, suppression of triforium stage in bay scheme of, 147; peculiarities of vaulting in, 147.
Peterborough, cathedral of, has a uniform system, 2; aisle vaulting of, 11; composition of the piers in, 33; archivolts of, 42; buttress of, 35; clerestory of, 37; corbel-tables of, 42; fan vaulting of, 201; florid character of this vaulting, 201.
Piers, Norman illogical adjustment of shafts in, 2, 3; composition of, 31-35; cylindrical form of, 34; Early English, continuity of, broken in, 134; composition of, on the ground story, 134; of Lincoln nave, 134, 135; of Salisbury, 138; of Beverley Minster, 142; of Worcester, 144.
Pilaster strip, use of, in Norman piers, 3; in Worcester choir, 146.
Pinnacles, of the Early English style, 224.
Planning, monastic modifications of, in Anglo-Norman architecture gave rise to no essential change in the architectural system, 1; the double transept of Canterbury a fortuitous development, 113; the same in Lincoln a derivation from Canterbury, 113; Anglo-Norman features of, in Westminster Abbey, 152.
Pointed arch, employed creatively for structural ends by the builders of the Ile de France only, 35; used elsewhere as early, 35; of Fountains Abbey, 46; of Kirkstall Abbey, 47; of Malmesbury Abbey, 49; of St. Denis, 50; of Roche Abbey, 51; of the Worcester west bays, 53; of St. Cross, Winchester, 57; of St-Mary's New Shoreham, 57; of Glastonbury Abbey, 57; of Wells cathedral, 57; of Ripon Minster, 57; of the Temple Church, London, 57; structural possibilities of, not fully recognized in the transitional Gothic of Sens, 103; E. A. Freeman on St. Hugh's use of, at Lincoln, 128; use of, in Durham nave, 25.
Pointed Norman architecture, begins about the middle of the 12th century, 1; the change from round-arched Norman to pointed Norman wrought no essential structural change, 45, 69; of the west bays of Worcester, 53.
Prior, E. S., *The Cathedral Builders in England*, 107; *A History of Gothic Art in England*, 120 (footnote); on Canterbury choir and east end, 167; on the vaulting of Lincoln choir, 120.

REIMS, cathedral of, influence of its east end on that of Westminster Abbey, 150; its apse peculiar, 150; engaged shaft in pier buttress of, 156; ground story enclosure of, 157; mullioned openings of, 159.
Church of St. Remi, combination of triforium and clerestory in, 172.
Ribs, use of, in St. Ambrogio of Milan, 27; in St. Etienne of Beauvais, 23; in Peterborough, 24; in Durham, 25; conformation of vault surfaces determined by the, 28, 29; function of transverse, 30.
Rickman, Thomas, *An Attempt to Discriminate the Styles of Architecture in England*, 220 (footnote); on the Early English style, 220.
Ripon Minster, likeness to French Gothic in parts of, 65; intended high vaulting of, 65; aisle vaulting of, 66; transept system of, 66; ridge ribs in aisle vaulting of, 66; nave of, 66.
Rivora, Sig., *Le Origine della Architettura Lombarda e delle sue Principale Derivazione nei Paese d' Oltr' Alpe*, on the date of St. Ambrogio of Milan, 26 (footnote).
Roche Abbey, organic system of, 51; strong French influence shown in, 51.
Rochester, cathedral of, influence of Canterbury on east end of, 129; description of, 129; vaulting of, 129, 130; supports of, 130; irregularities of, 131; survival of Norman tradition in, 131.

Romanesque, of western Europe, 2; widely distributed, 2; of two main types, 2; each of many varieties, 2 (footnote).
Burgundian, imperfectly organic, 2 (footnote).
Ile de France, fully organic, 2; far advanced toward Gothic, 24.
Lombard, first fully organic mode of building, 2 (footnote), 4, 26, 27.
Norman, imperfectly organic, 2 (footnote). *See* Norman Romanesque.
Rhenish, imperfectly organic, 2 (footnote).
Romsey Abbey, uniform system of, 2; apse vault of, 15, 16; piers of, 34; buttresses of, 35; triforium of, 37; corbel-table of, 42.
Roofs, timber, exposed to view internally in the Anglo-Norman and Early English triforium, 222; trussing of, 208, 209; English misapprehension of the use of the tie beam and king post in the Middle Ages, 209 *et seq.*
Round arch, survival of, in the vaulting of Canterbury choir, 74; in the cathedral of Sens, in the archivolts of Trinity Chapel, 100; in Lincoln nave, 133.
Ruprich-Robert, M., *L'Architecture Normandie*, his theory of the system of Norwich cathedral, 3 (footnote).

St. Albans Abbey, aisle vaulting of, 5; buttress of, 35; clerestory of, 37.
St. Ambrogio, Milan, its organic composition, 26; its early date, 26; Sig. Cattaneo on, 26 (footnote); Sig. Rivora on, 26 (footnote); the conformation of its vaults, 26; its rib skeleton, 27; its alternate system, 27; all parts of an organic system present in, 27.
St. Bartholomew's, Smithfield. *See* London.
St. Cross, Winchester. *See* Winchester.
St. Denis. *See* Paris.
St. Etienne, Beauvais, aisle vaulting of, 23; compared with that of Peterborough, 23, 24; far advanced toward Gothic vault construction, 24.
San Francesco, Siena, church of, its timber roof, 217; proportions of, 217.
St. George's Chapel, Windsor. *See* under Windsor.
St. Germain des Prés. *See* under Paris.
St. Germer de Fly, apse vaulting of, 18.
St. John's Chapel, Tower of London. *See* under London.
St. Mary Redcliffe, Bristol, vaulting of, 196; continuous imposts of, 196; composition of the pier of, 196; archivolts of, 196, 197; character of the openings in, 197; buttress system of, 197.
St. Michael's, Coventry, timber roof of, 216.
St. Paul's, cathedral of (the old church), French Gothic features in, 170; influence of Westminster Abbey on, 170.
St. Sepulchre, Cambridge, foreshadows the Temple Church, London, 44.
Salisbury, cathedral of, its date, 136; influence of Lincoln on, 137; plan of, 137; no organic principle embodied in, 137; essentially Norman construction of, 137; shafting of, 137; Early English style of, 137, its vaulting not Early English, 137; piers of, 137; continuity of arcades in, 137; bases of, 138; pier capitals of, 138; archivolts of, 139; profilings of, 139; triforium of, 139, 140; clerestory of, 140; crossing piers of, 140; vaulting of, 140; walls of, 140; restoration of, 140 (footnote); attenuated supports of, 141; compared with the cathedral of Amiens, 226.
Saxon architecture brought to an end by the Conquest, 1; a rude basilican type, 1.
Sens, cathedral of, vaulting and system of, 70–74; remodelling of, 73 (footnote); single vaulting shaft peculiar to, 74; the wall survives in the clerestory of, 80; apsidal aisle vaulting of, 95; survival of Romanesque character in, 103; vaulting impost of, 105.
Sens, William of, his appointment as architect for the rebuilding of Canterbury cathedral, 70; handicapped by the old Norman remains, 71; his fall and retirement, 89; the eastern extension intended by him, 90 *et seq.*
Shafts, illogical adjustment of, in Anglo-Norman architecture, 2, 3, 32, 33; none for groin ribs provided in the system of Durham, 27; logical use of, in St. Etienne of Beauvais, 24; in St. Ambrogio of Milan, 27; in the nave of Le Mans, 31; illogical use of single in St. Hugh's choir of Lincoln, 114; superfluous use of, 125; continuity of broken, in Lincoln nave, 134; use of, in the buttress system of Westminster, 155; excessively slender in the Early English style, 222; free-standing in ground story piers, 222.
Sharpe, Edmund, *The Seven Periods of English Church Architecture*, 178 (footnote); on the Early English stvle, 221.
Sherborne, fan vaulting of, 202; pier not developed in, 203; use of mullions in, 203; archivolts of, 203; clerestory walls of, 203.
Siena, cathedral of, its crossing analogous to that of Ely, 177.
Church of San Francesco. *See* San Francesco.
Southwell Minster, no vaulting members in nave of, 2; triforium of, 37.

Spires, none extant in the Early English style, 224.
Spirelets, use of in the Early English style, 224.
Stilting, of the transverse ribs in St. Etienne of Beauvais, 24; in Peterborough, 24; of the great archivolts of St. Etienne, 23; of the archivolts of the apse of Amiens, 158; of the longitudinal rib of Glastonbury, 63; of Worcester west bays, 53; of Roche Abbey, 51; of Wells, 64; of Canterbury, 74; of Salisbury, 137; of Pershore Abbey, 147; of Westminster Abbey, 152; of Amiens, 225.
Sutton Courtenay Hall, Berkshire, truss of, 214.

TEWKESBURY, Abbey church of, nave has no vaulting members, 2; apse vault of, 16; nave piers of, 34.
Tiercerons, of Lincoln nave, 132, 133; of Lincoln presbytery, 162; of Lichfield, 166; of Exeter, 170; of Worcester, 175.
Timber roofs, three kinds of, 208; principle of the truss, 208, 209; truss of Grasmere, 209; mediæval misapprehension of the function of the tie beam, 209; truss of Charney, Berkshire, 209, 210; Viollet le Duc on the function of the tie beam, 210; ingenious carpentry in, 211; roofs without collar beams or tie beams, 211; timber roof of Ely transept, 211; misuse of the hammer-beam, 212.
Tower of London, St. John's Chapel of. *See* London.
Tracery, early development of, in the Ile de France, 159; M. Demaison on, 159 (footnote); of the east end of Reims, 159; that of Westminster modelled on Reims, 159; use of, in the triforium of Westminster, 159; of the presbytery of Lincoln, 164; increased elaboration of in the openings of York nave, 174; sinuous and cusped in Ely choir, 180; of the great eastern opening of Gloucester, 186; of York choir, 186.
Transepts, Early English art attains its most admirable character in, 147; the Norman character retained in Early English, 148; Anglo-Norman development of, in Westminster, 152.
Transitional architecture, no structural transition ever worked out in England, 45.
Triforium, character of, in Norman architecture, 37; character of, in Lombard Romanesque architecture, 37; suppression of, in bay scheme of Pershore Abbey, 147; of York nave, 172; remarks of Willis on, 173; of Romsey, 37; of Canterbury, 79, 81, 100; of Lincoln choir,

125; of Salisbury, 139, 140; of Beverley, 142; of Worcester, 144; of Lichfield, 166; of Westminster, 156; of Hereford, 168.
Troyes, cathedral of, combination of triforium and clerestory in, 173.

UNIFORM system, reason for, in organic building, 3; logic of, not often observed in Norman works, 3; of Winchester, 2, 189; of Peterborough, 2, 33; of Romsey, 2, 34; of Lincoln, 120, 122, 134, 135, 136; of Salisbury, 137; of Worcester, 52, 122, 134, 135, 162; of Westminster, 153; of Lichfield, 166.

VAULTING, character of, in Norman building, 5–30; domical form of, 22, 23, 26 (footnote); sexpartite form of, 71, 94, 129; quinquepartite form of, 79, 122, 123; lierne, 179, 202, 203; fan, 199, 201, 202, 205, 207; apsidal, 15, 16, 18, 19.
Vaulting conoid, shape of, determined by the number and the curvature of the ribs, 171.
Vaulting shafts. *See* Shafts.
Vezelay, groin arch straight on plan in vaulting of, 11.
Viollet le Duc, M. Eugéne, letter in *The Gentleman's Magazine*, 128 (footnote); *Dictionnaire Raisonné de l'Architecture Française*, 210 (footnote); on the choir of Lincoln, 128; on the function of the tie beam, 210.

WALTHAM Abbey, alternate system of, 2, 3; triforium of, 37.
Wandwell Court, Gloucester. *See* Gloucester.
Wells, cathedral of, points of likeness to Glastonbury, 64; high vaulting of, 64; compared with that of Salisbury, 64; external character of, 64; profiling of, 64, 65.
Westminster Abbey, French features of, 150; influence of Reims and Amiens on, 150, 151; apsidal chapels of, 150; system of, not French Gothic, 152; Early English features of, 152; vaulting of, 152; vaulting imposts of, 152, 153; vaulting shafts of, 153; ground story piers of, 153; cross-section of, 153; triforium gallery of, 153; flat roof of the same, 155; abutting arch of, 155, 156; triforium arcade of, 156; clerestory of, not in French Gothic form, 156; partial survival of the Norman form in, 157; openings of, 157; clerestory archivolt of, distinct from the longitudinal rib, 157; clerestory ledge of, internal, 157; ground story enclosure of, follows that

of Reims, 157; apsidal archivolts of, not stilted, 158; the organic principle of construction imperfectly embodied in, 158, 159; openings of, derived from those of Reims, 159; Anglo-Norman profiling of, 159; internal hood moulds of, 160.

Henry VII's chapel, vaulting of, 204; tortuous character of, 206; four-centred arches of, 206; aisles of, 206; flying buttresses of, 206; compared with those of the choir, 206.

Whitby, choir of, system of, 146.

Winchester, cathedral of, uniform system of, 2; buttress of, 35; archivolts of, 42; corbel-tables of, 43; Perpendicular work in nave of, 188; Edington's work in, 188; William of Wykeham's work in, 188; influence of Gloucester on, 188, 189; Edington's brace profile in, 189; the Norman system of, 189; Wykeham's alterations in, 189–191; four-centred arches of, 191; vaulting of, 191, 192; buttressing of, 192; hood moulds in Perpendicular form of, 192.

St. Cross, vaulting of, 58; square east end of, 58; combination of French Gothic and Anglo-Norman features in, 59; direct French influence shown in details of, 61.

William of Sens, architect of Canterbury choir, 70.

William the Englishman, architect of Trinity Chapel and the corona, 90.

William of Wykeham, architect of Winchester nave, 188.

YORK MINSTER, transept system of, 146; new features in nave of, 172; vaulting system of nave of, 172; wooden simulation of vaulting in nave of, 172; combination of triforium and clerestory in, 172; comparison with St. Germain des Prés, St. Remi of Reims, Amiens cathedral, St. Denis, and Troyes, 172, 173; remarks of Willis on, 173; new features in window tracery of, 174; gables over arches in, 174; west front of, 174; Perpendicular work in western towers of, 174; Perpendicular features in choir of, 186; tracery in openings of, 186; great choir vaulting shafts of, 186; eastern enclosure of, 187; interpenetrations of, 187; external clerestory mullions of, 187; aisle openings of, 187; eastern façade of, 187; buttressing of, 187.